Café Oc

Café Oc

A Nomad's Tales of Magic,
Mystery, and Finding Home in the
Dordogne of Southwestern France

Beebe Bahrami

Shanti Arts Publishing
Brunswick, Maine

Café Oc
A Nomad's Tales of Magic,
Mystery, and Finding Home in the
Dordogne of Southwestern France

Copyright © 2016, 2021 Beebe Bahrami
All Rights Reserved
No part of this book may be used or reproduced in any manner
whatsoever without the written permission of the publisher.

Published by Shanti Arts Publishing
Cover and interior design by Shanti Arts Designs

Shanti Arts LLC
193 Hillside Road,
Brunswick, Maine 04011
shantiarts.com

The author has recounted events, locales, and conversations from her notes and memory. Some names and identifying details have been changed to preserve peoples' privacy. The author has made every effort to present respectfully and accurately the utterly enchanting nature of this place and its people.

A few vignettes recounted here appeared first in varied form in the *Pennsylvania Gazette* ("On Hearths Ancient and Modern") and in *Wine Enthusiast* (two Last Drop essays, one concerning the wine-whisperer and *le chabrol* and the other Jacques — really Jack — the Jack Russell with a weakness for corks and legs.

All photos are by Beebe Bahrami except for the one on page 122 of Beebe holding a frog, taken by Sophie Cattoire.

Printed in the United States of America

Revised edition

ISBN: 978-1-941830-41-3 (softcover)
ISBN: 978-1-941830-40-6 (digital)

Library of Congress Control Number: 2016959739

To Sarlat and the Dordogne

To the people of the Périgord

To family and friends everywhere
who all are part of this adventure

To the rouge gorge and the mésange bleue

To Mr. Stripes

To Miles

To home

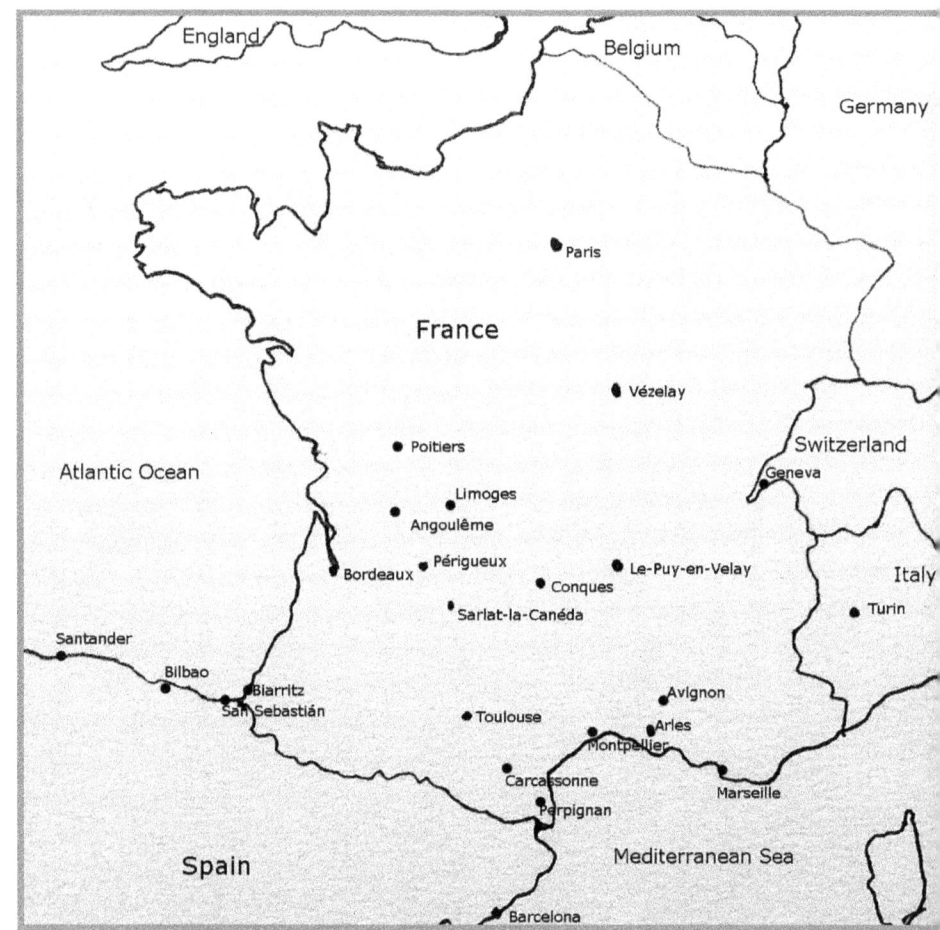

Café Oc takes its name from a group of warm and humorous people who meet once a month in Café La Lune Poivre, once called the Lébérou Café, a welcoming café in southwestern France in the town of Sarlat-la-Canéda. They meet to practice speaking Occitan, the old romance language of southern France still surviving today in the countryside and in revival movements in southern cities. Oc is the word for yes in Occitan. They call their meetings Café Oc. So do I, for my meetings with belonging, passion, magic, the ancestors and, best of all, home. This is the story of a nomad finding home and wholeness in Sarlat and staying on, leaving my tent poles anchored in place to that precious earth.

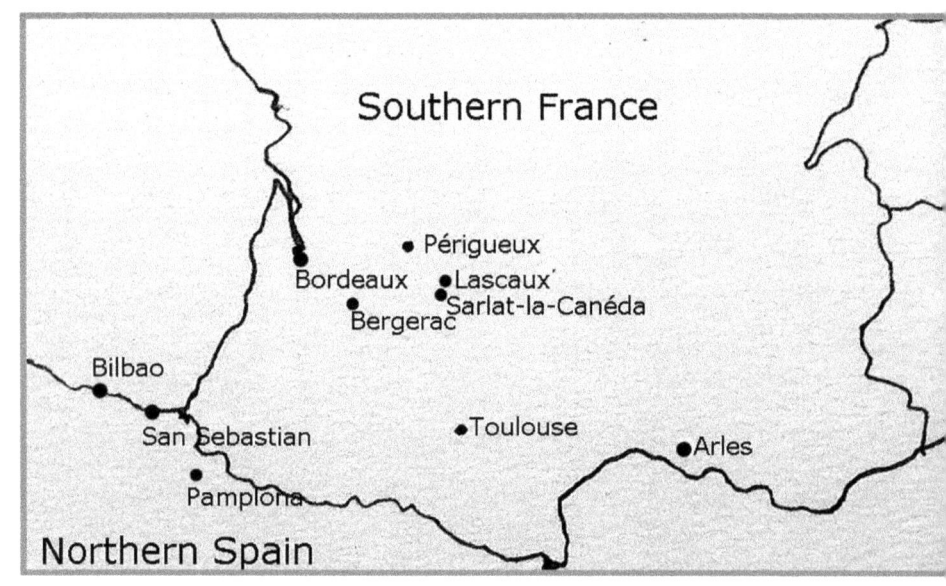

CONTENTS

FIRST WINTER	11
Arriving	13
Market	27
Vortexes and Olives	39
Café Oc	47
Caves and Cro-Magnon	59
Badminton and the Farmhouse	83
A Winter Feast	105
FIRST SPRING	123
Returning	125
Trekking with Early Moderns	141
Neandertal Fire, Troubadour Love	157
The Season	177
FIRST SUMMER	191
The Magic Flute	193
The Source of Sarlat	203
Recasting Home	215
FIRST AUTUMN	233
International Body	235
People in Black	253
The Dancing Flower of Temniac	271
SECOND WINTER	287
Hikes, Healers, Ancestors, and Spirits	289
Wednesday Market Café	311
Into Second Spring	325
ABOUT THE AUTHOR	336

FIRST WINTER

Les moins tendues et plus naturelles allures de nostre ame, sont les plus belles; les meilleurs occupations, les moins efforces.

The least distorted and most natural expressions of our soul are the most beautiful; the best vocations are the least forced.

— Michel de Montaigne (1533-1592), "De trios commerces."

Medieval Street in Sarlat

Chapter One

ARRIVING

An elderly man suddenly opened his front door and barked, "Bienvenue à Sarlat! Bonne journée!" He was an angel, dressed in a warm and dry cream-colored wool sweater and white dress shirt, and smiling broadly.

In spite of the heightening storm and downed electrical lines, the trains across northern Spain and into southwestern France were still running. Three days, four trains, and one bus later, I made it to the town of Sarlat-la-Canéda in the heart of the Dordogne in the depth of winter, a hurricane-like storm relentlessly on my heels the entire way. On my final leg, before boarding my last train from Bordeaux to Sarlat, I'd secured a little studio to rent. It was with the only person who responded to my last-minute inquiries for a place to stay in the off-season. I was sure it was the size of a closet and on the edge of town because it was a decent rent for what I was learning was a serious tourist destination. I had to take my chances. Getting to Sarlat had become a singular obsession.

I hadn't even seen a photo of the town yet nor had any idea of its physical appearance. I picked it based on a desperate late-night internet search using all the words describing my favorite things in life, the things I really, really, really wanted. I had no idea what Google would deliver, but the first item listed at the top of the page was beyond my expectations. It was an obscure academic article about Sarlat, presented at a conference on religion and spirituality in Bordeaux. Those articles rarely have photos, which it did not, but equally rare is such a piece containing all your favorite things bundled into one rational document, which it did.

Sarlat was at the heart of a spirituality movement. Its attraction was its very geography; it was situated within a place that was occupied by humans as early as 400,000 years ago, first Neandertals and later Cro-Magnons (us). Early humans were drawn to the rich, vibrant land for the same reason we modern humans were: good food, climate, and shelter. This was the article's opening explanation for why Sarlat and the wider Dordogne of southwestern France, also known by its older name as the Périgord region, had become attractive to such a diverse array of spirituality movements. These ranged from neopagans and shamans, to a more liberal and catholic Catholicism, to the land of choice for resettling Buddhist monks from Tibet.

I was ready to seize what mattered most. Several relatives and childhood friends had died in the prior year, and my mother-in-law had died just a few weeks earlier, bringing on a time of grief and a strange anchorlessness. My husband, Miles, and I became her caregivers and we suspended many things in our lives, the most significant for me being my own movement.

I was born a nomad, and walking and exploring are paramount to my sense of connection to the earth and have also become my modus operandi as a writer and anthropologist. My husband understood this well, similar in nature to me, and was the first to push me out our door in New Jersey when I had the opportunity to inhabit a remote Galician fishing town in northwestern Spain for the winter. The plan was I would go there, settle into local life, and write. It was a place that had magical possibilities. It was in a mythic green land dotted with dolmens, petroglyphs, caves, and Celtic settlements. It existed along a beautiful coastline that wove into an interior growing good food and caring for rolling vineyards. And, it was along an important tributary of my other passion, the pilgrimage road to Santiago de Compostela, the Camino, the Way of Saint James. To live on and write about a place on one of the pathways of this pilgrimage, while learning the local lore, was a long-held dream. Miles would join me for Christmas. "Go," he said, "find out what it's all about."

I arrived in a town tucked into a protective blue bay along the Atlantic lined with colorful fishing boats and surrounded by lush green protective hills. The highest hill overlooked the town and bay, best viewed from its precipice where stood a small granite shrine dedicated to San Roque, the town's patron saint. He was a pilgrim himself, a native of Montpellier near the Mediterranean in France, and now in his celestial state protected people from disaster and illness. I was enchanted by the promise of being there, going deeply, finding out what it was all about.

What it turned out to be about was a closed society, not interested in the outsider, in fact, a little suspicious of her. You say you're an American writer and you want to write about us? Why? Why exactly? It sounded wacky, unsubstantial, and suspect. And winter was a horrible time to be there. I spent months being pummeled by the cold, wet, windy Atlantic and largely ignored by the community in the village. I went for long walks along the pilgrimage trail and into the forest and along the coast. I visited San Roque often on his hilltop. I talked to him. An outsider himself, he understood. While he protected the town, he was kept on its periphery too.

It was such a beautiful place and had such a vibrant life, but not for someone from the outside who wanted to be included.

My last thread of hope to become a part of village life was dashed when another outsider, a woman who was actually from there but grew up in France, told me to give up trying, that even she was held outside the inner circles and treated as a foreigner. She was ancestrally from the region and was married to a local, so I could see that my chances were nonexistent. But I bonded with her, the only person who accepted my invitation to meet over a glass, and I began studying French with her. French. That was another piece of the big dream.

To me, France and Spain were joined in many ways, most enticingly through the aforementioned Camino that arrived along four major routes from across France, climbed over the Pyrenees, and entered Spain to join as one great snake across the north toward Galicia. Even that one great snake was called the Camino Francés, the French Road, given how many French arrived on it, settled on it, and built it up in the Middle Ages.

As my new friend taught me to speak and conjugate verbs, she also suggested I take a break from the cold shoulder and society and winter of this corner of northwestern Spain, go to France, and practice my newly minted verbs. That was when I did my weird late-night internet search ("prehistory, folklore, spirituality, good food and wine, warm social life, France, Chemin St-Jacques," the latter being the French for the Camino), and discovered the name Sarlat in the midst of that obscure publication.

I was so sure of this trajectory, so ready for new possibilities, that I never looked up one photo of the place, only train maps to get there, and packed a light backpack, leaving the other things to wait for me on my return, and then stepped through and closed the door of the place where I had been staying.

As I did, the strangest thing happened. I was hit with the strong scent of gardenias all around me. It was a rare and unusual scent for my apartment in Galicia but one iconic to my mother-in-law. It was a perfume she always wore; it felt as if she showed up to bless my journey and wanted me to know this. I might have also felt the gentle pressure of a hand on my shoulder, guiding my way forward, out that door and toward another.

Three days later, I boarded that final train that would take me directly to Sarlat. As the train left Bordeaux, it slipped through long sweeps of flat, hibernating vineyards with thick fog hovering two feet above the ground. Once we passed Bergerac, the flat vine-covered plains slowly began to clear of fog but began to mist and roll into forested hills. By the time we were a few kilometers from Sarlat, we were shrouded with the increasing presence and closeness of jagged hills covered in thick dark forests that ended in cliffs and sheer drops, the signature landscape of this fertile land framed between the Vézère and Dordogne rivers.

There was something in that close and intimate landscape that possessed a strong ancient presence. It was physically palpable, mysterious, haunting, and strangely pleasing. Like those pigment-blown stenciled handprints on Paleolithic cave walls, it felt as if ancestral hands were reaching out from inside the stone to touch me. It was clear to me in that moment that thousands of years ago our species had decided this was a great place to live. ("A vacation destination for 400,000 years," reads the tourist slogan for the region.)

Arriving in Sarlat, still wet from the rain that drenched me from Galicia to Bordeaux, I clutched like a talisman in my hopeful fist the now soggy slip of paper with my new address. I stepped out of the train station and made the one-mile walk downhill into the center of town as the wind and the rain resumed their freezing sideways whips of water that stung my face and further soaked my rain jacket and backpack. But I walked and I clutched. I was almost there. Soon, I'd be dry, and soon, I'd be in a new place, ripe for a new adventure.

I could hardly see anything other than the rain, the wind, and the gray mist lowering into the valley. There was no one out, and I felt I had arrived in an abandoned outpost. I almost fainted when halfway down, stopping to wipe the moisture from my glasses on the narrow sidewalk, an elderly man suddenly opened his front door and barked, "*Bienvenue à Sarlat! Bonne journée!*" He was an angel, dressed in a warm and dry cream-colored wool sweater and white dress shirt, and smiling broadly.

"Do you do this to everyone who arrives from the station?" I smiled back.

"Of course not, *Madame*," he lingered elegantly on the second "m," then continued. "Only for those who need it." I showed him my drenched slip of paper and he pointed down the hill and to the right, and made sure I continued in the correct direction before going inside and closing his door.

I forgot that I was cold and wet. In that split second, I received more enthusiasm and welcome than during my many weeks and months in that fishing village in Galicia. In fact, that was a more boisterous welcome than I think I'd ever received as a newcomer anywhere. I pushed on down the road, my heart singing. I don't recall if it was still raining.

Soon the modern street gave way to a modern square, and as I got further directions to my new temporary home, I found myself not walking on the outskirts but going deeper and deeper into the medieval center. I turned the last corner to my place and it was as if I'd suddenly wandered into a set for *The Three Musketeers*. The medieval town of Sarlat opened like a daylily at dawn, petals slowly expanding and stretching to allow the light's passage in.

My new home held one corner on the Place du Peyrou. Its three stories, swooping tiled roof, and golden stone face with pale, dusty blue shutters looked right onto its most imposing neighbor, Sarlat's cathedral, Saint Sacerdos, which anchored the biggest corner. It loomed protectively over my building with its Romanesque tower and Gothic stained-glass windows. At another corner was another famous stone celebrity: Étienne de La Boétie's house, the very place where in the sixteenth century he was born, where he wrote his humanistic prose, and where he died.

As I waited for the woman with the keys to arrive to let me in, I recalled her details. My studio was on the top floor and one of three apartments in a building built in the 1450s and of the same sculptable tan-golden stone as the cathedral. I immediately touched and fell in love with its great wooden door that was painted a saturated French blue and set with thick iron studs. I let my hand run over it, not minding the wet. When my fingers reached the mailbox flap, I ducked down and pushed it open and peeked in. There from the other side rushed toward me a smell that hit me hard and threw me back, back in time.

I was twelve and standing in my father's mother's impeccably kept, whitewashed, marble-floored home in Tehran. It was a comforting smell, one I associated with her and her expansive idea of hospitality.

When she invited my brother and me over for lunch, she would cook for an army. We marveled at the heaps of food that were for the three of us. Once I asked my mother, "Why does Maman June cook so much food when it's just us three?"

"Because she is a lady," she replied, "and she cooks only large quantities of food. What is left goes to the poor in the neighborhood. The food was in your honor, but not just for you." That day I learned that "lady" meant not how a woman looked or her demeanor but how she honored the obligations of her social station. And my regard and love for my grandmother deepened. I pushed my nose nearer the flap and took a deep breath, savoring once again the rush of fresh cut flowers, new paint, morning dew, and musty linen closets.

I came back to the present and stood up straight, hearing the mail flap click shut, when the Englishwoman who ran the bed and breakfast up the hill cheerily greeted me. She was doing the landlady of my studio a favor and meeting me with the keys to let me in. She took one look at my bedraggled state and quickly unlocked the door.

"The owner will stop by after you've had a chance to settle in to introduce herself," she said as she pushed the door open, "and you" she added humorously, "to the quirks of the apartment." I wondered what that meant but soon forgot as I was engulfed by the feeling of stepping into my grandmother's home, a sensation I hadn't experienced for over thirty-three years.

"You know, the place is just sitting empty in the dead of winter and the owner will be happy to have someone in it to heat the old stone walls and keep them dry."

My heart fluttered. *Old stone walls.* I followed her up the wide wooden staircase and noticed the warm golden stone on either side that framed our ascent. She warned me about the last step at the top, that it was higher than the rest, and I gave an extra big step up and soon stood at the door to my rental.

Now this is where reality will rush back, I said to myself. At the rate I was paying, even if in a most magnificent building, the apartment itself still had to be a closet. This was my certainty as the lady fumbled with finding the correct two keys to unlock and open the door.

We stepped in. I staggered.

Yes, it was one room, with a kitchen to the side, but it was a remarkable room. It was spacious and had a high ceiling, stucco engraved light mounts, and tall French windows, one in the main room and one over the kitchen sink that looked out onto the cathedral's north wall.

A defunct but beautiful stone fireplace held a large ceramic Buddha head on its wooden mantle, smiling beatifically and feeling like a long lost friend. The kitchen was small but well-equipped and oddly smelled of my other grandmother, my mother's mother, and her small kitchen in Tehran. I inhaled deeply as ground saffron, cooking basmati rice, chopped herbs, and homemade sour cherry jam mingled and came back to life. It all felt like visiting my family, not staying in a vacation rental.

The Englishwoman left me to settle in and dry out.

I dropped my wet pack in the entrance, kicked off my soaked hiking boots, peeled off my rain jacket, and went directly over to the French windows and opened them. I then unlatched the heavy, wooden, pale blue shutters and pushed their nine-foot stature aside until they clicked into their brackets.

The rain temporarily ceased and a small ray of light pushed its shoulders through the thick clouds. Like a stage set, it accentuated the comings and goings on the Place du Peyrou below. Some people went into Saint Sacerdos. Some stopped to chat with the woman in the linen shop on the corner below or to pick up a jar of foie gras from the producer next door. Boétie could have greeted me from his window just across the square or waved down to his close friend, Michel de Montaigne, as Montaigne walked down the street named after him, the rue Montaigne. That was the one and the same street on which I now found myself living, a street that descended from a steep hill and emptied level into the square, and that was all that separated my building from the cathedral.

Suddenly, Saint Sacerdos' bells began to swing and let out a deep, resounding clang. With each strike of the metal, the clanging turned into a mesmerizing hum that turned into a strong, resonant Tibetan-prayer-bowl-like ringing. It nailed me to the floor, the energy and sound were so penetrating and so pleasing. It felt as if its healing vibration was resonating through every cell of my body, shaking them awake to be at their best. Wet, fatigue, and cold all flicked off of me. The longer the bells rang, the more that scintillating resonance took purchase, like a Tuvan throat singer's double chord that underpinned the more prominent overtones.

As each ring went deeply into my chest cavity and made me feel warm and whole, it also made me feel a suspension of time and a rare knowing, one of those sublime moments we all recognize when the veils of our life have been momentarily lifted and we know exactly what it is we are here for, what we are really about. In that moment, I knew my life was going to be entwined with this place, I had friends here waiting for me, and I would somehow come back. I also recognized the telltale signs of love and affinity. I felt as if Sarlat was courting me, and I was answering her with a deep resounding "Yes."

There was a sudden knocking at the door. I popped out of my reverie, quickly closed the windows against the impending return of rain and cold, and went across the studio to open it. A spritely East Asian woman smiled and entered, gave me the customary kiss on each cheek, and said in a steady, unbroken stream, "I'm Nadiya. Welcome to Le Chardon. What we call this studio. It means The Thistle. A favorite flower from my husband's native Scotland." She went on to explain that the tough but beautiful thistles, *les chardons*, figured importantly in her husband's childhood memories of growing up in the Highlands. They represented a very Scottish idea, of being tough and tender at once. She added that she was from Thailand and that she and her husband met in Paris but then got married and settled here in Sarlat.

Nadiya then just as matter-of-factly showed me the mechanics of living in this particular place, an over five-hundred-year-old building that developed its own character and personality over the centuries. "You need to learn to work with it as a person, not push it around like a stack of stones."

My head swirled as I followed Nadiya's instructions. "Shut the shutters at night, before the sun goes down, to retain the heat. Open them during the warmest times of the day, when the sun is high, to bring in as much warmth as possible. Don't forget, market day is Wednesday and Saturday, and for those living on the square," she pointed outside and below, "it starts especially early, around five-thirty in the morning when the fish seller arrives right below your kitchen window to set up her fish stand. Lots of ice. The sound will ricochet right up the wall and into the apartment." She paused and smiled. "It's a natural alarm clock."

Nadiya then pulled open a map of Sarlat she held in her hand, placed it on the dining table, and began to mark her favorite spots in town with an X.

"Here's the grocery store for things you can't buy at the market." X. "Here's my favorite baker." X. "Here's the organic food store and here is where the organic farmers set up on market day." X, X.

Xs big and small began to populate the town as Nadiya's personal Sarlat emerged. "Here is my favorite restaurant." X. "You really have to try their fish soup. There's none like it, not even in Portugal."

I learned that she loved driving and would often drive across northern Spain to Portugal where she'd indulge in a few days of eating fresh seafood, another one of her passions, and then happily pull a long day or two driving home. She had done thorough research into fish soup. That she was also Thai, another nation capable of making a knee-weakening, heart-swooning fish soup, added to her authority on the matter.

"And if you want to try a good local wine, one you are unlikely to find outside the region, you really must try Pecharmant. Good bottles start at around ten euros, and you can get them here." X. She went on like this, the printed portions of parts of the map disappearing underneath her favorite world. Suddenly, she stopped and looked at me. "I think you'll come back here to live." X.

I felt it marked right on my forehead, where the third eye is supposed to be. Her one-liner struck a chord that was as resonant as that feeling I got in my chest cavity from the ringing cathedral bells. There was a theatrical air about it all, too. As she uttered this one sentence, I felt the lights temporarily dim and heard someone say, "Curtains!" from stage left.

My head swirled. My heart expanded. My spirit said over and over: *home, home, home.*

What a strange thing to say upon my arriving in a place about which I knew nothing. But to Nadiya, I just smiled and replied, "That wouldn't be a bad thing. I already like it here."

Later I would come to learn that loaded one-liners from Nadiya weren't random utterances. The lighting crew had been right. She'd get a feeling about something and lob a one-liner that often came to pass. And a few days later I would learn, as an offhand comment in a story she was telling, that her mother back in Thailand was a very real and very gifted medium. In that same breath I would also learn that Nadiya herself didn't trust such things and held them at arm's length. But she still spoke from her heart and spirit and would lob one-liners before even she knew she was blurting them.

But at this moment, on the first day of arriving, I didn't know any of this. All I knew was that the lights had changed, that time stood still, and that line — that exciting idea — had already existed unuttered within me only moments before.

I could feel myself shiver, which Nadiya took as my need to get into dry clothes. She left me to change, unpack, and explore the town now covered in Xs and buy coffee and milk for the next morning before the shops closed for the night.

As she closed the door, I stood in the middle of the big room and quickly stripped out of my layers of wet clothes. It was when I was down to my undergarments that a strong visceral sensation hit me, and I knew I was not only shivering and peeling off soaked garments, I was also dislodging an ancient layer of armor, heavy metal sheaths that I donned sometime in my distant adolescence without even being aware of them. Until this moment. A strange and sudden physical knowing hit me, thirty years after the fact and conscious for the first time: I wore armor. Its invisible but palpable sheaths peeled away from my skin — they at last arrived at their expiration date — and fell off with loud clangs. I was sure I could hear them hit the stone floor. As each piece of protective plating hit the ground, I also noticed that the lighting crew, a new and surprising backup team to better mental health, just cast extra illumination on the matter.

What the heck? How was this possible? Clang, clang, clang.

And then I knew. It was so obvious it had become unobvious. Something about this place triggered memories long buried. This, on top of the dramatic changes from the past year, seemed to have set me up for being ready for this moment, as surprising as it was.

Belonging. Belonging had been at the root of everything. My nomadic nature. My search for home but not finding it. In that room, now shivering in my undergarments and stunned by what was happening to me physically and psychologically, I was fifteen again and news of the Iranian Revolution had arrived. After what was an idyllic childhood, growing up in Colorado and visiting relatives in Iran in certain summers for long months, in one day I had to give up one of my two beloved homelands. I had been a nomad all along, but a healthy one, with a winter and a summer pasture to go to. Suddenly, one pasture disappeared. Far worse than this, the two peoples I loved most in the world were at odds with each other, and I was both of those peoples. I was American born and raised and felt American pain over the conflict. I was Iranian by ancestry on both sides and had been loved and nurtured by warm, kind relatives whom I would never see again, and I felt Iranian pain over the conflict. Over the years I would get news by phone and letters that one by one my beloved relatives passed away. While alive, I never saw them again, and in death, I was never able to go to their funerals or visit their graves. Unbeknownst to me, not being able to talk to the recently arriving Iranians nor Americans about this sadness — because they did not think I experienced loss — I donned that armor and went silent. Even to myself.

I began to shiver hard and rushed to put on warm, dry clothes as I dug open my wet backpack. Goodness, age fifteen was also the same time I became a full-blown nomad in earnest. Once I had lost one home, I had gone immediately in search of another. It was an ancient idea of balance, that one needed two places for harmony, the winter and the summer pastures. Only then would one's herds be healthy. This, to my mind, was a very logical thought. In that moment, one foot had pulled up from the earth and dangled, wandering and feeling around for another satisfying foothold. I'd been searching ever since, even thinking for a long while that Spain was that place, but not quite. I loved Spain in many ways, but still, it didn't quite fit my foot. Maybe it was as one Spanish friend said to me in a moment of deep reckoning and likely over-generalizing as we were figuring things out over a nice bottle of local red wine: "We Spanish are *muy sospechosos*. We're very suspicious," she said. "From Isabel in 1492 to Franco in the twentieth century, our psyches have been clobbered by too many leaders who fear outsiders and themselves."

Over the years, the whole search left me feeling incomplete, as if at any moment I would topple over, putting too much weight on one foot as the other held itself aloft, not settling. I did, however, have some pretty remarkable adventures when I went searching and unleashed the nomad onto the open road. But still, it took thirty years for all this to come to light. Geez. And what was it about **this** place that made it finally all come to the surface?

Fully dressed and feeling the comfort of dry clothes seep into my skin for the first time in three days, I heard one final clang. The last piece of armor fell and hit the floor. I knew something was now significantly different. I knew coming here was no accident. I knew I was meeting my present, my future, and my past all at once in a place that could handle it. I knew all this in that moment standing in the middle of that room, and I hadn't yet seen the town. I just knew. It was a deep, strange, bone-penetrating knowing, and I also knew I had to trust it. I knew that even that insular fishing village had conspired to direct me to my place in the world. And I knew I was now comfortable enough in my skin, thirty years later and so much older, to be open to this strange mystery. I committed then and there to finding out what was waiting for me. Here.

I pulled on one more layer of dry clothes, leaving my rain jacket on the coat hook to drip in the vestibule. I went out and found the little grocery store before it closed for the night and bought coffee, milk, eggs, apples, butter, and bread for breakfast. There was still a slight lull in the rain, but the clouds hovered so heavily that all I had a chance to see of Sarlat before the skies opened up again was the little street leading off from my apartment across the cathedral square as I went out, and the magnificence of Saint Sacerdos cathedral upon my return, with her Romanesque bell tower topped with early modern curves and bells. But it was enough for romance and dreams.

Coming back through the big blue door and heading upstairs, the smell of my grandmothers' homes — one at the entry, the other in the kitchen — was still there. It reminded me of the warmth of a childhood that embraced me with loving and protective arms. A childhood I often could not allow myself to remember for the grief. As soon as I was safely behind the big blue door, the skies opened again and cathartically dumped buckets of rain that continued to pour down all night.

I went to bed early. Tired from my travels and from this strange revelation, I was also giddy, for tomorrow was Sarlat's Saturday market, my first Saturday market in Sarlat. And I was in southwestern France. I wiggled my toes at the thought. I was going to market tomorrow. A French market. I wiggled my toes again, feeling so good, all warm and dry at last, and resting in fresh, pressed sheets. I was a happy girl, all whole and safe and on the precipice of an entirely new adventure. Without armor.

I slept deeply that night, more deeply than I had in a very long time. I slept in a new body, one lighter than it had been in three decades. I marveled at how the body knows things profoundly and honestly when the mind — the knowing organ — is often blind to these honest truths. But once acknowledged, this wisdom seemingly held in the cell tissue of the body could make a person whole and perform strong healing.

I had vivid and deep dreams, an aspect of life in this apartment on the Place du Peyrou that I would soon learn was part and parcel of the experience, not just the result of my rain-soaked epiphany. In those first dreams in that first night, I sorted through the threads and cause and effect that had brought me here to this uncanny moment of beginning to be consciously whole again. In those dreams, I knew it was time to go boldly forth, visibly and without armor, into unknown galaxies, or more accurately, deeper into this strange and beautiful mystery in the depth of winter. •

Fish at the Sarlat Market

Chapter Two

MARKET

The bread baker had arrived. He had the figure of a man who taste-tested all his creations, several times, for quality control. He was the paradox of the French Paradox. He had a basket full of chocolatines, those buttery croissant-like creations elsewhere in France called pain au chocolat, with a brick of dark chocolate slowly melting in the middle. I could smell them through the glass.

THE SWISH AND SHOVELING OF ICE AT THE FISHMONGER'S stand commenced like clockwork the next morning. At 5:30 the sound reverberated up the stone wall and into the tall window of my room. I had been dreaming a very lucid dream, so lucid I could not tell if it was a dream or some threshold reality. A young woman had stood near the bed, whispering the name Rafaea or Raphaela. She had a long flaxen-colored skirt and white high-collared shirt with lace finish. Her light brown hair was piled on her head in a pretty chignon. She felt like a person from the sixteenth or seventeenth century, maybe a contemporary of Étienne de La Boétie's. Rafaea?

I woke up more as the ice scraping and shoveling repeated and the image of the woman from another time faded. I briefly thought: *ghost*; then, *nah, can't be*. More ice. I was more awake but disoriented. Was I still in New Jersey? No. Galicia? I didn't dare move until I knew which bed I was getting out of and from which side. Then it dawned on me and a sudden jolt of excitement raced through my limbs. I was in Sarlat and it was market day, and I was feeling a whole lot lighter.

I reached over to my bedside stand and made a note in my journal, in groggy chicken scratch marks, of the dream image and the name. Then in the pitch dark of the wintry pre-dawn, I slipped out of the comfortable queen-sized bed in my high-ceilinged studio and went to the little kitchen and began making coffee, all to the rhythm of the fishmonger's ice.

As I worked on the brew, I looked out the kitchen window. It looked right onto the north Gothic face of Saint Sacerdos Cathedral. I craned my neck to see three stories below and at last glimpsed the fish seller arranging that day's catch. Fresh Aquitaine trout was on special, announced her blackboard, which was already set up in the Place du Peyrou, illuminated by a street lamp.

I looked again directly in front of me, at the cathedral's north wall, and saw three Gothic arched stained glass windows, faintly illuminated by soft lights, perhaps candles, from within the church. If approached from inside the cathedral, rather than from this pigeon's ledge view, those three windows would correspond to the first three chaplets to the left upon entry. From my vantage point, the window images told their stories in reverse.

One was of the martyrdom of Saint Philomena, a young Greek princess who chose Christ over marriage to the Roman Emperor Diocletian in the fourth century. Her whole family had recently converted to Christianity and it would have been a good move to marry, but she refused. The window showed her resulting punishment: she was whipped, drowned, and shot with arrows, all failing to kill her until she was finally beheaded. I squirmed and heard water boiling. I was happy that torture by boiling water was not on the menu across the street as I went to the stovetop, turned it off, and poured the hot water over ground coffee, hoping that when I was more awake, those scenes would seem less harrowing.

They were. The second row of panels of Philomena's window was peaceful: beheading complete, they revealed her spirit rising and transcending the world of illusion, like the Buddha smiling behind me on the mantle in the other room, and going to heaven. There, she was greeted by angels and God and, in my rendering, ended the cycle of reincarnation; she got to stay in heaven for eternity, offering a helping hand to us mortals still mired in desire and karma. She never seemed to have worn psychic armor. What a courageous girl.

There in that apartment, my interior life tumbled out into the open.

I had always striven to see the universal messages and continuities between faiths. Here, the Buddha and Christ held posts on either side of my kitchen and let my inner babble pour out into the room. I took a sip of coffee and looked down.

The bread baker had arrived. He had the figure of a man who taste-tested all his creations, several times, for quality control. He was the paradox of the French Paradox. He had a basket full of *chocolatines*, those buttery croissant-like creations elsewhere in France called *pain au chocolat*, with a brick of dark chocolate slowly melting in the middle. I could smell them through the glass.

Desire is a hard illusion to overcome when it comes in three dimensions with sensory enhancement. Not yet dressed or ready to go down and fetch a *chocolatine* — though the thought of lowering a basket out the window filled with coins did occur to me — I controlled desire a little longer, sipped my coffee, and looked up and across at the second stained glass window.

It told a local story, that of Saint Bernard of Clairevaux's visit to Sarlat in 1147 when he cured the populace of a plague with bread. "Eat this bread and you will be cured," were his approximate words. When a local priest said, "Believe and eat and you will be cured," Saint Bernard corrected him. "No, I said, 'eat and you will be cured.' There is no need for belief. They'll be cured." People did and they were. His faith was enough for everyone.

Apparently, the enigmatic tower, the lanterne des morts, that stands just behind the cathedral's apse — like a Buddhist stuppa towering to heaven with the flow of divine blessings — was built in his honor. Others say the lanterne des morts was a medieval funerary building, holding a lit candle after someone died in order to help guide their soul to the light and to heaven. Reinforcing this claim, tombs have been found all around it, but then, tombs are often found near holy sites because they offer prime real estate for those desiring the waft of perpetual prayer for the soul of the deceased. What was clear is that it was a holy site.

I looked closely at Saint Bernard's bread in the window. That did it. The desire to go down and bite into a *chocolatine* became the single strongest desire of the morning. It would be my first bread of Sarlat. If it afforded healing powers, *tant mieux*, so much the better.

The third window would have to wait.

I flew down the stairs so quickly that I forgot about the tall top step and my left hip plunged deeply before I caught myself for the remaining descent. Nadiya had told me that the top step was often called *attrape le voleur*, catch the thief. One false step and an intruder — or *chocolatine*-crazed visitor — would tumble to their death, or at least make so much noise as to be found out.

In truth that step was the result of the old style of building in the fifteenth century: a builder would make general measurements and then start from the bottom, cutting and placing the steps. By the time he reached the top, the measurements were usually a little off and that last step compensated for the rest and came out a little taller or a little shorter than the others.

Having plunged, adrenaline was pumping and I was now truly ready for that buttery cocoa croissant. I pulled on the heavy blue wooden door and a gust of wind finished the task. A brooding storm hovered and built momentum, as if the day before had been mere practice. Merchants still continued to set up in the Place du Peyrou. They reminded me of the hardiness of the merchants in Berlin's open air markets, setting up every week, all winter, no matter if it snowed or the temperatures plummeted well below freezing.

The pretty brunette fishmonger with strong brown eyes and a broad smile greeted me. She was dressed in a heavy brown fleece and olive-toned rubber boots and was surprised to find an inhabitant in the building near her ice. I cast my gaze upon her fish and alighted upon a tray of white anchovies marinating in herbs, lemon, and olive oil. Real white anchovies. I secured a hundred grams and moved on to her neighbor to her left, a boisterous cheese seller with a fast grin whose laugh cut across the small square quicker than the hurricane's wind when someone made her laugh. And the baker across the way made her laugh a lot. I wondered if her cheese and his bread ever got together.

Her cheese case was arrayed with varieties of creamy little hockey puck disks from the outlying region and I knew more research needed to be done. I felt a pang. My heart was already registering the future pain of departure and the hope of return. How did that happen so quickly?

From the cheese lady I purchased two small pungent disks of fresh goat cheese, *cabécou*, "from Rocamadour," she added with a knowing look, as if the nearby Black Madonna, Our Lady of Rocamadour, personally took it upon herself to infuse the herbs the goats ate on that magical mountain with divine luminosity. Here I was in a secular country, and yet on merely one cup of coffee, I already had Saint Philomena, Saint Bernard, and now Our Lady floating about my mind. I moved deeper into the square.

To the cheese seller's other side was a man with walnut oil and bundles of shallots. The oils were pressed from nuts from nearby walnut orchards after having been slowly roasted, offering forth a toasty amber-colored liquid. Beyond him, at the other end of the small square was a tall Dutch woman, with long blond hair piled atop her head like a Parisian *femme fatale*, who sold hard cheeses, a complementary offering to the soft cheeses of Our Lady. In her case was a six-month cured cheese from the Pyrenees with black specks from the local truffle. My mouth watered and behind her I heard a low, welcoming bark. It was the Dutch lady's golden lab, and he sat in his own waterproof doggie tent. He was the meet-and-greet committee of the two, and he offered welcoming woofs to friendly two- and four-leggeds as they passed. More cheese and my pannier took on the promise of a good still life in the making.

All that splendor was unfolding but a few meters to my left as I emerged from my blue front door on rue Montaigne into my own little cathedral square so full of life. I then turned to my right to meet the apple seller and his dozen varieties of *pommes* in all shapes, sizes, and colors, from pale yellow to fresh green to deep red.

And finally, a few steps away from the apples, right in front of me, at last, was the baker and his bread. I took in his big wheels of earth-toned rustic breads, his long, crusty baguettes, his raisin Danishes, and *en fin*, at the very end of the table, his warm *chocolatines*. I greeted him and greedily purchased two along with a raisin Danish and a rustic baguette. I unabashedly bit into a *chocolatine* as I turned toward the Place de la Liberté, Sarlat's main medieval square. Warm dark chocolate and butter melted on my tongue. The wind picked up.

The two squares, Peyrou and Liberté, stand near each other. A small cobblestone passageway filled with truffle and foie gras shops led the way from one to the other. I took it and stepped toward the larger public square. It was filled with colorful umbrellas, golden stone pavement, and sweeping amber-colored limestone buildings from the twelfth to the eighteenth centuries, hearkening to a town that recovered over and over from wars and pestilence to flourish as a regional center. This was why the town symbol was *la salamandre*, the salamander, a creature fabled with regenerative skills that emerged from fire again and again hale and hearty and ready for another spin in life. The Place de la Liberté was punctuated in the center by the town hall and surrounded by cafés, shops, and more stone passageways rising and falling into and out of the square like a beach blanket in the wind.

As I finished my bread, I stopped at the plaza's gateway, letting my eyes adjust to the animated feast of shoppers and vendors buying and selling local foods. I wanted to absorb the lay of the land. I also was looking for the telltale signs of the black truffle market, a specialized market within a market.

Nadiya had mentioned that the truffle market, operating in sync with Sarlat's Saturday market, was in full swing from November to February. Once in my life I beheld a whole, precious black truffle in person. It had been a Christmas gift to a Philadelphia foodie friend from her foodie husband. She had stored it carefully in a container of rice, waiting for the auspicious moment when she located the best recipe in which to apply the black gold. She carefully lifted it out from the rice grains and let me inhale its musty scent, an oddly seductive smell of sweaty-locker-room-meets-crème-brulée-and-hyacinths. It took possession of me for reasons I could not rationalize. I had no good explanation why an object that looked like a dried dog turd would make my mouth water while simultaneously evoking images of passionate kisses stolen in dark passageways.

Sarlat is the heart center of the Périgord Noir. The Périgord—the older name for the Dordogne—is further divided into four subregions that have color names: *Pourpre*, *Blanc*, *Vert*, and *Noir*. Each identify different nuances that respectively define its four corners, from Bergerac (wine country) to Périgueux (limestone plateaus) to Nontron (green valleys overflowing with chestnuts and heather) to Sarlat (dark evergreen oak forests and undulating hills with rich fertile earth). Here in Noir country I was also in the presence of another serious noir: black truffle country. Noir on noir. I had landed in the homeland of that seductive dung-like fungus, and I wanted to smell it at its roots. And maybe, just maybe, purchase one and take it back to Le Chardon and let it seduce me in the kitchen.

I stepped into the square. At the same time, farther west, a hurricane-like storm touched down in Galicia, strafed its forests and took down half the old pine trees that surrounded the shrine dedicated to San Roque on the hilltop. Fishermen were lost at sea. From there, it moved east to southern France and flattened the pine forests along the Atlantic coastline of Les Landes. As those winds were rushing inland toward us, I wrapped my rain parka more tightly around me and dived into the Place de la Liberté where the majority of the market vendors anchored their canopies and carried on commerce without skipping a beat.

I saw one of the organic farmers that Nadiya had marked on the map. He cheerily greeted passersby as if it were a sunny day as wind and rain whipped back his already wet gray-speckled brown hair and sun-dried wrinkles. Immense piles of just-harvested winter spinach tumbled over the back of his truck. I purchased a large bundle, received his recipe for sautéed spinach with *lardón*—that crazy French-style bacon cut into thick match sticks to sauté with anything that demanded smoky, fat flavor—and then moved on to the next organic farmer, a grumpy organic lady who cheered up when I gave her exact change for her robust carrots with their green tops still attached. I then moved on to a big stand right in front of the town hall ruled by a flirty male brunette with a classic Périgordine full mustache with wing shaped tips that flew off the side of each cheek. He was the happier sidekick as with his partner they played a game of good cop bad cop with an elderly woman who was maneuvering to talk down their artichoke prices. The brunette joked while the other merchant looked sore and insulted. They finally settled on a price, lobbed a few colorful jokes at the woman's expense, which she took gracefully for she had just saved a healthy handful of centimes, and looked at me expectantly.

I gulped but pushed out of my mouth verbs and nouns that resulted in my becoming well endowed with ethereal oval red-white radishes, rainwater-glistening chanterelle mushrooms, various herbs, endive, clementines, and shallots. I didn't dare bargain. It was just sinking in that one of their off-color jokes at the lady's expense, a woman twenty years their senior, had something to do with her wearing them out in other places too, the *boudoir* being heavily implied.

My pannier swelled. The still life was ready for my countertops. I set it down to tighten my hood and scan the glistening golden stones of the large square for a vendor of the famous dry-cured duck breast, when the primal scent of rutting nailed me between the brows. I looked at the market man and his mustache and I blushed. When I recovered, I got to the business of tracking down the scent like any self-respecting dog or pig of the Périgord.

It came from my right. I turned and followed, and there, in big black lettering on a banner over a storefront, were the words to the illicit but legal magical kingdom: *Marché des truffes*.

The truffle market was housed in a dry, protective space, a storefront with large picture windows on a prominent corner on the main square. As I opened the door and stepped in, several things happened at once: my eyeglasses fogged over; I felt the warm, lurid scent of truffles; and five hands pushed the goods toward my nose before I could orient to the direction of their owners, each holding a truffle and saying, "*Venez*, come, sniff mine. See for yourself the superior quality. *Non, venez*, sniff mine ... here ... "

I suddenly understood what it felt like to be a new dog entering a popular dog park. This may not have been quite as intimate as the greeting dogs offer, but the gesture felt as intimate, as if my nose was being presented with the most seductive private parts a nose could be offered. As the five saucy sellers enticed me with their dark clusters, my reptilian brain took over and swooned in the thick air. I became a player. I perused and sniffed each attentive and extended hand. To my novice nose, they were all superb. How did I proceed from there? I didn't want to skim the periphery or be a tease; I wanted to go home with one of them, the *truffes*, that is. I inhaled and blindly dived in, letting my intuitive feel settle on a woman in a quilted vest and thick, cable-knit, wool sweater and curly, black hair that was growing curlier in the musty air. She had dark eyes and a sweeping smile that made me relax enough to inquire, flirt as foodies do to learn more, and ultimately purchase a good little *truffe*.

She had three baskets of truffles of different sizes and qualities. I quickly learned that I could get a small, experimental truffle without going into debt. I sidled up and sniffed some more, chatted amiably with her as her husband stood back and smiled. I finally committed to a little black gem the size of a small walnut in its shell for seven euros. Though it was of average grade, it smelled great and looked good, as far as turds can look: well-formed and solid with a consistently strong black color and a clear vein pattern.

As I paid and she handed me my little prize in a small, brown, paper sack with the picture of a truffle stamped on the outside, I realized I knew nothing about the care and feeding of my new specimen. How do I store it? When do I cook it? How and what do I cook?

"Your truffle," she explained, "will peak in a couple days. Don't cook with it until Monday, and then be sure to use it within the next two to three days. Store it with your eggs in the carton on the kitchen counter." (Eggs don't get refrigerated in France. It reminded me of my year in Morocco where many of my friends didn't have a refrigerator and did not need one. Their eggs sat on the counter and all their food was purchased daily from markets similar to this one. It was one of the things I loved about living abroad — learning what others deemed necessary and unnecessary from my own familiar life.) I made a mental note not to forget to buy eggs before the market folded.

The dark-eyed lady then smiled. "Listen, a truffle will make anything taste good, but it is best to handle it with simplicity."

"What are your two favorite recipes?" I asked.

She licked her lips. "My absolute favorite is to scramble eggs and grate the truffle—the entire truffle—on top. My second favorite is sliced thinly and layered on toast with foie gras."

I licked my lips. "And the wine?" I forgot to be nervous about speaking French. There was something about talking about food that relaxed the mind and opened the language skills. It helped to have passionate and amiable folks with whom to speak.

Her husband jumped into the conversation. Wine was a more manly discussion. "Any good red wine," he said, "a good strong red." He made a muscle gesture with his upper arm. His wife nodded, her eyes glistening. The air thickened with pheromones.

Before I left, I was dying to know how they gathered their truffles, how they knew they were ready for market. This time the husband and wife fused and finished each other's sentences in a rush of enthusiastic love-making.

"The dog will tell you," said he, hands both opening to the sky as if receiving divine grace.

"He just knows," said she, left hand sweeping left as if it is an act of fate, something to trust.

"Simply from its smell . . . " he went on.

"It has a certain fragrance, you know . . . " She smiled.

"When it is finally ripe . . . " He.

"Ready to eat..." She.

"You can find truffles in the spring too but..."

"...they get more concentrated and mature in winter."

They paused. The wife then smiled, individuated again, and added, "You know, I have a third favorite recipe: Fresh tagliatelle tossed with butter, fresh cracked black pepper—not too much—and the grated truffle."

I was undone. My mental note grew longer: Eggs, red wine, butter, tagliatelle, and then home to a porcine feast. We had peaked.

I do not recall how I managed to stay upright and leave the truffle market. The heavy truffle scent had intensified, and clear cognitive activity was impossible. But once I did exit, the whipping rain slapped me back to my senses, and I managed to finish my shopping right before the storm arrived in earnest. All the while I coddled my new truffle in its brown paper wrapping like a newborn infant.

The market folded early. I hunkered down in Le Chardon. Once safely behind the big blue door, the skies opened again and dumped buckets of rain all night. The wind rattled the windows. I closed the shutters early because the sun was invisible in the swirl of menace and gray that lurched in the streets above and below. Businesses closed, cafés shut down, and no one left the warmth and protection of their homes.

Holed up in my own new home, I contemplated my visceral experience from the market. It had revealed the town's personality: people here were not harried nor overstretched for time like so many of us in the United States. The people of Sarlat, the Sarladais, also did not have the underlying suspicion of outsiders I'd experienced in Galicia. They were warm and welcoming, interested in the newcomer, and remarkably international in their outlook, even that pipsqueak lettuce man who only spoke to me in Occitan and inspired me to try harder. And they had all made a decision to be here. Some came to Sarlat as adults, others decided to stay after birth and freewill kicked in. There was something in this society unlike any other I'd visited. I could already feel it. It seemed to be happiness, real, rooted happiness.

There was another balance here: of humans and nature, nature and nature, humans and humans. People lived by the seasons and close to the land. And the land was profound. It was deep, ancient, and ancestral. One truffle hunter in the market had alluded to it, joking that Cro-Magnon clearly was a gourmand for settling here. He was tapping into the reality locals here lived, that there was a viscerally daily and direct connection to Cro-Magnons and Neandertals via the land and how people still lived on it.

I couldn't wait for the storm to pass and to go back out into this new Old World. I already loved this little town. With two markets a week, I could test drive some of these market theories on Wednesday. And in between there were other adventures and mind-expanding experiences to invite into my life. I swooned in this waking dream, of having at last found a vibrant society and wildly ancient landscape, a place that at last could meet these desires and so openly take me in.

I decided that as soon as the storm died down and life in Sarlat resumed its public activities, I was going to scour the town for those signs of the spiritually inclined that the obscure academic article promised was here. My own spiritual journey had just deepened and this made me hungrier to find the external signs, which naively I assumed looked like other spiritually-inclined places, with New Age book stores, crystal shops, tarot readers, neoshamans performing rituals in the caves. Right?

Night fell. The winds grew stronger. I covetously stared at and sniffed my truffle. Two days? As desire again did its dance of I-want-it-now versus the sweetness of delayed gratification, I received a call from Nadiya. Was everything fine? Had I closed the shutters? It looked like we were in for a really big storm. Once it blew over, one day next week, did I want to meet her for coffee at her favorite pastry shop? Yes, yes, and definitely, yes.

Then she asked the question that the lady from the B&B up the street ominously said Nadiya would ask. "Would you like to come to my badminton club and learn to play?" I shrugged off the B&B lady's warning of pulled hamstrings, sore muscles, and compromised moments. She knew Nadiya was always looking for new victi—, that is, partners.

I should have been nervous, wondered why, but instead, I thought of the chance to meet locals and to work off the calories from that favorite shop, and the *chocolatine*, and the butter-coated tagliatelle, not to mention future follies with foie gras. It also was a break from the norm for me. All the sports I went for were solitary — surfing, running, hiking, and yoga. Badminton was going to require group cooperation, an understanding of the rules, and most frightening of all, a command of action French. Nadiya, content she'd found a new guinea pig, changed the subject quickly and instead gave me the address of the pastry shop, and hung up. •

Olives at the Sarlat Market

Chapter 3

VORTEXES AND OLIVES

I tried to get used to that particular sensuous scent during the year I lived in Morocco, where a pass through a market or grocery store alike would offer up some thirty-six varieties of olives. Here it was again. Here, in a place nothing like Morocco. Here, in a place that was using my sense of smell like a family photo album, calling me home one smell at a time.

THE STORM TOUCHED DOWN. IT UPROOTED TREES AND tossed them helter-skelter everywhere. Many roads were temporarily blocked. The next morning I peeped out of the apartment during a brief lull in the wind, clouds, and rain, and ran to a little café down the street that had opened only briefly to serve up coffee and company. I ordered a café crème and listened in as locals marveled over how little damage occurred in spite of the strewn trees. Reports of havoc and destruction were pouring in from coastal Les Landes, where whole forests were flattened along with people's homes. They speculated that it was the undulating hills around Sarlat that protected us.

Those hills were hard to nail down. They were like the shifting staircases at Hogwarts' School of Witchcraft and Wizardry. Each day they appeared to have moved, innocently looking on as if they'd been in their new position for an eternity. That hard-to-conceive landscape with its many hills at odd angles and varied heights helped to break the storm's wind, to slow it down, so that by the time it rushed across Aquitaine to undo us, we undid it. But not before damage to trees and homes of proportions hitherto unseen here.

Others added to the hill theory, saying that the special energy of this land, the sacred vortexlike energy, protected us. Locals also said that His Holiness the Dalai Lama chose the Dordogne as a place to live if he ever needed to leave Dharamsala, in Himachal Pradesh, India. This led to the speculation, one that locals had felt for a long time, that this place had good vibes, maybe was a power spot, and truly a good place to be.

And there it was, that spiritual vein I had been seeking. While I tried to find outward signs of a spiritual movement — New Age stores selling crystals, incense, or pagan amulets; pamphlets distributed throughout town; or any of the other usual signs of a spiritual movement in a place — here instead it was in the people, in café conversations, a part of the daily folklore and life of the place. It was low key and real and this fact made it feel even more real. I also knew I had to give it time. I knew it was here in deep roots. I could feel something in the earth itself, blatantly telling me a strong old sacred vein ran through this land and drew people to it.

I left the café and walked to the small grocery store for a few more provisions. Run by a high-strung couple, the wife had that middle-age, middle-class French woman's style, with frosted blond and black, fashionably short hair, gel-spiked in places for drama. She had the favored French designer glasses, with wiry angles that also strove for accentuating drama around the eyes. I liked this fashion. An eyeglass-dependent person myself, for whom contact lenses are eye torture from the past, I could easily embrace a culture that turns a necessity into a sassy accessory.

Behind her eyeglasses were eyes that could throw darts. My French faltered when I went in, but all she would offer me was a *bonjour* and an *au revoir*, so in a sense I was safe. Her husband was a little more forthcoming, but not much. It felt as if Madame kept a tight reign on her domain.

A bottle of Pecharmant, a bag of organic tagliatelle, a block of butter, and oh, what's this, a jar of wild cèpes in truffle sauce? Wild porcini in truffle sauce? Really? Yes, that too, and a liter of milk, and I headed back to Le Chardon well endowed as more gray clouds heavy with rain gathered on the horizon and swiftly flew nearer in a darker, slate-colored sky.

I put my groceries away and eyed my truffle with one day left to peak and was glad, in spite of the B&B lady's warnings, that I had signed on for badminton with Nadiya. I had left the world of olive oil behind and entered one thick with duck fat, cream, and butter.

I slept deeply again that night and the next, and the next. I did not awaken to a ghostly visitor or recall what I dreamt. But early Wednesday morning I woke up thinking about the Dalai Lama and about the possibility of earth vibes and power vortexes. I sat up and looked at the Buddha on the mantle, and at the same moment heard the swish and shovel of the fishmonger. I opened the shutters to a dark, pre-dawn morning on the Place du Peyrou.

At last the string of heavy, stormy weather passed. People were already busy setting up down below for the Wednesday market. I quickly splashed water on my face, dressed, and skipped down the stairs, not noticing the extra lunge of the top one, as if in the span of five days my body had already written the map of this place into its pacing.

I purchased a chocolatine from the paradox's paradox-figured baker and made a mental note that I'd have to back off his buttery bakes soon. But not today. I then entered the main market space and took a seat and a café crème at an outdoor table in a café on the square. As my coffee steamed and the rays of a warming sun splashed across happy market goers, another nostalgic scent assaulted me.

Olives. A thousand varieties, I was sure. It was a seductive pull, different from truffles that clobbered you over the head with pheromones. Olives like these were like a silk robe over a naked body just out from the bathhouse, clean, scrubbed, and skin bright and alive. I tried to get used to that particular sensuous scent during the year I lived in Morocco, where a pass through a market or grocery store alike would offer up some thirty-six varieties of olives. Here it was again. Here, in a place nothing like Morocco. Here, in a place that was using my sense of smell like a family photo album, calling me home one smell at a time.

I finished my coffee and followed the new trail. It took me to a stand rife with color. There stood a handsome man in his sixties wearing a broad black fedora and a broad smile. A red winter scarf wrapped about his neck, he picked up a spoon and offered me a taste of the long, moss green olives my eyes first set upon.

"This is the Lucque olive. My wife drives everywhere for the best. They are from northern Italy." I took the offering. Its meaty and lush flavor gave me courage to try out my new French verbs, interspersed like the flecks of herbs on the olives, with nouns, prepositions, adverbs, and adjectives.

"*Je voudrais*, I would like, a small sack, *un petit sac*, of these, please, and the black ones, *à la Grecque*," said the tag. He waited patiently, smiling all the while, a warm smile, one that spoke of friends already met.

"*Pas sac*," he said, "*poche*. You mean to say *poche, une petite poche.*"

A little pocket. I liked the way he corrected me; it was kind and sincere and the only way I'd ever improve my French. "And *une petite poche* of the piquante, too, *s'il vous plait*." Clever boy. French lessons loosened my purse strings.

He bagged the little pockets, and as he handed them to me asked, "Where are you from?"

"*Je suis une Américaine*," I uttered confidently, nailing the last "n" with a flourish. Wasn't that the first sentence I'd ever learned in French?

That elicited a big grin, which was already stunning, but then he suddenly switched to perfect English and said, "I learned to speak English from Texans in Saudi Arabia. They were a lot of fun."

Texans? Saudi Arabia? Exactly who was this olive seller in the Dordogne?

Jean, he explained. Jean from Greece. *À la Grecque*. Jean was from the island where *Captain Corelli's Mandolin* was filmed. But truly, he grew up in Istanbul and loved all things Turkish, except that he loved all things Persian even more.

I told Jean that in my experience, he was a very odd Greek, which seemed to delight him rather than offend. In graduate school in Philadelphia, I spent a year eating in a dining hall near my graduate student housing that catered mostly to law students, and my table was often the one where all the exchange students from law schools in Greece gathered. They didn't know what to make of the Iranian-American anthropologist who knew very little about law but a whole lot about obscure things that people do with culture. Comfortable in their group feeling, they often liked to remind me that Alexander the Great conquered Persia. One day, in a pissy mood myself, I shot back that Persia conquered him, that he married a Persian, and that for

Iranians the fact of marriage claimed Alexander as Persian from there on out. This made them irate. How dare I mess with their history! They had no sense of humor whatsoever, and as much as I was giving them their own medicine back, and with more levity than they dealt it out, what I naively didn't know is you don't mess with other people's identity, especially people who insist on asserting a very defined and certain one.

So Jean sort of caught me off guard. I was ready to be reminded of how the Spartans kicked Persian butt, but instead, I'd met someone who longed to be on the other team. I told him that was a very interesting perspective, and for the record, my parents were Iranian, and though I had been born and raised in the USA, north of Texas — so I therefore knew that the English he learned was colorful and idiomatic — I also grew up speaking Farsi — Persian — thankfully, because my parents both spoke it at home. For the first five years of my little life, I actually thought that English and Farsi were one language, not two. I was narrowly rescued from special education classes when one astute teacher noticed that my classmates were learning my alien gibberish mixed with English, which to his ear sounded more like another language than a learning disability.

Apparently, the two languages in my head also made me slow to learn to read and write. With a good tutor and time, I learned to sort out my one intimate language into two public ones and to read and write in English. (Curiously, that was around the time my grandfather began teaching himself English so that he could write me letters telling me how important it was to learn to read and write Farsi. In that hard-working gesture, he taught me he was not a hypocrite, that he would push his agenda on my turf, through my language and culture.)

Jean's smile managed to grow wider and exceeded the wide rim of his fedora. "My wife Petrus is running errands, but when she comes back, I want her to meet you. If she likes you, we're taking you home." He then quickly added, "for lunch," to be sure I didn't misunderstand.

As we waited he explained that he had been an oil engineer and work had taken him and Petrus all over the world. In Saudi Arabia, they had the best time. They loved the classical Arab culture, they loved the contact with the rowdy, flamboyant Texans, and they loved restoring antiques they'd find in bric-a-brac markets.

Petrus arrived a few minutes later. I'd never seen a person embody perpetual motion as much as she did. She was the Eveready Bunny with Swan Lake and Kermit the Frog wrapped into one, ever moving, this way and that, grace, energy, elegance, and fun bouncing off each movement. She chatted away, her graying, long blond hair swishing this way and that as she switched between French, English, Dutch, German, and Spanish to the international flow of olive, spice, and dried fruit customers. We liked each other immediately. They were taking me home.

We arranged that I would return to their stand on Saturday when the market folded and drive with them to their place. We would make lunch in their walk-in fireplace in the medieval stone farmhouse they restored together. Jean wanted to talk about Persian mystical poetry. Petrus had a few things to tell me about the spirit and energy of the land. I would also meet Minicat and Ferdinand, added Petrus, the famous feline progeny of their former cat, Isabel.

"A house is not a home without cats or dogs," she said, and added, "but cats are better. They keep the rodents in check and look after themselves if you need to go somewhere overnight." We shook hands and with these parting words echoing in my head, I went deeper into the Wednesday market and pinched myself.

Was I dreaming? I was giddy with the realization that soon I would attend a real farmcountry lunch here in the Dordogne. And before that, I had coffee and badminton with Nadiya and the beginning of explorations in the Périgord's prehistoric caves. I secretly began to idealize Cro-Magnon, thinking he was one clever boy to have made this place his home.

Back at Le Chardon, I boiled water and threw in the fresh tagliatelle as I sautéed a minced shallot in butter, salt, and pepper. I threw in a splash of dry white Bergerac wine and let it reduce. I then added cream and at last added the coveted black truffle thinly sliced, folding it in and tossing it all with the pasta.

I uncorked the bottle of Pecharmant red, plated up my creamy dish, opened my balcony window, and sat and savored the visceral, full immersion of living in the Périgord, from its physical fungal roots to its lofty spires of the medieval cathedral outside my window, nailed down with a glass of wine.

I was fully alive. I was fully visible. I was fully engaged. I was fully unarmored. I was experiencing my life on an entirely new level. I was in love with the place that did this to me. Sarlat. I could now even say the "r" then the "l" without losing one in the other, and even without sounding too handicapped, drunk, or swollen-tongued. It felt like a homerun. Home. •

Café Oc

Chapter 4

CAFÉ OC

With its ancient caves and thick, dark, mysterious forests, this place is special. The people here are special because they take an interest in everything and engage everyone, even me. Here, it's as if the place cultivates the people and the people cultivate the place. Everything, land and people, feels whole and healthy. I have to find out why it suits me so well to be here.

I CLIMBED UP THE NARROW MEDIEVAL COBBLESTONE passageway in Sarlat-la-Canéda's historic center and saw my destination, Café Lébérou, at the precipice just as a blast of frigid wind whipped through the streets and stung my face and froze my breath. I sucked in the cold air and wondered why I hadn't stayed home, nice and warm, on this glacial winter's night.

Because, I said to myself, as I gripped in frozen fingers the newspaper page with its little square ad at the bottom right, I had to find out what Café Oc was. The ad said, "Café Oc, the next monthly meeting to speak Occitan is at the Café Lébérou. The participants will enjoy sharing little histories, whether true or not, from today, yesterday, and even *d'un cop éra*. All who are interested are cordially invited." That one phrase stumped me until after several Google searches, during which I repeatedly had to insist it not change the spelling to *coup* or to *etat*, a Catalan source translated it as "once was." Interesting, I thought. From a time that once was? Once upon a time? Occitan and Catalan were pretty close and here this Romance language was alive and well all across southern France, not just on the Mediterranean side but also the Atlantic. And here it was, a little square ad inviting me to the beginning of a fairytale. That doesn't happen often so I pushed on against the brittle wind toward the café at the top of the hill.

The café's name also held Occitan nuance. It was named after a legendary animal of the Périgord. Depending on who you asked — and I had asked a few people by now and they all had a serious opinion — the lébérou was half-man and half-hyena, or a rough-and-tumble hairy man wearing the fur of a creature with a rabbit's head and the body of a wolf. He was not quite a werewolf, though his tendencies and temperament had similarities. He tore across forests on full moon nights when his nature surfaced, but he didn't kill. Instead, he troubled, he trickstered, and he disrupted the peace.

He could also be a she, local lore acknowledging that women as much as men could have a wild, smelly side. And yes, he or she didn't smell so good and was in such a rush to maximize the full madness of the moon that if you ran across the lébérou on its rampages, you'd risk becoming a mule to the wild human who would jump on your back and demand that you carry him or her for the rest of the night from one place of havoc to the next.

There is only one way to break the lébérou's predicament. He or she, or you if you've been lassoed into transport, must visit seven churches and ring each of their bells within the span of the evening before sunrise. If you so succeed, the lébérou will snap out of its curse. If you've already imagined those undulating hills and little valley pockets and large swaths of dark forest around Sarlat where villages huddle with their churches, you can appreciate that no one as of yet has managed such a journey in one night to seven such places, especially not with an odorous, hairy, wild human on their back. But seven is an interesting number, an old mystical number that smells of fairy dust and magic.

As I searched for the meeting place and thought about its name, I knew this much: the lébérou was not someone I wanted to meet on this particular night, nor on this partially lit street in midwinter where dark shadows and ice reached too closely from engulfing stone walls. It would be a long, cold night for me if I did, and it was a perfect night for him, or her, to be out.

But then I saw the café. Its light and mirth poured out from its windows and onto the cold and dark and dispelled my icy thoughts and invited me in. I pushed the door open and at once warmth and a boisterous chorus of greetings rushed at me. *"Benvengudu au Café Oc!"*

My God, they were just like that old man on the train station hill in his warm, dry, cream sweater from my first day. I looked around and saw that ten other people had come out from their warm homes on this chilly night for the sheer purpose of speaking Occitan, the ancient Romance language of the region. They called their circle Café Oc.

Oc is the word for yes in Occitan, the language that got officially bumped by those maneuvering northerners who say *oui* when they mean yes. Through a long, complicated process beginning in the Middle Ages and finalized in nineteenth-century politics, *oui* finally trumped *oc*, but in the south, no one had forgotten. They know, and are happy to tell you, that the reason the north wanted to dominate the south was because they are more interesting down south. Their food is better. Their wine is superior. (Don't try to debate the merits of Burgundy in Bordeaux country if you want to leave a party early.) Their culture is more colorful. They laugh and they joke. And they have sunshine and that special light. And here, in the southwest, they have Neandertals and Cro-Magnons, two early humans who declared this the best place to live in Europe, giving it the Most Beautiful Caves designations from their prehistoric press people. And up to World War I, dialects of Occitan were the mother tongue of most French people south of Limoges.

I looked around the room and realized I was the youngest by about a decade and a half. I apologized to them that I didn't speak a stitch of Occitan but hoped that between my Spanish and efforts in learning French, I might understand a little and learn. They assured me that I would get the hang of things because Occitan was related to both. A kind woman in her sixties came and sat to my left and patiently and slowly translated everything from Occitan into French for me for the rest of the evening.

We sat in a circle and introduced ourselves while Franck, the café owner and a local man who'd grown up with parents and grandparents who spoke Occitan at home, came around and took our drink orders. We were farmers, homemakers, business people, artists, and builders. All but the homemakers and artists were retired. Homemakers and artists don't retire, they quipped. All had grown up with an intimate experience of Occitan, be it their parents or their grandparents who spoke it exclusively at home as the first language. One woman grew up when Occitan was forbidden and came to it as an adult. Another had lived in Catalonia for several years and said how easy it was to go from Occitan to Catalan. Another added that Occitan takes on added color in Gascony further south where people in the countryside speak a patois of Occitan and Basque. Now, young people study it in school but don't speak it or find an application for it unless they are working with older folks in the countryside.

When we finished these preliminaries, everyone looked at me, and everyone had the same question. Why was an Iranian-American writer interested in speaking Occitan, and what was I thinking of coming here in winter, the worst season to be here? Didn't I know the season begins in April?

The season referred to when the population swells here, when tourists from all over the world come to see Sarlat's extraordinarily well-preserved medieval section that had been featured already in over fifty historic films; to visit the famous nearby prehistoric painted and engraved caves, such as Lascaux and Font de Gaume, and the stunning twelve-hundred-plus castles and châteaux; to eat roasted duck, cured duck, duck confit, foie gras, black truffles, and walnut cake; and to imbibe as much Bergerac and Bordeaux white, rosé, and red as possible. So why on earth had I picked winter to be here when everything was gray, dark, wet, cold, and mostly closed?

Well, answering that last question was easy, so I began there. Winter, I explained, was the season I was already here. I had just come from northwestern Spain. I had picked that town, as this one, in part, because it was on one of the pilgrimage roads to Santiago de Compostela, one of the tributaries of the Way of Saint James. To me, the Way is one great big smiley face that splashes across southern France and northern Spain. It's my favorite place on earth. It makes me smile to think of it. It had become a primary mission to live on it. I skipped the long story of how I picked Sarlat — and how it picked me — and returned to why winter.

Winter, I told the gathered crowd now sipping beer, wine, coffee, tea, and juices that Franck had placed in our hands, was the one time of year when local life came to the surface, when locals themselves, living in a town of six thousand, weren't overtaken and hidden by the mind-boggling bulge of over two million visitors a year, mostly from March through October. It was the perfect time for a writer to learn about real local life. And I'd discovered that local life here was profound, intact, unaltered by the virtual and fast-paced modern world. It was a region that had never been industrialized, and life was still lived close to the land.

The group smiled at this. They seemed to appreciate that I had tapped into what made their region special. But not to be distracted, they waited and held a pregnant silence that demanded I answer the other whys that preceded winter.

I realized that night that here the art of conversation was still wedded to the art of listening. As gifted listeners waited, I knew I would not get off the hook as usual and be able to brush past cause and effect. And, I'd have to do it with newly birthing French and stabs at non-existent Occitan.

I felt the answers were in layers further down, so I began to dig toward the roots and I began to travel in time. This went back, much farther back, beyond the decades of donning and shedding of armor.

As a child, ancient things fascinated me. The older, the better. The bigger the mystery, the more exciting. Born and raised in the Rocky Mountains and the child of Iranian parents who had immigrated there in 1960, I grew up in a milieu that spanned ancient Colorado to ancient Iran. My childhood included seventy-million-year-old seabed fossils and remnants of the Clovis and Folsom cultures going back some 12,000 years, as well as the realm of ancient Persia, the old crossroads of the East and West and the homeland of the world's first farmers about 10,000 years ago. In a strange sense, this heritage of two vastly different but equally magical places turned me into a time-traveling, semi-nomadic character in adult life, perhaps just like Cro-Magnon.

Every three or four years in the 1960s and 1970s we would spend the summer visiting relatives in Tehran. Like going to the summer pasture, my mother, brother, and I would be there for over three months, and my father would visit during his two-week-a-year vacation from work. There I would hear stories of the Turkmen and the Qashqai, along with other nomadic Iranian peoples, and how they had been forced to settle down because a population on the move, one without a permanent settlement, was hard to control and, even worse for officialdom, nearly impossible to tax.

I began to form romantic ideas in my mind of being a Qashqai girl, knowing also that Qashqai women were remarkably self-determined and empowered. I also lamented what I called the end of nomadism, deeply saddened by their forced settlement at the hands of bullying modern nation states. It had to have been torture when the open horizon and its possibilities were encoded in your blood.

I felt the echo of desire for the open horizon in my own blood. Sometimes it would hit when I saw a shepherd pass with his sheep down the narrow streets of my grandparents' neighborhood in Tehran heading to some unknown pasture beyond the city. Often I felt it when we journeyed to villages and towns in the northern mountains and along the Caspian Sea's coastline, encountering a diverse array of peoples in whose eyes I could often see traces of the distant horizon, indicating a recent past connected one way or another to the old nomadic ways.

In Colorado, what I saw as my nomadic winter pasture — most appropriate since winter can last nine months in Colorado — also held ancient traces of a semi-nomadic way of life. Colorado had become the necessary recipient of Native Americans fleeing the incursions of Europeans from the east. Much earlier, it had also held the bones and art forms of the ancient ancestors of those same peoples, reminding them and us of the ancient migratory routes across the Bering Strait, following game and new horizons well over 13,000 years ago.

Why, when I left that fishing village in Spain and landed three days later in Sarlat, had I felt like being home, grounded, both feet rooted to the earth for the first time in thirty years? Why did I feel this way to the very center of my bones? Why now and why here?

To the elders around me and their expectant silence, I tried to offer a brief, stripped-to-the-bones answer. I went to the root of the bigger story, bigger than I, but still about this place.

"Coming to Sarlat is the first time in all my adult life that I felt all of me fully engaged. Coming here brought everything together for me." I then got a bit woo-woo because I saw people nod, and I saw they expected me to go on. "I feel there's some invisible corridor, a very ancient one that predates the pilgrimage road, one that maybe connects to the original prehistoric peoples who traversed it some 30,000 years ago, that sweeps from southern France into northern Spain, and I feel that Sarlat is at its heart. I feel this place is special. With its ancient caves and thick, dark, mysterious forests, this place is magical. The people here are special because they take an interest in everything and engage everyone, even me. Here, it's as if the place cultivates the people, and the people cultivate the place. Everything, land and people, feels whole and healthy. I have to find out why it suits me so well to be here. And this is the reason I want to speak Occitan."

I was finished. I had gone on too long. But instead of yawning or looking at me like a weirdo from outer space, they nodded and began an animated discussion about all I had just confessed. What I said made perfect sense. Yes, the world out there moves too fast. It has lost its roots. This place is both open-minded and flexible but also deeply connected and nourished by its roots. Yes, of course. We get it, they said collectively, some with words and all with warm smiles and bright engaging eyes.

They nodded and agreed and added that this was also the very same corridor traversed millennia later by medieval pilgrims and troubadours. We all concurred that something rich and inviting to humans existed along that sweep and they kept traversing it, keeping fresh and current the leylines — vibrant, feel-good, invisible earth energy lines —that connected them. How delightful. They were now getting a bit woo-woo too.

No one of Café Oc cared one iota that I didn't speak Occitan. They knew that through exposure, I'd eventually learn. I never wanted to leave this universe. To speak Occitan was to speak a language of the corridor, a language dominating the traditional geography of that smiley face across southern France and northern Spain, with Sarlat at its engaged and vibrant crown.

An eighty-something man, whom I would later consider the ringleader, looked seriously at me and asked in Occitan, "*Perque*, why, if the French president speaks English, the American president doesn't speak French and Occitan?" He waited, willing a grave expression to remain cemented on his face, but a second later the trickster spark raced across his eyes and he burst out laughing, taking everyone else with him. No one expected an answer, and everyone knew the French president didn't speak Occitan; he was a northerner.

The trickster then added, "You know, in Baton Rouge, in your Louisiana, there is also an Occitan-speaking culture, and they say *oc* instead of *oui*. Just so you know, we really like that."

The woman to my left chimed in. "Even so, it might not be possible to understand Baton Rouge's Occitan. The Occitan language in the Périgord has changed so much in each generation that my first two children speak a different dialect from my last three children."

I had heard that there were as many dialects of Occitan as villages in Occitania and wondered about the many larger variations of the language. It is essentially the old language of southern France, still spoken and understood today anywhere south of Limoges and in seemingly infinite dialects. Like French, Spanish, Portuguese, Italian, and Romanian, it is a Romance language based in Latin, but is among those, such as Galégo-Portugais, Asturiano-Léonais, Aragonese, and Catalan, that through political competition and machinations in various times past lost out and was pushed aside from official status. It became more the language of the people, as they could retain it. And they seemed to be successful in doing so, even against all odds.

What is striking about all these marginalized Romance languages is that together they were the languages of song and poetry in the twelfth and thirteenth centuries, interwoven across kingdoms by wandering troubadours. They are beautiful languages, still spoken today in various surviving forms, some with remarkable trends toward resurgence and still strong in the hearts and minds of their speakers. Their modern survival exists in the same places they were spoken during the Middle Ages, creating a sweeping corridor from all along northern Iberia, across the Pyrenees and all across southern France into northern Italy. When you hear these languages today, you can still hear the melodies hearkening back to the music of medieval European minstrels.

I got caught up in the romance of all this that night, and the next two hours were a whirlwind of Occitan with conversations made up mostly of jokes and reminiscences deeply connected to the land, revolving largely around truffles, fishing, hunting, harvesting grain with traditional tools, and how to outsmart neighbors on mushroom hunts during cèpes, or porcini, season. Normally the wealth of porcini occurs in September and October, but they may appear at other times depending on when and how much it rains at any time of year. When it rains here, people aren't thinking of the inconvenience, they are calculating when in the next two days after the rains they will be able to sneak off and search for newly sprouting brownish tan fungal caps pushing out from the humus. Then they are planning how to sauté it and scramble it with eggs and eat it with fresh rustic bread and wash it down with a glass of red.

"A few days after a good rain, you get up very early in the morning," divulged conspiratorially an elderly woman sitting across from me, "when it will still be dark for at least a couple more hours." She paused so the woman to my left could finish translating for me while the others, in a mock hushed tone, pretended to be new to this public secret.

"You take your basket and cover it with a kitchen towel," she continued. Everyone nodded in accord as I wondered what was so special about the towel. She looked at me and answered my unuttered question. "The towel is very important, not to protect the mushrooms, but to hide that you have them." Everyone laughed. "You then walk to the forest edge — never take a car, it's too obvious — and get down on your elbows and knees and shimmy to the areas you know from times past have cèpes, and quietly fill your basket. Then you shimmy back the way you came, and once back on the road, dust off the dirt and act as if you are just beginning your porcini hunt and have so far found nothing." It's so coveted a mushroom that competing against and outwitting neighbors is a part of the hunt.

Everyone grinned at her in approval. The ringleader said, "Don't believe a word of this. When you have twenty fishermen and twenty hunters, you have forty liars because they all tell fish stories about how big and how hard they had to try to get their fish, their cèpes, or their wild boar."

Cepes naturally led to black truffles, the other famous fungus from the Dordogne. It was my neighbor to my left who spoke this time.

"We weren't wealthy," she said, first in Occitan and then in French for my benefit, "but we would find truffles on our farm and a good truffle season meant that we would have a good winter and a festive Christmas." People around the table nodded their heads, knowing exactly what she meant. They had grown up on a farmer's subsistence economy.

"I would walk to the market in Sarlat," she continued, "carrying my basket laden with truffles. After I sold them, I could afford to buy holiday foods and gifts. In really flush years when we found a lot of truffles, we would keep some for ourselves and make canapé of fresh sliced truffles on buttered bread with a sprinkling of salt and pepper. A glass of brut champagne wouldn't hurt, either."

Our mouths watered. One woman softly said, "*Oc. Oc.*"

As we left the Café Lébérou that night and bid each other adieu, the group beckoned me to return. One woman asked if I needed a ride to my apartment. I declined but joked, "Are you afraid the lébérou will get me?" She laughed and pointed at the crescent moon in the sky. "No danger tonight. It's only during a full moon that you need to worry." As much as she said it with a twinkle in her eye, her statement was so matter-of-fact that it gave me pause to wonder about the truth harbored inside legends.

That evening I did not feel the winter chill as I walked home along the dark cobblestone streets that had wind-whipped me hours earlier. I reflected, with a constant smile on my face from my warm-hearted evening with people living close to the land in such an ancient place, that I had come a long way since thirty years ago, even if I still had a long way to go and even if none of this had been planned.

In fact, how I found this place and how this place claimed me was still like the realm of legend, not reality, from the moment I'd stepped off the train at the station at the top of the town's hill and tumbled down to its center in a winter storm. I knew I had to play this story out, find out how it continued, and perhaps, how it ended, if it had to. What I knew so far was that this place spoke to me of home. The alchemical brew found only in this place did things to my body, mind, and spirit that no other place had done. It had called me, it had enacted a healing on me that I did not even know I needed, and now it asked me to hang up my nomadic ways and weave myself into it.

How would I pull this off? How would I honor this strong pull of the spirit like none other I'd ever felt in my life? All I knew while stepping along those centuries-old foot-worn cobblestones was that I had to. I had to gamble, to try my hand at coming as often as possible, having one foot in New Jersey and the other planted firmly, for the first time in three decades, in the Dordogne, and directing all my resources and energy to this singular effort, risking everything to do it. While still here on this first visit, I knew I had to gather more experiences and dig deeper. I had to visit the caves. I had to seek the original inhabitants of this place and ask them what they knew. I felt they held a key to helping me understand my own mystery. •

Combarelles Cave Entrance

Chapter 5

CAVES AND CRO-MAGNON

> The cave had evidence of human presence going back 150,000 years. It also exhibited some of the first human art, dating back some 40,000 years. It was overwhelming to stand a few feet from such antiquity and realize that thousands of years ago someone stood where I now stood but had a completely different life.

A YOUNG AMERICAN WOMAN STUMBLED OUT OF THE cave and took a big gulp of air. I was right behind her and was afraid she was fainting, maybe from claustrophobia. The Font de Gaume cave wasn't as tight as others, but it still had narrow passages that made you feel as if you were passing through the Earth's birth canal.

Her mothers rushed past me, hip women from San Francisco in form-fitted, black leather jackets and fashionably faded blue jeans. Like lionesses defending their young, they ushered their only daughter to a rock and grabbed a bottle of water. They were visiting France in winter while their daughter spent a year teaching English in Bordeaux. Today they were sightseeing together throughout the Dordogne.

Our guide, a Cat Stevens look-alike with long, salt-and-pepper hair and a black, cable-knit, turtleneck sweater and cave-worn jeans, ran over to assist. We were all worried. For someone so hale and hearty, she looked deathly pale.

The young woman shook her head and took another deep breath, "I'm fine. I'm fine." She looked at her worried mothers. "It's just that . . . I'm . . . overwhelmed . . . by so much time."

She glanced up apprehensively at me, the only other person on this little tour and a stranger, but she relaxed when she saw me smiling. I thought I understood what she was feeling: life seemed normal up until now, but then she came face-to-face with something from 17,000 years ago and life no longer was normal in any reasonable way.

The Font de Gaume was narrow throughout, and when we encountered an engraving or polychrome painting, its impact was immediate and intimate. At one point we halted at a handprint found underneath a stone ledge, at knee height. Our guide said it was the left hand of a woman. Given our audience, we were excited but also skeptical. Hadn't cave art specialists of the past insisted these were masculine spaces?

"Experts think it was a woman's hand," he explained. "Our earlier ideas of prehistoric artists or shamans as being men is off."

I liked him.

As we moved on, we were treated to engraved and painted animals. The Font de Gaume is one of the very rare prehistoric caves with polychrome paintings that is still open to the public. The guide took us reverently into this world, explaining that all the animals found in the Font de Gaume, his old friends by now, were in a state of peace. There was no image of hunting or killing. This has some thinking that it was a place of great power, where the animals depicted were revered. He reinforced this idea by stating that no plants, no trees, no humans, except for hands, are depicted here, just large animals, mostly bison, but also horses, a mammoth, some rhinoceroses, and reindeer, though the deer are the least depicted of the big animals.

And while this is so, the most emotionally moving image in the entire cave is the one of the two deer, the *frise des rennes*, where one bows before the other who licks its nose. The tongue is clearly there, engraved, gently licking the face of the other. It feels like a seventeen-thousand-year-old expression of love and affection reaching out from the walls to touch our hearts again. It might have been this vision that began to unravel our young companion's sense of belonging on Earth.

My first prehistoric cave experience had been a couple years earlier, south of Santander in northern Spain's Cantabrian region at the cave of El Castillo outside of Puente Viesgo. The cave had evidence of human presence going back 150,000 years. It also exhibited some of the first human art, dating back some 40,000 years. It was overwhelming to stand a few feet from such antiquity and realize that thousands of years ago someone stood where I now stood but had a completely different life.

My first glimpse of the old pigment-outlined handprints created an odd out-of body feeling, like someone was standing next to me. Beholding the elegant elk and bison, worked three-dimensionally onto cave walls chosen for their contours as much as for other unknowable cave feng shui, was like being pushed up into a higher threshold of mystical experience. Something in my brain got it, something that has been around all the while, replicated generation after generation in our DNA, but I lacked the words to state it or the experience to explain it. My head swam, and I was no longer able to gauge my own tiny life span. I was also tackled head on by an awe that filled the breathable spaces of that cavern of ancient human ancestry. I was overwhelmed by time.

The rest of that day existed in a dreamy, time-suspended state. I had a glass of wine in the nearby village café, which I thought would relax me, but paradoxically I was already beyond the point of relaxation and was easing back into just how small I was. Rather than causing anguish, such awareness made me let go of a lot of contemporary what-life-ought-to-look-like baggage. Suddenly, I was simply there, fully in the present, breathing, and savoring the journey.

I visited that cave with two friends. One of them disappeared from the café where we silently sipped our wine. Her bag was still on her chair, her wine untouched. Worried, I finally got up to see where she had gone and found her standing at the back of our rental car, the back hatch up. She'd broken open her watercolors and was sketching and painting the images we'd just seen in the cave. She had a dreamy expression on her face, a time-traveler's expression. When she saw me approach, she simply said, "I needed to ground myself after that. I was overwhelmed by how old and how fresh our ancestors' images are." I said nothing. There was nothing to add to that. I looked at her painting. Over and over, she had painted in charcoal, mustard yellow, and ochre red the outlined images of hands, forty-thousand-year-old hands pressing through the stone to meet us from the other side of the veil.

Overwhelmed was the one word we all used.

The young American woman at Font de Gaume smiled back. "Being from California, I've never come in contact with time, you know? I've never been near anything human that is so old. It's moving and unsettling. I need to adjust to the fact that I'm just a speck in all of existence."

To be with someone so young confronting mortality, and it not being a near-death experience, was magical.

Her mothers and the guide relaxed and let her be. She took another deep breath and leaned back against the cream-colored limestone walls of the cave's exterior as if she was trying to absorb some of its sturdy longevity. Overhead I could see the mineral striations of the stone, from ferrous red to magnesium black to golden ochre. Inside, these minerals had been ground and used as paint for the animal figures and the handprints. Everything was so immediate, even though it had taken place many millennia ago.

What grounded all of us was our passionate guide, who was in the rare position of having entered the cave almost daily for over two decades. His knowledge was more profound than that of the best trained paleoanthropologists because he was there everyday, presenting the place, feeling the presence of the past, studying every subtle contour, turn, and color, all 17,000 years of it. Even though he would not say it, in order to remain objective and professional, I believe he also felt the spirits of the place. It was hard not to. They reached out palpably as we moved through the dark passages, some subtly with brushing fingertips and some with grasping arms. That might have been part of the overwhelming sensation for the young Californian; something intangible but real reached out from the stone's interior. It felt like the ancestors, like ancient humans leaving their spirit here for eternity to speak to those who came after, as if their stenciled handprints were actually their hands pressing from the other side.

Ironically, this region, with its oldest of expressions from humanity, both Neandertal and early modern humans, Cro-Magnons, had a pull that made me feel almost immortal in the face of my mortality. I felt like both the little speck of dust the young woman described and also like a part of some great and eternal thing. It left little doubt that these works were sacred and magical efforts on the parts of the people who settled here some 40,000 years ago. I wanted to tell the young Californian that, after a while, the feeling of small-speck mortality would expand into a wondrous knowing that even after you are gone, you somehow remain a part of all this.

As we climbed down the side of the cliff to the ground level and parking lot, I saw my new acquaintance, Philippe, waiting for me while leaning against his four-by-four. He looked at us and had a knowing smile. He'd seen that same wonder on other visitors' faces and he never seemed to tire of it. He adored where he lived.

Philippe drove a local taxi and was a prehistory and history buff who enjoyed designing tours to the caves and medieval villages of the region. I discovered that hiring him was a better value than renting a car, as it also came with local knowledge, an indispensible natural resource. I told him my interests and left him to propose a plan for a half day of driving about and visiting places. When I first called him in that blustery, icy winter month, he'd laughed heartily over the phone, "I'm like a bear in winter and your phone call has brought me out of hibernation. Business has been very slow with this freezing weather."

When I first saw him walking across the square where we were to meet on the designated day of our tour, I realized his analogy of a bear was more than just for seasonal sleeping habits. His was a towering bear figure lumbering toward me, with a long below-the-shoulders brown and gray ponytail that swished back and forth as he walked. He gave me a bear's handshake, rattling my arm to the shoulder, and then we were off, heading toward Europe's highest concentration of prehistoric art, all along the Vézère river valley.

As we drove out of Sarlat, I discovered that Philippe loved to cook and eat as much as he loved history and prehistory. By the time we drove into Les Eyzies and toward the Font-de-Gaume, we were already swapping recipes and in a contest over who could make whom hungrier.

"I have a surprise for you," he said as I buckled my seat belt and we left Font de Gaume behind us. "I want to show you old Monsieur Magnon's hole."

Quoi? I gave Philippe a sideways glance. We'd only just met and I wasn't sure I wanted to see some old guy's hole.

We'd been speaking a mixture of French and English, he humoring me because his English was far better than my French, but still, sometimes he said things that were odd in English and unintended, just as I did in French.

I asked for clarification and Philippe bust a gut. A big bear gut. When he stopped laughing, he said, "No, I really meant hole. 'Cro' means 'hole' in Occitan, similar to *le creux* in French. It's how Cro-Magnon got his name. Mr. Magnon lived right here in Les Eyzies."

We drove into town as Philippe explained how, in 1868 when they were working on a road through town and along Mr. Magnon's property, a worker uncovered bones. Work halted, which has always been a risk when you go digging in a place as old as the Dordogne. Specialists unearthed five human skeletons belonging to three men, a woman, and an infant, plus animal bones, and flint tools. All the human adults but one were in their thirties. The eldest, in his fifties, had died from a rare degenerative bone disease. Carbon dating showed them to be around 27,500 years old. We laughed. They were old enough to free old Mr. Magnon of any accusations over dead bodies in his side yard. Moreover, it placed his humble abode on the map and gave our ancient ancestors, early modern humans, his name.

In 1868, the world was on the cusp of a period when exploration, discovery, and expansion would reveal much information about the prehistoric world that had until then been left quietly alone and hidden. It seems prehistoric humans loved this valley so much that any turn of a spade or plow could turn up some evidence of their settlement. There is incredibly deep ancestry in this small region. Like Mr. Magnon's, many traditional houses in the Dordogne are built up against the back of a rock shelf, so that the only way to expand is sideways, along the rock shelf.

"It's a very clever building style for defense and warmth," said Philippe, as if reading my mind as I gazed upon the entire village built against a great limestone cliff wall. I recalled the homes he'd shown me on the drive along the Vézère to get here. Most of the building dated to the Middle Ages, but the same rock shelves had been occupied for thousands of years. If you lived there, you could see anyone approaching from the valley below or the plateau above. Before they could climb up to your entrance, it bought you time to decide whether to invite them up for wine or pour boiling oil down onto them.

Some of these old rock-shelf houses were still occupied by farmers who enjoyed the cozy, high perch after a day of working farmland lower down in the valley. Local lore describes a farmer's find nearby, in St-Cirq. He lived in such a place and had decided one day to expand his cave to make a special cave for storing wine. As he cleared the fallen debris from a small cavern behind his house, he discovered he was not the first human to mark that little spot as special, for there he discovered two of the most enigmatic engravings in the world of ancient cave art. Dating to around 15,000 BCE, one was a rare image of a human being with a huge head and a very large penis proudly unfurled for full disclosure. The other was of a human head facing and staring warmly into the eyes of a bear or wolf who stared back in the same sweet, chummy manner. That humans are generally the least depicted animal on prehistoric cave walls has made this cave particularly important. Called Le Sorcier, to describe the guy with the huge fifth limb, it is still privately owned, and the farmer's house is now a small museum and visitor's office from which they arrange guided tours.

We parked on the road passing through the heart of the village of Les Eyzies and walked a few meters up a small unassuming dirt path to a humble stone house. To its side sat the famous "cro." Its small protective rock shelf of liquid sun-colored ochre swept over the ancient grave marked with a small cairn-like pile of river rock. Though that was it, there was something beautifully eerie about standing at the site of such an old burial ground.

The debate rages as to whether Neandertals really buried their dead or if this is a ritual enacted only by us moderns, us Cro-Magnons. Whatever the truth is, to stand next to a 27,500-year-old burial spot was another chance to be authentically overwhelmed by time and humbled by life.

Feeling the gravitas of my mood, Philippe then said, "I have other surprises for you. Would you like to see the geese of the Périgord, and one of the most beautiful villages of the region?"

I did want to see the geese, the famous foie gras geese, who also have a fairly ancient presence in these realms, from ancient Roman and Visigothic goose feasts to mysterious connections with a medieval Templar-associated board game emblematic of life's labyrinth, the Game of the Goose, *Le jeu de l'oie*. Indeed, we were deep in solid goose country, but at the time, I wasn't thinking any of this. I was thinking how odd it was for all us tourists to come so far from home to gawk at tonight's dinner, to look at and ultimately eat a bird whose throat gets excessively crammed with corn everyday so as to engorge its coveted liver. But I really did want to see them. And the pot-stirring part of my soul wanted also to liberate them, to open the gates and let them run, run, run away.

But no such agitating luck. When we arrived at a pretty, free-range goose farm, it was clear those birds had bought the system so thoroughly, had perhaps been genetically selected for Borg-like assimilation, that they came running to us goose-eating humans with what I could only call glee. It felt as if I had walked into a Pavlovian experiment where human = corn = food = no need to work hard in life, even if one's liver is engorged and you are a dead bird in the soon-to-arrive end and eaten with fig jam or caramelized onions on delicate little toasts with trimmed crust.

Apparently it's the goose's own damned fault. Food history surmises that the ancient Egyptians observed migrating geese gorging themselves before making their lengthy seasonal flight. They also noticed that the bird-about-to-migrate tasted better than geese at any other time of year, and moreover, they had a particularly large and buttery liver.

An Egyptian tomb wall painting from the Fifth Dynasty depicts the entire process graphically. It shows humans stuffing the geese's faces with rolled olive-size balls of wheat and water dough. It shows the geese lining up for the forced feast. It shows them getting fatter, and then it shows them being enjoyed at a great sumptuous feast. Apparently, Egyptian geese were a delicacy and often a gift from Egypt to Greece. The Greeks may have passed on a passion for goose liver to the Romans, who cultivated it throughout the natural goose regions of the empire.

Southwestern France has long been a natural goose region. It is curious that some Neolithic images of the great goddess, possibly the supreme being for Europe's early farmers, were of a woman with a bird head. Some theories wager that Mother Goose comes from these more archaic associations. Basque folklore, with their Great Goddess, Mari, a cave- and spring-dwelling divinity associated with birds, reinforces this vein of thinking. And that the Basques also inhabit nearby parts of France and neighboring Spain and also are known for their goose dishes, makes for some intriguing goose connections.

And here they all were, running toward us like long-lost friends. We politely greeted them and then drove on before the farmer came out and offered us one of their livers. Through rolling hills and craggy cliffs, foie gras ruminations led to other culinary associations with my new foodie friend.

"What do you think about the black truffle?" I asked.

I was expecting a bard's delight waxing poetic about the little subterranean fungi, but instead I got that quintessentially French poof-shrug. Philippe even did it without loosening his grip from the steering wheel, which I found impressive as I still have not mastered the poof-shrug even with my arms and shoulders free.

"Why so little to say?" I prodded.

Again, the poof-shrug, and then, "Listen, when I was a kid, we'd find truffles all over the forests here. We'd find really big ones and play soccer with them. They were everywhere." Sure, he went on, people cooked with them, but they weren't demanding the kind of gold prices they do today. He felt it was an urban fashion, a Paris thing. "Nine hundred euros for a kilo?" He went on, warmed to the topic. "Food should be simple. Food should be affordable."

His opinion echoed part of mine. A few days earlier, when it had finally been time to eat my truffle, my anticipation had been high. Its smell had filled my apartment over the brief days since I'd bought it and with a scent so strong that it was hard not to be hungry all the time for all sorts of things. On the day, at last, that I'd made that simple truffled tagliatelle in cream sauce, I ceremoniously seated myself at Le Chardon's great window overlooking the Place du Peyrou as winter tourists from Australia, Germany, and America gazed at Boétie's home below. I raised my glass of Pecharmant red and toasted to the health of all and took a sip. I then paused only long enough to set the glass down, pick up my fork, and shamelessly attack the dish. I vigorously twirled my fork into the pasta and formed a glutinous noodle nest which I unceremoniously stuffed into my watering mouth. Oh yeah, it was excellent, truly excellent, but . . . but when the experience was over and I had eaten a few euros tossed with pasta and butter, I sat back feeling a bit confused.

It was a great experience, but it wasn't as great as the smell had promised. That smell is an enigma: it promises so much, yet when it comes down to final delivery, the promises aren't as golden, nor as tasty. I realized that there must be something in the truffle that really plays with the smell-taste ratio. True, we taste a lot with our sense of smell, but I think the truffle hordes more of that. And once it hits the tongue and brings the taste buds into play, its smoke and mirrors efforts are exposed.

Not that I'm complaining. This is hardly suffering or disappointment. But I agreed with Philippe. That same handful of money could have bought a truly good bottle of local red wine or a beautifully cured whole duck breast studded with black peppers and thinly sliced to eat like Prosciutto, or a whole little crate of just picked chanterelles that, opposite of the truffle, are mild on the nose but deliver a punch on the tongue in exploding, earthy pockets.

Philippe was now so deep into simple foods poetics, caramelizing onions, mashing potatoes with butter and cream, explaining the perfect steak haché ("minced steak not hamburger, please"), and discussing his passion for gardening and fresh, local ingredients, that I just watched him gesticulate, the image of this bear man kicking around a truffle as a soccer ball dancing in my head.

He then stopped the car on a bridge and went silent. I turned and looked out at a place that surely cannot exist in reality. There sat the fairytale image of St-Leon-sur-Vézère, *sur Vézère* saying exactly what it did, sitting enchantingly along the banks of the Vézère river. A lyrical limestone Romanesque church offered its twelfth-century tower to the skyline as forest danced beyond on the other side of the river bank, and little stone cottages huddled like good friends at a pub over food and cheer. It was just in the right nook of the curve of the river, a green forest stole around its shoulders, and it rested in the perfect dip of the valley. It was the sort of place where a Hobbit would want to live out his days, enjoying the river, eating wild mushrooms, working a small garden in the dark fertile soil. It was Cro-Magnon's paradise.

"We humans really picked the best places to live early on, didn't we?"

"Yes," Philippe said reverently. "This is why I love it here. As a boy we would come from Versailles in the summers to be here. It was magical then. It is still magical now."

He knew the pull then that I was feeling. This land was like Odysseus' lure of the Sirens' song, too beautiful and too impossible to leave. Thankfully, death was not the alternative, and there was a fundamental element here lacking in Odysseus' journey, but central to his return home: here, there was an inexplicable sense of deep ancestry, mine and everyone's. I still didn't have the words to describe it, but I knew Philippe felt it, and I was certain others did too.

"But, I have to confess," Philippe looked at me sheepishly, breaking the Siren's song long enough for ordinary time to flow back into the car, "my favorite dishes are actually Moroccan and Algerian. I absolutely love merguez, couscous, and a good tajine."

He laughed at himself, here in the land of foie gras and truffle cuisine, and then told me about his North African friends in the Dordogne with whom he regularly enjoyed these dishes. He then went into a litany of spices and seasonings — cumin, chili pepper, fennel, sumac, garlic — that went into the lamb and beef sausage. He then had to go into grilling it, with vegetables, and laying it on that fluffy bed of buttered couscous. Now we were back with Odysseus, only this time at Circe's table.

"My mouth is watering," I said.

He laughed. "We have the same expression: *J'ai eau à la bouche.*"

"*J'ai eau à la bouche,*" I repeated three times to commit it to memory.

We drove on. Food remained the topic at hand. The landscape

spoke food, food, food. From fat geese running toward us, to the walnut orchards found in patches between small family vineyards, to fields of grazing sheep and cows munching on herbs that defined their milk and cheese, to evergreen oaks whose roots were symbiotic with black truffles in forests where wild boars foraged as happily as we when they came upon a wild cèpe, porcini, that grows abundantly around here.

Then there were the apple orchards and pear orchards and strawberry fields and rivers full of trout. As I ate the passing landscape, I felt shamefully gluttonous, seeing the edible possibilities in every bend. Unknowingly pushing gluttony over the brink, Philippe said quietly in a dreamy voice, "But sometimes, all you want is a good steak frites." He looked over at me so seriously. "You know?"

I laughed and nodded my head. "*Oui. J'ai eau à la bouche.*"

We arrived in Sarlat, and Philippe dropped me off at the Place de la Liberté. We gave each other a big bear hug as if we'd known each other all our lives. We certainly had broken a lot of bread in a manner of speaking, the magical bond of humanity since the first shared roots and roasts. I was both exhausted and starving.

My phone rang.

"Nadiya? Coffee tomorrow? Sure." And before she signed off, I quickly asked, "By the way, where can a person get a really good steak frite in Sarlat?" She laughed. My question had caught her off guard. She was used to visitors asking for the best grilled duck breast or foie gras and those restaurants were in the medieval center of town where all the tourists ambled.

"You'll have to go to the edge of town, to the workers' cafés. They'll make the best. That's where the locals eat and where they demand good, solid cooking. But they're only open at lunch time."

So, it was another delightful game of delayed gratification in a universe lush with options. In spite of my raging appetite after a day with Philippe the Bear, the dusk hour had turned the medieval town aglow, and I forgot fatigue and hunger and followed its golden lines. The last of the day's sunlight grazed the steep and heavy stone-stack layered rooftops, locally called *lauze*, and the emerging street lamps began to light up and illuminate the amber stone walls as if they were translucent and held flames within. All the light-kissed lines led the eye magnificently to the cathedral, Saint Sacerdos, with her golden bell tower signaling home. Before I went up my flight of stairs across the street, I was pulled into that line and walked straight to the tower.

The cathedral was still open and light inside the church brought out the cobalt, red, and yellow of the stained glass windows that were fast becoming my friends. That made me realize that I had never gotten back to that third window. I stepped in. The spacious Gothic cave had sandstone pillars along the nave with a raised and carved spiraling pattern. Spirals to heaven, spirals to earth, a great journeying tunnel right there perennially engraved on both sides of the center aisle.

I turned left, and there stood the third window to the left of Saint Bernard and Saint Philomena. A single candle burned, intensifying the cobalt of a kneeling Bernadette at the little grotto in Lourdes with the Lady in white smiling beautifully down upon her. My spine tingled.

Though my parents are from Iran, Saint Bernadette is a very important personage to my mother. During World War II, when Russians took her father as a prisoner of war, my mother was sent to a boarding school in Tehran, a Catholic school run by Italian nuns. For two years she lived away from her family. Many of the other girls who arrived at the school were Polish refugees and had made it to Iran as a safe haven. It was a very frightening and lonely time, even in the company of other girls with whom she shared a lot of concern. To comfort her, one of the nuns told my mother the story of another lonely but brave girl, Bernadette. She gave my mother a Bernadette medal from Lourdes, and my mother cherished that little piece as a protective talisman. Anytime I saw images of Bernadette, I thought of my mother.

But today, having also just come back from the caves and now here looking at another cave experience, it established an unbreakable connection between the two, from Lascaux to Lourdes. Another tingle traveled along my spine in a pattern similar to the spirals on the cathedral's pillars.

I had recently read about Bernadette's history in Graham Robb's book, *The Discovery of France*, which described the more local account of the event, not the official church account.

In the early days of these otherworldly visions, Bernadette reported seeing a small female figure, about Bernadette's own height, dressed in the folkloric attire of a fey from the Pyrenees: a white dress with a blue sash and yellow roses on her feet. Bernadette called this figure *uo pétito damisèla*, a little damoiselle, the local Occitan term for a forest fairy who was a force with which to be reckoned, who could alter the weather and make unusual things happen. *Damisèlas* lived in caves near springs. They sounded a whole lot like the Basque Great Goddess, Mari, as well as divinities called xanas further west in northwestern Spain. They were ancient representatives of a time when the face of God was very likely female. Damisèlas, xanas, and the Basque Mari are all likely related survivals of the Neolithic cultures in the same areas of northern Spain and southern France, with the Pyrenees as their central corridor, that held a female divinity as the primary creative force. She lived in caves, especially ones with sweet water springs.

I heard the cathedral's doors scrape against the stone, my signal that the priest was beginning to close things up for the night. I quickly dropped coins for a candle and lit it, feeling it was an important final touch to this day all about caves and magical local life.

I crossed the little street and went up to my studio, taking in the top step without thinking, as if I'd been doing this now for years. I fixed a dinner of market greens dressed in the local toasted walnut oil and layered with a few slices of cured, dark burgundy-colored duck breast. I poured myself a glass of the local Bergerac red. I silently toasted Philippe as I gazed out my kitchen window onto that third window. The sole candle I had lit was enough light to illuminate the kneeling Bernadette and *uo pétito damisèla* we all now take as Mary, a sweet surrender of goddess to goddess, tradition to tradition.

I grew very sleepy, but just before turning in, I checked my email. Like celestial clockwork, there sat an email from my mother, one she'd sent hours before, sometime right after I'd set out to meet Philippe for cave adventures.

"I wish I was with you," she wrote, "when you go to the caves. One of my memorable dreams from years before we came to the States was of a cave with a flowing spring in it, and I saw my grandmother's shadow sitting very comfortably by it. When I was waking up, I thought the shadow was really me."

I sucked in a deep breath and let it slowly out in near disbelief. Her words hit a deep chord of connectedness, not only of a mother sharing a part of her inner life, her past, her own psyche, but also of how oddly alike her dream was with the lore of ancient women sitting by cave openings, a stream flowing by. It spoke of a beautiful and haunting chain of transmission from one generation to the next, not just women in my family from my great-grandmother on, but in all women, and men, who came before, who participated in this more ancient archetypal spirituality of the mother goddess as the source of water, earth, and sky, the source of creation and balance.

I took another sip of the Bergerac red, leaned back, gazed out the window at the blue sky of twilight, and wondered. Was my mother's dream, and the timing of her email, tapping into some ancient, ancestral, archetypal image wired in the brain? Or was my clever Cro-Magnon brain making meaning out of lots of disparate pieces?

Whether logical or not, her email arriving at this time deepened my sense that I was tracking something profound and ancestral in my own life by being in this place that opened its heart to me in a home that smelled like my grandmothers' homes. I closed my eyes. I fell into a deep sleep with all these strange and delightful ideas dancing on in my mind, my Cro-Magnon brain that had been to the very caves where the original Cro-Magnons had been. I too was overwhelmed by time, by time and ancestry. I awoke with a start as Saint Sacerdos rang out her resonant beats for ten o'clock. The sky was now pitch black, and the cold winter air made the stars in the sky shine more brightly above the bell tower. It had been a sunny and warm winter day, so my failure to close the shutters at sunset was less egregious this time. I closed them now and took myself to bed. I fell asleep as soon as my head hit the pillow.

The next morning I met Nadiya at her favorite café. It was in the center of the main commercial street, the Rue de la République. On entry it was a chocolate and pastry shop and in back a snug hidden café. I passed on the sweet desserts overflowing from the case and decided a comparative study of the town's chocolatine bakers was in order. Research was a rigorous business but it had to be done. I ordered one and a café crème. Nadiya, a petite woman and muscular from all the badminton she played, and also, I was soon to learn, from visiting the shooting range a couple times a week, took her coffee with a lush cream pastry and a stack of thin butter cookies curved upwards like wings or demonic smiles. "They're called tuille."

"Those terracotta roofing tiles?" And also apparently the hinge plating on suits of armor.

"Yes, they look like it don't they?"

They did on a small scale, and as I nibbled on one, I discovered they tasted far better, of caramelized sugar and tons of butter straight from the farm.

I then attacked the chocolatine as the café lady set down my coffee, dunking and chewing. I tried to be ladylike, given the delicate pink atmosphere of the café's current décor preparing for February romance, but I quickly forgot it as the chocolate croissant transported me to my own sensory heaven. This might have been as good as the baker's bread under my window. I made a note to gather more data. I dunked.

"Okay. Tonight, you will come to badminton," Nadiya served. The birdie landed in my coffee next to my just dipped croissant.

"Tonight?" I held the soggy bread over the cup.

"Yes, we have a match, with the team from Bergerac, but there will be a few courts open for practice for those not in the match."

I lost my appetite. I was going to expose myself for the first time on a badminton court, and I had to do it in front of the top pick from Bergerac? Nadiya ignored my growing paleness and the fact that I had now set down my chocolatine. My appetite slipped under the table with the flaky crumbs.

"And I have a pair of shoes for you. I saw yours, they are hiking shoes and have black bottoms. You can't wear them on the court." There was no way out. Her feet were the same size as mine. As she closed all escape routes, I thought of the B&B lady's warnings. I was also learning that Nadiya was not only a dedicated foodie, placing culinary Xs all across maps of the town and the region, but also was in possession of an impressive collection of athletic gear, especially shoes.

I nodded meekly and sipped my coffee, flicking the birdie aside. My evening was settled then. She'd pick me up at quarter to eight. Nadiya began to tell me about some of the people I would meet.

There was a man, a local electrician who had vivid dreams, so vivid he could wake up and sketch them and sometimes paint them, which he did, if the topic was pleasant. Some of his dreams were premonitions. These, he didn't paint. Then there was the local fine artist whose watercolor landscape paintings were in galleries and homes across the region because he so precisely evoked the hidden but omnipresent spirit of this place. There was a teacher of English who looked forward to chatting with me. There was the daughter of a family that owned several small businesses. There was a young restaurateur whose family-run establishment in the neighboring village offered excellent communal home cooking. As she went on, I realized that I would meet a good cross section of the town, all through the seemingly humble sport of badminton.

I told her how different this all was from my time in Galicia, about how hard it was to make friends there. She was thoughtful and then said, "Here, if you really take time with the people, listen to their stories, they open up warmly and easily. They'll open their homes and hearts and do a lot for you. When my husband and I got married, the locals got together and helped, providing things for the wedding and refusing to be paid for them."

She had marveled at their generosity. That was years ago and they had been living in the area only a month, but people got the sense they really loved the community, and so they stepped forward and insisted on contributing to the wedding celebration. One person provided all the foie gras. Another hunted for wild mushrooms and provided huge quantities of them for the wedding feast. Others gave beautiful flowers and many others helped set up and throw a great wedding party. Another, a shepherd, slaughtered one of his own sheep and grilled the cuts out on an open grill right at the wedding celebration.

I regained my appetite and finished my chocolatine. We were safely away from the topic of badminton. I then learned that Nadiya had been married before, in Thailand, to a Frenchman. Both were working, but when the government changed its employment laws and her husband was no longer allowed to work in Thailand, they decided to come to France with their two little girls and start a new life here. "But people change, the culture changed him. It was different here for us than back in Thailand." They decided to split up, and today they remain good friends.

As she had done in Thailand, Nadiya worked in hospitality, managing a hotel in Paris. One day her future husband walked in with that charming Scottish swagger and lilt, saw her warmth and beautiful smile, and both were smitten. By and by, city life appealed less and less, and as they traveled and visited friends around the country, they arrived in the Dordogne and both knew from that moment that this was home. I suspect it had a lot to do with the people, along with the beauty of the land. There was just something here that seduced people and locals deepened that seduction by being so nice.

I thought of me. I thought of Philippe. Now, I was hearing the same story of pull from Nadiya and her husband. This reinforced my non-logical feeling that I had to find a way to come here again.

As I was thinking this thought, it happened again: that lighting crew showed up from stage left and then that look arrived on Nadiya's face. I took a deep breath and waited for the one-liner.

"You come, you do."

"Pardon?"

"You come, you do. You know. Like that movie, *Field of Dreams*? You came, you'll do something here." Ahh.

Nadiya is beautifully fluent in English and French, and still, a Thai logic guides it. I was learning that I had to think of what she was saying beyond and between the words. And her words mattered to me, considering their timing and the shift of light.

"How do you do that?"

"Do what?"

"You come up with a one-liner that echoes what's firing unfettered and unspoken inside my head. The lights change, your face changes, and you get all Delphic."

She lowered her chin toward her chest and looked at me through the upper rim of her eyelids, smiling a sweet, demure smile. "My mother in Thailand is a medium. A real one. She's good. People depend on her and she helps them. But . . . "

"But what?"

She jutted her chin forward and her face went perfectly perpendicular again. "I don't go for it. I respect it but I don't go that way. I don't go for that myself."

"Yet," I pressed, "you do have an uncanny way of seeing what I'm thinking about and saying it out loud."

She lowered her eyes and was quiet for a moment, thinking things over, then looked up again. "I see from my mother's life that when the spirits ask you to work with them and you accept, they will call at all hours of the day and night. She must listen to them and respond when they speak. I don't like the hours. And like I said, I respect it but don't go."

Though I was intrigued by the skeptic-believer divide within her, I knew I had stumbled upon a mother-daughter issue that was intimate and best left alone. I also thought of her electrician friend and his prophetic dreams. That was a huge responsibility, one I also would not wish to take on. What if you dreamed something difficult or sad about someone you loved? Would you tell them and look like a fool or be silent and have to deal with hindsight and regret if things turned out as seen? I'd probably make the same choice as Nadiya: no, thanks for the job offer, but I need to find employment with hours better suited to my life.

As we readied to leave, Nadiya told me her husband worked for an oil company in Algeria. He was there one month and worked 24/7 (kind of like her mother but for a different cause), then home one month (unlike her mother, who never got a break). His work life was like a game of badminton, back and forth over the net of the Mediterranean. Before we said goodbye, she said I was in luck; he was coming home at the end of the month, nearly upon us, so I'd get to meet him.

We both then went back to work. She, a Thai woman married to a Scotsman working in Algeria and living in France, back to manage some building improvements; and me, an Iranian-American nomadic writer having found home in Sarlat with a husband back in the USA cheering me on, back to carefully read over the proofs of my book on sacred Spain that was about to come out. The publisher had sent it right as I was leaving Galicia for the Dordogne and I had been spending early mornings, late nights, and any space of time not devoted to my new love poring over them.

As I walked across the small Place du Peyrou, the sun came out and the clouds burned off. I heard a shopkeeper call to her neighbor that we were going to have an uninterrupted sunny day. I decided on the spot to delay getting back to the proofs for a bit. I wanted to go for a walk, a good long walk into the forest. The air had that fresh, just scrubbed quality only possible after heavy rain followed by reviving sunshine.

I ran back to Le Chardon, smiled at the Buddha on the mantle, and put on my Nadiya-rejected but wonderful-for-hiking, black-bottomed cross trainers. An extra sweater, a map, a bottle of water, and south I went.

I left Sarlat proper and entered a green way, a *voie verte*, toward the village of Carsac. Eight kilometers from the center of Sarlat, I could get to Carsac and back for a late lunch, then suit up for my evening badminton debut. I was quite sure that hitting a little birdie across the net, compromising as it could be, couldn't be all that taxing. I reasoned that I'd have plenty of energy for it all.

The *voie verte* was a defunct railway that locals turned into a car-free path for bikes and pedestrians. Around twenty-eight kilometers long and going south then east from Sarlat to Souillac, it passed several beautiful villages, meandered through thick forest and small narrow gorges, and came out into rolling hills, farms, and cliffs, with the river a constant companion.

As I left Sarlat behind, I entered a deep, dark green canopy of oak trees rising and falling on either side of the path with vines and moss dripping off the trunks of trees that leaned over into arches. Their roots clung to the rock surfaces, some ground level, others off the face of rising rocky gorges.

The deeper I went, the more a mysterious Middle Earth landscape drifted in like a low thick mist. There were shape-shifting moss-covered rocks and trees set in winding mazelike passages, little caves, ferns growing out from the sides of rock walls, old trunks overtaken by man-eating vines, and shifting ground over drops with nature-made trap doors. Just as odd, I came in and out of pockets of air that were one moment warm and then stunningly cold. It was a microcosm within a microcosm, little universes of diversity next door to each other. It was alien, exhilarating, and alternately brightly lit with kaleidoscopic light and colorful energy to then plunge into a seething, green-gray darkness and spine-chilling mood.

At one point, the path narrowed so much that the trees on the rock face above had leaned over and grown into a closing arched canopy. The stone edges encroached upon me and shut out the last of that glorious winter sun. Before I went farther, I went back a couple hundred yards, back toward the cheerier dappled light behind me on the path.

I pulled out my topographical map and saw, further ahead, a familiar name: Pech de l'Azé. It came from my days as a graduate student in anthropology and archaeology. One of my professors, Harold Dibble, showed us numerous slides of this place where he had dug. It was a Middle Paleolithic Neandertal site. I have never forgotten the enchantment of those images, though I saw them a long time ago, and I couldn't believe that I was here now on the very spot we had spent so much time discussing.

I was in Neandertal country. To me, saying or reading or hearing the word Neandertal was sheer enchantment. And this realization really hit me here, not the day before so much, even as with Philippe I had gazed across the Vézère river to the cave of Le Moustier, a Neandertal cave that had given the village's name in which it sat to an entire stone tool-making technology, the Mousterian. It was enchanting and its forty-five-thousand-year-old age designation was enthralling, but given the kilometer or two that still separated us, it was not yet fully absorbed.

But here, now, with the green and craggy Middle Earth closing in on me, the trees moving like old spirits, a rock appearing one place then not, I felt the ghosts of people so old that we are still debating how closely related we are genetically, if they had a fully-developed language, if they made original art, and if they buried their dead. It was certain they were a whole lot like us in that they made their own beautiful and complex stone tools. Here in this terribly ancient place, I felt time slip back to some 400,000 years ago when these fascinating other humans first lived here all on their own, before we Cro-Magnons arrived around 40,000 years ago.

I got another chill. But to get to Pech, I first had to push through the pressing darkness.

Suddenly, out of the bush to my right came a rustle, a crackle of twigs, and then a big, black, bursting figure rushing toward me. I had a proverbial heart attack and then my mind and vision cleared, and there was a black dog the size of a grown wolf standing jolly in front of me and bumping his body into my thigh in greeting. I wanted to collapse but pushed back to stay afloat.

He was blessedly friendly. He had a collar. I looked around, but his human counterparts were nowhere to be seen. I continued to walk, and he came with me. As worried as I was to have someone else's wolf dog come along with me, I was equally relieved to have good company to dilute the eerie passage up ahead.

He wove in and out of the forest and back to my side as if he was the warp and woof of a tapestry on a handloom. He seemed almost as happy as I to have a companion for this stretch of walk. I proceeded back to the brink of darkness at that narrowest stretch and stepped inside, trying to remember to breathe. To my side were natural but grotesque formations of moss and squirmy cliff walls with sudden gaping holes that went into the ground or deep into the rock. It felt like being plunged into a glass of ice water as a darkness and a chill struck a final death knell to any warmth from the dead sun.

I felt a prick of disquiet, maybe even a tinge of fear, and in that very moment, the black dog came closer to me and stuck to my side. He didn't seem to like it either. I felt vindicated that it wasn't just my imagination. And I was grateful to him. We passed the cold, narrow, and dark place together in utter silence. Clammy vine fingers reached and grazed our skin. I realized no birdsong followed us in, something that had been riotous only moments before. Faces shifted in the rock, looking at me, looking away. It felt threatening, as if something had happened here in this narrow grotto, and it lingered still, leaving a film of darkness.

I recalled days earlier an older man in the market in Sarlat had told me that the land here has potent energy, both of light and dark. It seemed to absorb and remember everything, and depending on what spot you stood on, a feeling of light or dark could alight upon you.

That darkness could have been really old, something prehistoric, or it could have been from the Hundred Years War, the Wars of Religion, or the tragedies of World War II when Nazis occupied the Dordogne because of its abundant food supply. The Resistance here had been strong. One could only begin to imagine the seeping depths of horror and sadness the soil absorbed from that terrible time. This frightening image was further accentuated by all the caverns and crevices where people could hide as easily as disappear.

The dog and I were somber and swift. As soon as we exited and returned to the light, air, and birdsong, he resumed his cheery temper and went off again on his usual weaving explorations, checking in occasionally. I wondered about that place, why it had made us both feel so unsettled. Had it just been me, I would have shrugged it off to foreignness and fantasy in my own mind. But a dog's instincts I trust.

The forest was fresh and light and interspersed with life-affirming farmers' fields and small stone cottages with kitchen gardens. To my left, I sensed we were just passing under the four caves, three of which were occupied by Neandertals anywhere from 35,000 to 180,000 years ago. Though my topographical map marked them as Pech de l'Azé, no physical marker did so on the ground. Everything was covered in thick undergrowth, but with the thinning of winter foliage, I could just make out one large dark eye looking down upon me. It had a fence in front of it that protected the cave from modern treasure hunters. I took in a deep breath, imagining mingling Neandertal molecules with mine and eventually continued along, the dog bounding to and fro.

The mood lightened more and more the closer we got to Carsac. It was a vibrant little village with a twelfth-century Romanesque church built over a twenty-five-hundred-year-old Celtic era, druidic forest and spring. Its homes of yellow light-glowing stone were either nestled in the valley around a burbling creek or along a sun-kissed limestone wall topped with forest. It was the sort of place that made you want to settle down, live there, and begin to plant your garden and sip a beer at the local pub, which I looked for and discovered, just beneath the path I was on. It was a perfect little place.

At that moment, the dog disappeared. It happened in a blink of an eye, and I have no idea where he went or in what direction, but I was grateful for his guardian-like presence. At the same time, I saw clouds moving in and shivered at the thought that I had to walk back the way I'd come without my friend.

I spent a little more time in the church, trying to imagine the druidic forest and what went on here then. Outside, a white stone statue of Mother and Child stood framed against the brown, orange, and green of Carsac's limestone cliff walls. A woman was weeding her vertical garden next to her little house as a white goat straddled the slope behind her, eating anything she missed. I thought of Mr. Magnon and his cro. I took a deep breath and rushed back. That one stretch was still as dark and as chilling as the first time, but in contrast, the rest of the way was perhaps more beautiful and cheerful.

The rain didn't arrive until I clicked the heavy brass latch of my blue front door into its groove and was snug and warm and installed in Le Chardon. This place not only shed me of my armor but also seemed to protect me and expand me at once. I next enjoyed a late lunch, poured over proofs, and even had a little rest before my evening trial in white-bottomed shoes. I thought of that dark place, the magical dog, the Neandertals, the return of birdsong, the rain, and the immense overall beauty of this place, all wrapped into one footpath south of Sarlat. A chill of elation rushed several times along my spine. It intensified when I realized that the evergreen and oak forest through which I walked had been rich with truffles and neighbors shimmying on their elbows and bellies for cèpes. Neandertals, like Cro-Magnons, had been very smart folks to live here. I hoped to do the same. •

The Dordogne River

Chapter 6

BADMINTON AND THE FARMHOUSE

As I stood inside the fireplace and pondered all the culinary possibilities, Petrus told me the meal plan for the day. "I think I'll roast a leg of lamb for dinner, along with grilled leeks and artichokes, but do you mind roasted duck with an endive salad for lunch? It's just a simple little meal."

"Let's warm up," Nadiya said after we'd already run a few laps around the court. "I'll serve first." She hit the birdie. I hit it, but not back. The racket was so light, the birdie was nothing with its little plastic feathers. It seemed that more muscle was required, not less, to deal with all this nothingness.

"It's all in anticipation and the angle. Anticipate where it will go, then get behind it but not too close. Give your arm room to maneuver and hit it square, then don't hit too light or too hard." She served again, this time she hit the birdie as she normally did in a match. It was coming right at me with the sound effects of a gun that had just discharged a bullet. I tried to anticipate, to get behind it, and it stung me on the arm. It hurt. I also wondered what she could possibly have meant by "not too hard."

"What about the rules of the game?" I asked as I rubbed my arm and went to gather up the two spent birdies. "Shouldn't you tell me a bit about the rules before I begin to play?"

"You do. You learn. Don't worry about the rules. Worry about hitting the birdie."

To think this was my sweet landlady who loved coffee and pastries in fragile pink settings.

I returned the birdie. This time she was gentler, hitting it so that it would not leave another welt on my arm upon contact. I began to adjust the force of my racket, the distance I struck from, and got into the realization that you pretty much needed to be always in motion or ready for it, even more than tennis, because the lightness of the equipment all around made it move faster and more unpredictably.

That was the challenge and passion, I think, for this game and why all these people in a small town in southwestern France had signed up for three nights a week of this.

As my heart rate and breathing increased and sweat was running down my nose, more blood must have been getting to my brain because I relaxed around French. True it was still just Nadiya and me, but I was so determined to hit the birdie that language was no longer the point but the vehicle of expression.

For better or worse, depending on one's position, as we hit the birdie back and forth, I let loose a litany of French curse words I didn't even know were in me. I was shocked, both for the unknown source from which they came as well as for what others were now going to think of me: the vulgar American. But rather than shock, my desperate spew made people putting on their shoes on the sidelines laugh. Their favorite seemed to be the archaic *sacré bleu*, literally sacred blue, which appears to come from referring to the color Mary wore. Hardly racy material, and honestly it makes little sense to my Anglo-Saxon-Iranian logic. But once, in the Middle Ages — and in any Hercule Poirot novel — it was a terribly nasty curse. Now, it is out of vogue. Harder stuff has taken its place. Where on earth had I come upon it?

I realized I had heard it repeatedly in the car when my father was driving. In Colorado, he and I commuted together, I to school and he to work. Slow traffic or bad drivers earned it, especially the variety that sped up just to hug your backside and didn't pass and stuck to your speed whether you sped up or slowed down. They really drove him nuts. "*Sacré bleu!*" he'd bellow into traffic. "What does that mean?" I'd ask him and he would shrug, "I'm not really sure but I think it's the equivalent to taking God's name in vain." Later in life he explained to me it really took on a softer meaning, "like 'unbelievable' or 'fiendish.'"

Sacred blue? Really? Adults.

The question I really should have been asking was: *why was my Iranian father cursing in French in a car in America?* I'd known somewhere in the recesses of his youth in Iran he had studied French, but that was all I knew. All I'd heard was that it was just for a couple of years. From my Spanish language education in Colorado, I'd been pretty sure two years was hardly enough for fluency, and I certainly had not learned much cursing, other than *mierda* and *caca*, which most of us know without language classes. But French and my father as a French speaker were still alien to me, so I shrugged and relegated it to the weird world of adults.

Only later in life when I seized my lifelong dream of studying French and began studying it with my one friend in Galicia did I send an email to my father and ask him more about his relationship with French.

He told me how his father had planned his education with iron-fisted direction. As his only son he sent my father to the best grade school in Tehran, which was a Zoroastrian school, so the first years of his education were under Zoroastrian instruction. Though he was excluded from the religious observations at the school, he was intrigued by Zoroastrians and heard a good deal of Avestan. That may have opened him up to a curiosity about other languages.

Later, when my father entered high school, his father deemed that his son should study French in preparation for studying medicine in France. My father threw himself into French and learned it with a vengeance, a skill he had with languages in general and that he would apply to English a few years later when his father changed his mind about French medical school and decided the wave of the future was university training as an engineer in America.

But for the duration that my father prepared for France, he became wildly fluent, so much so that French women's magazines publishing in Iran asked him to translate their articles into Farsi. My father took to the task with great skill, and intrigued by the world of women, he decided to write a few articles and pitch one to one of the most important daily newspapers in Iran. The subject was the many varieties of kisses, which caused him to set out, the burgeoning adolescent investigative journalist, observing anywhere he could, within reason and in public, the different types of kisses human beings bequeathed upon each other.

The day his piece came out in the press, his father, a famous writer on politics, history, and poetry in Iran, called him to his office. My father was sure this stern patriarch was going to give him a tongue lashing, which he did severely, but embedded within it my father also received some sideways praise for his chutzpah in going out and writing the piece.

When the tide shifted to English and America, my father nevertheless held on to French, which he loved. He also learned English as fiercely and to this day loves word play and puns, sometimes bi and trilingual ones.

Even though I did not know this history until later in my life, I think it colored anything French in our household and, subconsciously, I picked up a love for French, even though in eighth grade the only language class I could take was Spanish. Even then, as I absorbed Spanish and enjoyed it for the doors and windows it opened in my life, in the back of my mind, from the very beginning, I vowed one day I would also learn French. I didn't realize it would mostly be self-taught and earned through Spanish and sometimes on a badminton court in the Périgord.

French added another layer of important family history when more recently my father had a stroke, one that hit a large part of his cerebral cortex where language lives. He temporarily lost his ability to speak English. In the hospital, as we tried to communicate with him, my mother naturally went into speaking Farsi, and he responded immediately. Once he even replied in French. I tried my beginner's French with him, and he responded. It was English, also a near native language to him but one acquired a little later in life, that he wasn't able to get to in those first frightening moments. As time went on, he regained his ability to speak fully in English again. In part, it may have helped that he had French and Farsi, older avenues to the same information in his brain's road map; they may have helped create a detour as he repaired his communication system.

Nadiya was called to begin her first match. She wasn't sweating or out of breath. I was drenched and speechless. As I wondered what to do next, having no rules and just beginning to hit the birdie back, a woman stepped onto the other side of the court and said she needed to practice her serving skills, would I mind? She was actually quite skilled, like Nadiya, but saw that maybe I needed to be eased into the game without too many welts. With her I learned to gain control over my body, my racket, and a bit more over the birdie.

Conversation went back and forth over the net during our game, and I learned she worked in a restaurant right on the Place de la Liberté,

Sarlat's large market square. I recalled it. It was one of the charming places that set out tables on the cobbled stones with a chalkboard announcing that day's menu. Duck always figured prominently, from its breast to its liver and giblets. She was petite and pretty with black hair and blue eyes and a strong, upright posture that spoke of both athleticism and professional restaurant work.

After a few minutes, she also was called to join the match. I watched her go, seeing Nadiya just beyond in the heat of battle. I relaxed further; no one from Bergerac or the Sarlat team playing them ever looked my way. I began to walk off the court, wondering, again, what the rules were, if I had overstayed my turn on the court, when another kind woman approached and asked me to practice with her. She then went to join another group on the neighboring practice court and as she did, another woman stepped in. I was beginning to feel a tight pull in the back of my legs but stayed with it. I really wanted to learn. I really wanted the duck fat and butter I'd consumed this week to burn off.

Before me was yet another sweet and patient young woman, the one Nadiya had mentioned whose entire family were restaurateurs and had been for generations. This woman ran a legacy of a restaurant in Carsac that offered regional home cooking savored by locals and visitors alike. She helped me loosen up even more, and we laughed a lot at our folly over such a little plastic feathered creature. I found that though I was tiring, I was reaching a high, one of elation at so many kind people, at being able to use what French I had without others flinching, and at being treated like a normal, local element in this new place in which I'd alighted. The restaurateur moved to the next court and I stepped off to take a break, heading out to the entrance hall where I found a drinking fountain.

When I returned, a D'Artagnan look-alike of about forty approached me and asked if I'd join him and the other two women, my last two partners, in a match. I fumbled for words. He threw me off entirely. Not because he was a French man, for goodness sake, though that wouldn't be a bad guess if you had seen him with his thick long salt and pepper hair, his black-silver designer glasses, his gregarious and generous smile, that quintessentially long and slightly bent Gallic nose, his deep, sparkling brown eyes, and the fact that he towered over me and every other person in the gym into the past-six-foot range. A Viking D'Artagnan and wouldn't you know it, he was from Gascony. That wasn't what undid me. What undid me was that I actually recognized this man. *Sacré bleu.*

It all came rushing back. I'd had a dream about him. It was a dream that made no sense.

I had woken from this particular dream with the Viking before me a month earlier in the fishing village in Galicia and scribbled it in great detail into my notebook, including making a sketch of the surrounding dreamscape, before returning to sleep. I then entirely forgot the dream, until now.

I smiled and acquiesced to the invitation, while inside my mind I drove hard trying to pull out any more details from that dream.

Dreams are taken seriously in my family, both as inner compass material as well as for the occasional epic dream that seems to speak of things to pay attention to, things that may come to pass.

My mother once told the story of her paternal grandfather who'd had a dream that he looked at a clock and its time announced the moment of his death. The dream also told him the day of his death, which alarmingly was not too far away. On that day he refused to get out of bed. He said if he were to die that day, it would be easier for everyone if he stayed in bed. But in the late morning, he heard the desperate cry of his middle son who had fallen into the garden's pool. Many traditional houses in Iran had gardens arranged around a square courtyard with a pool for all manner of water access in the center. His son, my future grandfather, was drowning. He leaped out of bed and jumped into the pool and pulled his son out, pushing the water out of his lungs and giving him resuscitating breaths. When his son regained consciousness and opened his eyes, my great-grandfather had a massive heart attack and died. The clock struck the hour at that moment. It was the same hour he'd seen in his dream.

Now, some in the family said it was a self-fulfilling prophesy because he believed the dream so much. Others said dreams are a gateway to the soul and are important to listen to; they are a special communication line with an invisible benevolent force. I think both are correct but some dreams can't be self-fulfilling. They're just weird in their foretelling of details that are alien to the dreamer at the time of the dream but do come to pass. I realized now that I was in possession of such a dream, thankfully a happy one, with no death involved but instead a new life in a new place. That much I could recall. I really needed to go look it up when I got home.

The dream man's name I soon learned was Cédric. The restaurateur and I were on one side of the net and he with the other woman across from us. We began hitting the birdie back and forth, he initially being gentle and making it easy for me to hit back. I studied him. He was a good five or six inches taller than the other men. He had on the same glasses, the same smile, and the same hair, right down to the length, cut, and coloring that I remembered from my dream. He made me chat about myself as we played.

"You're a writer from America? What do you write? Are you writing about us or are you on vacation?"

I tried to answer his questions. As I did, he slowly maneuvered closer and closer to the net, hitting the birdie harder and harder at me each time so that my hits grew harder in return. He then was almost right at the net and he stopped my fast and furious birdie with a light little tap and it died right there, limply falling on my side of the net, just like a dead bird from a tree. Bastard.

"You must only give just enough. Don't overdo anything." He smiled.

Those were words he seemed to live by in everything. He loved to eat and drink and socialize and flirt but all in moderation and just enough. Life was to be enjoyed. That one had to work was enough pressure. Let the rest be enjoyed, from family to having kids to playing badminton to making friends. Keep it steady. Keep it even. Pace it with just enough to carry it and then plunk it at the lip and go home happy and not overly spent, ready for the next thing.

The crazy thing is that I kept hitting too hard, and he kept showing me up with little flick-of-the-wrist maneuvers that controlled the birdie just enough, without too much running about, and deposited it right over the net before I could do anything about it.

If we attract people we have the most to learn from, then Cédric was my antidote to trying so hard and being so serious most of the time. As we hit back and forth I also learned he was a trickster who loved nothing more than to make puns and language play, to turn all sorts of straightforward French phrases into sets of words that were funny, often risqué, and had double meanings. French is ripe for all manner of double meanings, especially when spelling and pronunciation are so vastly different.

"That hit," I said, miffed, "was dangerous, *a été dangereux*."

"No," he replied with a demonic grin, "*a été d'ange heureux*, it was a happy angel."

Bastard.

Before I'd arrived at badminton that night I'd truly worried about being able to play well and about not making a fool of myself. All my life I have enjoyed athletics (thank you Title Nine), and the team sports were the most challenging for me. I slowly gravitated to the ones that made me happy, not stressed, and found myself in a sea of solitary sports: surfing, yoga, hiking, running, and kayaking. As a writer, my livelihood further reinforced the solitary approach to life, not to mention my foundational nomadic nature. At best, I resisted and was nervous about playing team sports in English. To do it in another language seemed total insanity to me, until this moment in Sarlat.

There was something strange happening to me here, something that told me the risk was worth it. I had found a place worthy of falling flat on my face, one that would be too important to me to want to retreat into safety. I was going to dive in, get messy, maybe get judged, but I was where I felt I belonged for the first time in a very, very long time.

After the matches, everyone showered and gathered in the great entrance hall of the club where the Sarlat team members had each brought food and wine to share with the Bergerac guests and the rest of us. A side counter was arrayed with different varieties of locally made cured sausages and foie gras. Some had brought Epiphany cakes, round rings of brioche-like dough glazed and stuck with crystallized sugar and candied fruit. The cakes' interiors each hid a ceramic trinket and the person who got it in his or her slice got to wear the gold cardboard crown it came with and be queen or king for the rest of the night.

Red Bergerac wine and fruit juices flowed, and I delighted in how different this scene was from my gym back home. I tried a sausage with wild mushrooms and a glass of red, and it momentarily made me forget that my hamstrings were tight, stiff, and screaming. But my entire body glowed in the aftermath of exertions with such gregarious people. My French fell terribly short, like my birdie, in their native sea of babbling away in familiarity with each other, yet many slowed down and took their time with me, a couple even offered little language lessons along the way. Cédric continued to make double entendres, of which I understood none. But his grin said it all. He was all mirth and kindness in his own ornery way.

Nadiya dropped me off at Le Chardon. It was cold outside. It was late. It took me a long time to make it up the stairs to the top. That last stair, I remembered it, but it really killed me. My legs were so stiff, my hamstrings so tight, that to lift my legs an inch higher was like asking them to climb Everest. I had underestimated badminton. It was a terrific workout. And between the constant motion and need to lob fast words in French, I was exhausted, body and mind. Yet, my soul was quite content. *This is what I've wanted all along*, it whispered as I climbed into bed. I was nearly asleep when I remembered to look up the dream. With effort I reached for the journal on my bedside. I found the entry and slowly read.

It was unusual in that it was full of details that normally I would forget upon waking, but these were vivid, like an epic feature film in full color. I was walking through a medieval square. I now knew it was Sarlat's main medieval square because even the image I'd sketched along with the details that went with it were exact. But at the time of my dream, I hadn't yet seen images of Sarlat. And medieval towns in Spain are very different. I had nothing to influence or compare this with, only my words about golden buildings with roofs shaped like the capital letter A, thick with stone-stacked *lauze* roofing, not shingles, and engraved lintels like those found on Boétie's house or one on the Place de la Liberté from the same era. All these were somewhat unusual to Sarlat and yet here they all were.

I was walking through a medieval square of golden toned buildings. I then reached a café table, and a man with long salt-and-pepper hair — exactly Cédric's glasses and his hair, eyes, nose, and grin — stood up and greeted me like an old friend and said, "Welcome." I knew the welcome meant, "Welcome here, welcome to this place." It felt like an invitation, an initiation. Behind him, the medieval buildings of the square framed his head, with one particular enigmatic tower right behind him. He was tall and so I had to look up and I saw only the buildings from that upward glance as their upper floors and rooftops met the sky.

And now, matching detail for detail, I knew exactly what towered building that was: it was in the Place de la Liberté, right as it narrowed to enter the passageway leading to the Place du Peyrou, the gateway to my new home in Sarlat. The building had a neighboring A-shaped building, but its texture was unique: it had red brickwork that filled the space between cross-timbers. It was also on the corner and its side had a tower, a tower just like the one from which Rapunzel must have thrown down her long hair. In my dream, I even noted the passageway that narrowed and that it ended at another tower, the one that I now knew belonged to Saint Sacerdos' bells, the very bells whose voice was like Tibetan prayer bowls opening my spirit each time they rang.

I think we all have prophetic dreams at one point or another in our lives. Whether we recognize them or not may be as simple as jotting them down in that freshest of waking moments or letting them slip into nothing again. I had been lucky that I had managed to capture this one, grabbing it by the tail as the light began to fade, scribbling seemingly nonsensical details, and then forgetting them until a month later when my dream stepped off the page onto the badminton court.

Was it prophesy, or was it more a sort of time warp where for a moment in the sleep state my spirit raced forward to the future and glimpsed it? Or perhaps I'd experienced the nature of time described in some mystical traditions, where everything is happening simultaneously, but we are consciously planted on only one time coordinate. Sometimes, however, when we go around the spiraling bend of time, we come close to seeing our future self in a narrow turn as our present self is wheeling out of view. And how often do we have a greeter on the spiral? This time, it was appointed to Cédric and he was welcoming me home.

I slept after that, ten long hours without dreams. When I woke up, I nearly fell out of bed. I'd forgotten the state of my legs. They needed a little longer to mobilize, but a hot shower and a hot café crème as I stared out at Saint Bernadette and the Lady readied me for heading into the Saturday market, this one unmarred by high winds and freezing rain.

It was blinding. After so many days of wet and gray weather, the sun made its stunning, cloud-free appearance and lit all the market tables into jewel-toned feasts. Though the temperature was still blustery, everyone was feeling the good cheer, their somber moods lifted into flirtatious boisterousness, whether it was over paying for a cup of coffee or pondering a pound of spinach.

I passed through the narrow passage connecting the two squares and greeted the two A-shaped buildings and the tower. The market had expanded to its more normal Saturday market size, with food, clothing, and craft merchants setting up everywhere along the central streets of the medieval town. The main street in town, Rue de la République, simply called *la traverse* by locals, cut Sarlat's medieval town in half like the two halves of a walnut. It ran perpendicular to the two market squares with their fresh foods and expanded the market into a full-blown buy-everything-you-need-here market. The long road was a bazaar colorfully animated by merchants and their stands, selling clothing, crafts, books, prepared foods, ceramics, leather goods, kitchen goods, linens, lingerie, and jewelry.

The prepared foods alone were a festival. On one end was a chicken rotisserie with dozens of birds spinning, while *pommes Sarladaises*, those pan-fried potatoes in goose fat, garlic, and parsley, collected the drippings below and kept warm and crisp. At the other end was a great paella maker, a huge pan of saffron and espelette pepper-seasoned rice arrayed with colorful shrimp, mussels, langoustine, clams, and roasted red peppers. In the middle was a maker of apple fritters, churros, and crêpes. Where did one begin?

Midway, before I made any decision about what foods to sample, and past the fritter maker, I met Emmanuelle, a salty-tempered salt-and-pepper-haired twiggy who sold elegant Italian sweaters and sweater dresses at her outdoor stall. They were arrayed as if in the finest boutiques, and their grace drew me in, but her personality kept me there. Like her sweaters, she was elegant and earthy at once. She spoke s-l-o-w-l-y and e-nun-ci-at-ed clearly, telling me it bugged her more than anything else the way some natives mumbled in French without opening their mouths or stopping to make a vowel distinct from a consonant.

"It's like dragging your feet when you walk. Why?" She told me I could practice French with her anytime, implying that I must also look at her clothes, which was an easy deal. I already coveted a couple sweaters but had to tame the consumer desire. Everything I owned still needed to fit into the backpack with which I'd arrived. I told her sl-ow-ly that I would be back.

Setting up used books next to her was a salt-and-pepper-haired and chisel-faced man with sparkling eyes. Vincent, he was, the seller of used books. He was at that moment organizing New Age books next to historical novels while telling a woman about energy healing and chakras. I stepped into his stand of two long rows and stacks of books on several end-to-end joined tables just as he was finishing an explanation about the fourth chakra. He then shifted from chakras to dowsing rods, essentially shifting from the body's energy system to that of the Earth. He next described a pair of L-shaped copper wires, the short end of the L set in a hollow cardboard tube that formed the handle.

"You just hold them like this," he said and held imaginary wires before his chest, one in each of his fisted hands, arms bent at the elbow, "and just walk around your home." The woman nodded for him to go on. "When the wires cross or spread away, you've hit an intersection of the energy grid." The woman nodded again. She didn't need further explanation, so the conversation shifted back to the chakras and energy medicine. But I was stuck back at the earlier discussion. Copper wires, energy grids?

As he talked intensely to her, I also noticed he had a good bottle of whiskey and two crystal tumblers under his table. I decided to ask Petrus if she knew anything about copper wires but also wondered who got to share a splash of the golden winter tonic and when. Vincent was now making his way up the Kundalini flow to the crown chakra. I decided to move on, noting that good whiskey coupled with my love for books, especially old obscure ones on legends, myths, and other esoteric themes — and Vincent seemed to have a seriously good collection of those — were reason to come back again to his stand.

I had the morning to dawdle in the market and soak up its personality before meeting Jean and Petrus for our lunch date. They were busy sacking olives and spices at their stand, which on Saturdays moved from the central square to the edge, at the back corner of an old church that was now converted into the town's covered market. There merchants sold the classic regional products, from walnut oils to foie gras, truffles, duck and goose in many varieties, wild boar sausage, cèpes, and strawberries.

A stone's throw from the old church was a fountain dedicated to Mother Mary. Its water flowed from a subterranean source that emerged briefly there before returning underground and meandering underneath the medieval squares toward the cathedral and beyond. The Mary fountain sat in a natural cavern where the water burbled to the surface from the rock.

I had learned from prehistory that towns with subterranean streams and dedicated fountains to them usually sat on several layers of ancient settlement, often going as far back as the Paleolithic to Neolithic through to the Iron Age and on to medieval peoples, many who primarily assigned the caves and springs as dwellings of the goddess. Sarlat was such a place, and the goddess, as in so many ancient places, had simply taken on the most current name for her, Mary. Her image stood here atop a high, moss-covered stone at the back of the cavern, looking thoroughly perfect in her element. *Sacre vert.*

I made my way to Petrus and Jean's olive stand just as Jean had placed the last folded table into the old market van. He climbed in and slowly made his way off the market square with other merchants' vans in a row and onto the road north out of town.

The van was piled high with great containers of olives, spices, nuts, and dried fruits that could keep a man going for months if he ever got lost in the remote Massif Central. The smell inside was ten times the intoxication of Fez's market, so how Jean could drive and think straight seemed a marvel to me. As he inched away, waiting for the passage to clear of people and other merchants packing up for the day, Petrus and I went the opposite direction and walked to her little blue car, the dashboard of which she stroked like a good horse as soon as we got in.

"We've been together since 1976, this car and I. Oh, and the adventures we've had!" She then recounted all the drives across Europe she or she and Jean had made in it.

"We even found Isabel in this car on a trip to Greece." The kitten had apparently insisted on going home with them and they drove her back to the Dordogne, where she has since become the cat of legacy. She was successful in creating generations of healthy and sound progeny. Moreover, Petrus explained, Isabel the cat and her progeny were working cats. No one lounges about at the farmhouse. Everyone is industrious. The cats were never fed cat food but instead given table scraps and then left to clean up any rodent situation around the house.

As we left Sarlat, also on the road north, Petrus began to tell me how she and Jean had been in the Dordogne for nearly thirty-five years. Before then they lived in Holland, France, Saudi Arabia, and Indonesia, but finally decided to settle in one place and give their two sons terra firma.

I was curious how they'd chosen the Dordogne as their permanent home.

"We were driving through the southwest of France and came around a bend, and we just felt something. Our car also had trouble so we had to find a place for the night. We were in Terrasson. We found a place. We found help for our car. The locals came and shared their food and wine with us and acted as if we were long-lost friends."

Petrus took her eyes off the road long enough to look at me and smile. "How often does one pass through a place and experience that?" She stroked the dashboard again. *Good horse, you found us home.*

I had been thinking the same thing. How often? Not very. Though a lot of people seemed to have found just that when they came here. Was there something like resonance fields that were left by the first humans? These resonance fields were something I'd read about years earlier in the work of biologist Rupert Sheldrake. He called it morphic resonance, a sort of resonance pattern that evolves, and he discovered that all living species lay these down and that they are transmitted through generations without obvious genetic involvement. Could the morphic resonance for *Homo sapiens* be especially thick and rich in the Dordogne given our long presence here?

Well north of Sarlat by now, I looked east and could see the vista of the Massif Central unfold in its entirety. It was France's south central volcanic mountain plateau that separated the east from the west. It was a stunning millefeuille, a thousand layers of hills, colors, and changing contours. A cloudbank seemed half hidden, ready to spring unexpected precipitation on the inhabitants down below. It reminded me of where I grew up in Colorado, right on the edge of where the plains became the mountains. The mountains always half hid cloudbanks that were far bigger and menacing than one suspected. Many a late spring day had begun sunny and dry only to end with inches of freezing rain or snow.

We then turned off and drove through a sizeable village and then onward through a narrower road that began to snake and wind to the hamlet near their farmhouse. "It's a very old place," said Petrus as we coasted through, passing a beautiful little Romanesque church and five houses huddled around it. "All around us are Gallo-Roman ruins, Merovingian tombs, and even dinosaur fossils."

The hamlet's name actually came from a variant of an archaic Latin word for "ancient" that ended with the suffix "-ac." This tacked on yet another and older ancestry. This suffix, a holdover from the Gallic language that made its way into the local Latin, meant "place of." Many locales in France, most concentrated in the south, have the suffix "–ac" that identifies it directly to places inhabited by the Gauls who lived there before the Romans, such as Bergerac and Carsac, and Carnac up north. But as ancient as the Gauls are, my mind reeled further back to the most ancient inhabitants.

"Dinosaur fossils?" I asked, sitting up straight and looking out the window, as if that would help me see them better.

"You'll see. One day we'll make a walk and I'll show them to you."

Saint Sacerdos' spiral pillar pattern rushed up my spine.

We next turned off the narrow road onto a narrower one. Through oak and pine forest we went, passing a pigeon tower with medieval Romanesque faces carved under the lintels that looked like school children who pressed their noses onto the window and made faces at passersby. We made a final turn into a long driveway leading to a twelfth-century ruin next to a restored fifteenth-century one. Beyond the stone buildings was a kitchen and flower garden and then elegant sweeps of rolling hills extending beyond them. A horse nearby was grazing in one of the fields. She looked up at us and neighed, then went back to the serious business of eating winter grass.

"Welcome to our home," cheered Petrus.

The twelfth-century ruin was the original farmhouse. Petrus and Jean's oldest son was rehabilitating it stone by stone.

"We found that the fifteenth-century central portion was the most habitable, so we camped there as we fixed it up, rebuilt the stone walls, restored the floor, replaced the decayed roof . . . "

"You just camped here?" I asked as Petrus opened the front door to the central space.

"Sure," she smiled that engaging Kermit-Swan Lake mix. "It was fun but not easy. The place was covered in brambles and had plenty of snakes."

I felt a different sort of chill go up my spine, no spiral, just a straight, freezing shot up.

"Look at the fireplace," she went on, "who needs any other room?"

I walked to it and my head cleared the stone overhang without needing to duck. Inside, chains and a hook waited for a black kettle pot filled with stew. Leaning against the back stone wall were various iron and copper cooking pots, pans, and implements. Petrus did almost all her cooking in this great fireplace. She even had a specialized iron for burning the sugar on crème brulée, giving it that final candy caramel cap.

As I stood inside the fireplace and pondered all the culinary possibilities, Petrus told me the meal plan for the day. "I think I'll roast a leg of lamb for dinner, along with grilled leeks and artichokes, but do you mind roasted duck with an endive salad for lunch? It's just a simple little meal."

A simple little meal? I was speechless. I nodded two enthusiastic yeses, and my eyes fell upon an inlaid mosaic floor. I had been so drawn to the walk-in fireplace that I'd neglected to look at the splendor beneath my feet. There in the center of that great room lay a large circle in stone filled with concentric patterns forming a Maltese cross. The whole thing was the size of a decent throw rug. The overall pattern gave a rippling effect of a stone plunked into the center of a still pond. Petrus saw where my eyes had fixated.

"Can you believe we didn't know the floor was there? It was covered under centuries of dirt. When Jean cleared it, he saw the pattern. Then, patiently and painstakingly, he removed the stones and reset them, filling in the bald spots."

Jean walked in from his adjoining workshop at that moment, from the wall behind the fireplace, smiling proudly. "The stones are oblong river rock, four to five inches long." He indicated that the mosaic showed the small tip of the stones, that beneath our feet were vertical river rocks standing at attention, making the inlaid work several inches strong and deep. Nothing would alter that floor for centuries. In that moment, from floor to fireplace, I understood the self-sufficient and enduring satisfaction of existing in a place that had known centuries and millennia of constancy, even if through wars and pestilence, of which the Dordogne had plenty.

Indeed, Petrus later told ghost stories of this place and others connected to much turmoil, hardship, and death. And she wasn't the only person to tell such stories. I'd already overheard Vincent mention them and had heard about them in the cafés as well by the same old-timers who spoke about power vortexes and the Dalai Lama as they adjusted their Perry Mason sweaters and took a sip of wine. Spirits were part and parcel of the life of this place. I thought of Rafaea, my possible ghost visitor my first night in Le Chardon and wondered if this was how she fit in.

We worked together in the kitchen making lunch and prepping dinner. The kitchen was at one corner of the great big room with the fireplace, and all along the old stone walls hung copper pots, ceramic vessels, and cooking utensils originating from around the world. A broad wooden counter framed the kitchen's view out onto the fireplace and allowed visitors to sit on bar stools on the other side and participate in the culinary madness therein. I sat on just such a bar stool and noticed that every imaginable tool was there all around us and, upon saying so, learned how much Petrus loved to cook, having grown up with a mother who did the same, with a good deal of adventure, skill, and intense enthusiasm.

She placed legs and thighs of already-cooked duck confit in a pan, set them over the fire, and directed me to rinse the endive salad, separating the leaves and arranging them in individual salad bowls in a sunflower pattern. Back on the other side of that thick wooden counter, Petrus next turned to tying the ankle end of a leg of lamb to a string that had a half lemon strung on it like a bead, the juicy cut side facing down toward the lamb. She pushed fresh rosemary and garlic into the meat all around its thick fatty surface, rubbed it with olive oil, salt, and pepper, and hung the leg by the string from the hook over the fire. Satisfactorily suspended in midair over the blazing flames, she gave it a spin and from there it took care of itself, dancing a waltz to the crackle of fire music, twirling this way, then that, thermodynamics and lamb in a synchronized swim. To one side of the pyro-dance, the duck continued to warm and crisp, making those little sizzling and popping sounds that make one's mouth water while giving off a succulent almost nutty fragrance of dark meat, fat, and salt.

Now was when the cats made their appearance. Ferdinand was a feline after my own heart, with his tiger-striped gray and black fur and his take-charge-I own-you manner of alighting upon my lap and settling in after he established that I would tend to his ears and back. He spoke clear good French, and we spoke to each other as he sat in my lap and leaned his head against my shoulder so I would rub it. A bit cheeky. I was in love.

Minicat was more concerned with social etiquette and jumped up onto the empty bar stool to my right and stared at me with a litany of greeting meows. Soon both slipped away, their welcome greeting complete, and established themselves on the stone floor four feet from the fire as lamb and duck dripped and sizzled. Both sat firmly on their haunches, backs straight, tails swishing left then right, staring without blinking while licking their chops. They had their own synchronized meat-cooking song and dance.

In one bow to total modernity, on the counter sat a food processor, which I immediately learned Petrus employed in making dipping sauces with herbs, varieties of nuts, oils, and just the right splash of spices and vinegar or lemon. She made such a dip for the fresh endive by pulverizing almonds, adding paprika, sea salt, pepper, lemon, fresh aromatic herbs plucked from her winter kitchen garden out front, and healthy splashes of walnut oil.

The duck was ready, and the lamb began to give off its agrarian herb-fed cooking smells. As if on cue, the cats moved a foot closer, still patiently but covetously waiting their turn, one mesmerized into a trance by the swinging-twirling pendulum of lamb leg over the fire.

Lunch and dinner bled into each other. Petrus explained that market days were like this, a late lunch followed by dinner. In between there was a punctuation mark of a small siesta, a mandatory practice allowing Petrus and Jean to recover from the demands of the market.

We ate our crispy roasted duck and our endive leaves dressed in the nutty dip. Jean brought out a special rosé from Greece, one that had a slight resin from the Retsina but dry and full like a rosé from Provence.

We contentedly ate and drank and, as our tummies filled, the eyelids of my two hosts grew heavier and heavier. After a long day of hard work and delayed eating, they took their siesta, and I set out on foot and took the narrow road in to the ancient hamlet half a mile away. I went right to the church at its center, pushed open the solid wooden door, and sat in the small chapel. I wanted to reflect and pray and feel its old stones, and to see if, as the locals told me, it would reveal its stories.

It felt old, older than its eleventh-century construction, a beautiful early Romanesque structure of local limestone. Just before I entered, I noticed a carved wolf over the entrance door that stood alone and was unusual in grin, posture, and form, almost certainly speaking of a local and lost legend from long ago that meant something to people here and nowhere else. I thought of the Lébérou. Could this be? The grin suggested, yes. The smile broadened. I blinked a few times but he held it firm. Not. Your. Imagination.

Inside, to the right side was a stone tomb, its lid off. I got up and wandered over to it. A plaque explained that it was one of the Merovingian tombs found when they dug in the village center to do public works and found numerous tombs, all undisturbed, all around and under the church. The tombs dated to the seventh century. Until then, residents had thought their village was as old as the eleventh-century church, but these sepulchers pushed the age back four hundred more years. Most stunningly, the human skeletons inside were whole and still dressed in their burial clothes and adornments. Several were taken to Bordeaux for study and preservation. The vast majority were still underfoot, a few feet under, everywhere in the central square of the village church, which was essentially the entire hamlet.

I walked out, gingerly, thinking of the inhabitants below and then walked back to the farmhouse to find the household waking up. It was time to launch into more serious bread breaking over conversations about Greece, Iran, Holland, France, America, and about poetry, mysticism, music, and painting.

The lamb leg was ready and the cats had behaved well. They had at last curled up and taken *une sieste* as they waited from their spot three feet away. Occasionally, Ferdinand opened one eye to check on the appendage. I'm sure he donned the occasional grin, like the wolf of the village church.

The cats' patience would be rewarded with scraps offered freely later, after we'd eaten our fill. This was why they behaved. They knew good form delivered good results. It seemed a scene not far off from the earliest of times when cats and dogs may have actually domesticated themselves, rather than with help from us, given our Paleolithic trash heaps and fire pits. They were content to cast their lot with us some 10,000 years ago. (Possibly even earlier, especially for dogs, whose connection to us humans is now thought to go back as many as 40,000 years.) In this way, they diminished the need for pure hunting for food with a steadier food source: us. Petrus and Jean's cats were walking in the ancestors' footsteps too.

Petrus stepped back into the kitchen and set to work on the artichokes. As she trimmed and scooped them out and rubbed generous amounts of garlic into the hearts, I was put in charge of trimming and cleaning the leeks. As we worked side by side, inedible leek and artichoke leaves flying into the compost, I asked Petrus about what I'd overheard from Vincent the bookseller about those copper wires. "What was that all about?" I asked.

Very matter-of-factly she explained that the earth has electromagnetic energy, and it is patterned; it forms a grid. "You can even map it, like with the device Vincent described. It's a really good idea in your home because you don't want to sleep or sit on an intersection in the energy axes."

We briefly interrupted the conversation to arrange the artichokes and leeks on a grill over the fire. The grill was two-layered and had a hinge that allowed it to open so food could be placed between bars, leaving enticing grill marks on both sides. Also, with one flip of the attached handle, the device could be easily turned. Petrus gave the lamb another twirl because it had slowed in its rotations.

She then went on to explain that you could almost always tell where these energy lines are simply by watching dogs and cats. "Cats love to sit on the intersections of the energy grid." She glanced at Ferdinand and Minicat who hadn't budged even when she went past them to place the artichokes and leeks. "But for humans and dogs, that feels like negative energy, and we don't want to be in it. If you can't sleep well, you might discover that you've placed your bed on one of the negative energy spots. So, just move it a couple feet in any direction and see if your sleep improves. Get it off the intersection. You'll also notice that cats will love that spot, but dogs will never lie there. Avoid as a rule where the cat is sitting, but put your chair or bed where you find the dog."

I didn't know what the science of all this was but I knew exactly what she meant about cats and dogs. Sometimes cats seem to sit in the most sinister of places, and dogs will have nothing to do with those spots. Petrus went further.

"Cats are also energy clearers of negative energy. Often they'll be sitting in a place with dark energy and quietly clearing it. It's a wonderful thing that they do." She laughed. "When you see a cat sitting, looking wickedly busy without moving a whisker, he's likely working very hard at clearing energy. Maybe it feeds him in some way."

You have to admit, cats are wiggy creatures compared to dogs, who are terribly vulnerable and transparent. I was glad to have such a clear explanation because the fact was I had heard more people than Vincent speak of these energy grids. They were woven into the cultural lore of the region and whether one partook or not of this lore, it was important to people here and spoke of their intimate relationship with their earth. It offered one reason among several as to why they were more respectful of the Earth and its health than many people are elsewhere.

Jean came out from his rest. As Petrus put finishing touches to dinner and the lamb reached perfection, he selected and uncorked a bottle of robust earth-red Bordeaux and invited me to sit by the fire. Ferdinand took his cue and leaped into my lap. As the striped cat spoke French to me, demanding ear caresses, Jean and I talked in English about Greece and Iran, wine and food, his history, my history, our families' histories, and arts and crafts.

I learned that Jean was a master craftsman and worked in wood and stone and restored historic houses in the region, a lyrical move for an engineer with a passion for the past. He spoke about the stones and wood he worked with as incarnated with spirit. He took his time. He respected the soul. He didn't take on any work for which he didn't feel a spirited connection. He was also sensitive to the energy of places and the energy that flowed in those grids. It's a form of consciousness in construction that is missing today in building our homes. What if, whether one believed in these energy grids or not, we built with awareness, with respect and presence? Would it not change the energy of our abodes and how we lived in them?

This conversation continued through lamb, grilled artichokes, grilled leeks dipped into another nutty-spicy dip, garden plucked salad, a cheese plate, and digestive lemon verbena herbal tea.

Before I knew it, it was late at night and time for Petrus to take me back to Sarlat. She had offered for me to sleep over, a new toothbrush and a freshly made bed at the ready just for me, but I had left the shutters open at Le Chardon and remembered Nadiya's admonitions about the care and feeding of medieval stone buildings. I had not anticipated my lunch to last so delightfully long. I had to get back.

We drove through dark forest and a sky so black I could see the Milky Way. The only movement outside of ourselves was the occasional flitting of a deer or the possible distant shuffle of wild boar. Back home, as I began to close my shutters, I looked out from my third-story windows onto the Place du Peyrou as a group of German tourists gathered beneath and around Étienne de La Boétie's sixteenth-century home. It was lit up by theatrical lights mounted on the square's rooftops. The Germans craned their heads up to take in its romantic carved designs of cherub faces, hearts, ropes, and geometric forms, temporarily turning their backs to the medieval cathedral.

Every day so far, I had watched new sets of just-arriving visitors get their first view of the medieval magic of this place. I loved the expression of awe on their faces as they took in for the first time the unfolding beauty of the well-preserved medieval town, slowly peeling its petals back for fuller revelation the deeper they walked in. Sometimes the tour group was Japanese or English, American, Spanish, Dutch, or French. Rarely did they look up and see me, making my perch both a bird's-eye view and a fly on the wall. It had to be one of the best seats in town.

I felt warmed by the generosity and hospitality of my new market friends. I was still glowing from my time with the Badminton Club of Sarlat. I was still absorbing the impact of my dream. My mouth was still watering from my drive with Philippe le Taxi and my lunch and dinner at Petrus and Jean's. And still, there were yet more wonders to come, I could feel it in my bones. For a moment, I am sure, I saw La Boétie walk past the upper window facing mine and smile. Just in case, I waved. I then closed the shutters and went to bed, sleeping that deep sleep like none I'd ever experienced anywhere else. •

Winter Mushroom Harvest

Chapter 7

A WINTER FEAST

La mique was originally cooked in a big, thick, black iron kettle hung over the fire, like the fireplace at Petrus and Jean's farmhouse. It conjured up images of witches' cauldrons bubbling over an open fire. It was filled with all the vegetables of the season, a huge chunk of meat (beef, lamb, or chicken), all manner of sausages, wine, herbs, salt and pepper to taste, and then covered to seal it with a lid made of kneaded bread dough. It was hung over the fire for hours until the bread fully baked and took on an outer golden hue while its underside sealed the pot and absorbed the simmering juices and rising aromatic vapors inside.

Lascaux's hill was covered in deciduous forest and the mellow bird song of winter. The place seemed to glow with a palpable but inexplicable energy. It was a luminescence that I imagined had been here from the beginning, when early humans first arrived. The earliest were Neandertals who some 70,000 years ago inhabited this hill and left fossils, animal bones, and stone tools. Around 17,000 years ago, Cro-Magnons chose a cave in this hill with long, underground, intestine-like chambers in which to paint a stunning chapel of animals, color, and movement. The two areas of Lascaux hill — the Neandertal site called Le Regourdou and Lascaux cave — are about five hundred meters apart. The hominid morphic resonance on this one hill was thick and deep.

But today Lascaux and Regourdou were closed, something I learned only after Nadiya and Aidan, the latter having just arrived from Algeria, dropped me off on the hilltop twenty-eight kilometers northwest of Sarlat. They then continued on their way to run errands in Périgueux, just north and the provincial capital of the Périgord. We all thought the hill was open today and that I had a couple hours of visits ahead of me before they returned to pick me up. Knowing I had a few hours of waiting, I decided to do all I could to absorb just being here and to feel that resonance.

I turned to walk back up to the top of the hill where I'd been dropped off, and voilà, Aidan and Nadiya were still there in the forest-canopied parking lot. Aidan had received a phone call shortly after I got out and ran downhill to the ticket office before discovering it locked. While I was communing with the resonance and killing time, he'd turned off the engine, gotten out of the car, and was pacing back and forth as he trouble-shot some pressing technical details of oil and engineering on the opposite shore of the Mediterranean. Their delay was my grace.

I approached the car. Aidan gesticulated with his free hand as Nadiya got out and stretched her legs. She smiled when she saw me. "I had a feeling," was all she said. I was beginning to get used to this.

At that moment a fourth visitor joined us, all of three inches high when legs were extended into his little hops. He was not a forest fairy, though the magic of these hills had me believing in them. Before us bopped a very social little red-breasted European robin. He was a quarter of the size of an American robin and had a round compact body. Indeed, he and the American robin are from different families, but their similar coloring has given one the other's name. He had a melodious song that sounded like Pan playing his pipes from the leafy depths of the forest.

He also exhibited strangely doglike behavior. He flew right toward us, landed inches from our feet, and hopped about our legs as if in greeting. We had no food and this did not seem to be his motive, nor his deterrent once this fact was established. He remained hopping about us in a warm cloud of magic.

I crouched to look at him more closely, and he obliged and hopped toward me. For long moments we regarded each other eye-to-eye just inches away. I lowered my camera to the ground and clicked. He smiled. In that magical moment of trance, I was transported to the bird image in my mind's eye of a very similar bird painted mere meters away from us some 17,000 years ago within a vertical tributary inside Lascaux cave just below. It was of a man with a bird face or bird mask lying on the ground next to a spear and a staff topped with a bird carving. This bird, I swear it. They had the same tight, round shape and the same sense of getting along with us humans.

Yes, perhaps it was all in my imagination, but that bird of Lascaux above ground in the parking lot felt like he was tying a very ancient thread to us, one connecting the man and the bird below. Morphic resonance, of birds and of humans, and where the twain met, like those energy grids of Vincent's copper wires.

Ever since I saw that stunning image in a full-color spread in a book many years before, an image that also has a disemboweled bison lying on the other side of the reclining bird man, I'd wondered about the relationship between bird and man, and bison and man, and bird and bison, for that matter. All three were woven into an eternal dance that to this day no one understands. We may never understand it, but there are many theories. Some see it as hunt magic or fertility magic (the reclining birdman has a very erect, pointy penis) or both. No one seems to understand the bird other than to say the man may be a shaman and is in his altered-consciousness flight or his shape-shifting state of mind. No one knows if he is in a trance or dead.

I have always felt he is in a trance, or why bother with the bird face and its big open eyes? I also agree that there must be fertility magic and hunt magic at work but I'd wager that the bird staff coupled with the bird face are saying something about an even larger context of the interconnectedness of life and spirit.

I come upon my amateur's opinion from looking at later Neolithic engravings from around 8,000 years ago. These were of prevalent images of birds and bird-headed people, this time mostly of women who seemed to represent a supreme Goddess. And this Goddess seemed not only to represent fertility, but the life force in a broader stroke for all that life is, including the cycle of death and birth and maybe even rebirth.

One explanation is that the bird best represents these cycles. Birds show their fertility externally, visible through egg-laying, unlike us, who take a while to show our pregnancies. They show their regenerative skills through migration and molting of feathers. And they exhibit their ability to navigate earth, water, and air, and even sometimes fire as expert alchemists of the elements. (The serpent shares many of these qualities, and often these two are found together in symbolic art and are the most commonly depicted magical animals for humans.)

What if this even more ancient prehistoric bird-man image here in

Lascaux is a precursor, maybe even showing both sacred male and female fertility in concert with each other in one person in order to keep the cycle of life moving forward? What if the shaman is representing both genders, with a bird head and an erect penis, and being the intermediary between the power of the bird staff (life force) and the downed bison (life sustenance)? What if it takes both the divine male and the divine female to pull this alchemy off, not just one or the other? There is a lot about prehistory we don't understand and probably never will, but I was deeply enchanted by this little bird who was unafraid of us on Lascaux's hill. He made me consider more widely the possibilities of the past.

That little bird hopped about us for a long time, mesmerizing us. Nadiya whispered, "This bird is called a *rouge-gorge* here, a red throat. They are very friendly, but this one is unusually friendly." Aidan had been off the phone for a few minutes before we realized that all three of us were squatting and being quietly woven by the movements of that bold little bird, his brown wings and puffy red-orange breast, and little round body, and pointing beak. He finally hopped on a branch just within arm's reach of our heads and began to sing his territorial song, that sweet Pan melody, and whatever the words said — *you're mine now, this is my land, hello friends, bring food next time, yeah, that's my ancient relative down below on the cave* — they were as enchanting as his little body dance a few moments before.

But Lascaux the cave eluded me. It had with Philippe Le Taxi and it had again today. Nadiya told me not to worry. She had errands to run in a few days in Brive-la-Gaillarde, and she would bring me back and drop me off on her way. Moreover, it would be right after the winter feast. Did I want to join them? What a rich question. Yes was the only answer, and off we went for a day of errands in Périgueux. The days flew by. Before I knew it, the day of the feast arrived.

André stood and kissed me on the top of my head and began to refill our empty wine glasses. The first course had not yet arrived and we were already enjoying getting into our cups. His kiss and the table's *joie de vivre* catapulted me more deeply into the intense warmth of community and belonging I had sought for so long. His wife across the table smiled at me warmly rather than exhibit any reserve over the attentions of her husband. Besides, the entire exchange was downright avuncular; he was very much a doting uncle introducing me to the delights of his world.

Of course, we'd only just met. André and his wife were retiring here to their second home after long urban work lives in Toulouse. This was their heaven of choice.

André now filled our glasses with a red Bergerac wine. The aperitif, a kir with cassis, and a local white was finished, as were the appetizers of duck terrine canapés and bowls of nuts, and the first course of the winter feast was about to arrive. André went off to help the cooks in the kitchen. He soon emerged with a train of others delivering steaming hot bowls of thick pumpkin soup. He set a bowl before me, and I placed my nose in the center of the rising thick, orange steam, rich in local herbs, butter, and garlic.

A quick *bon appétit* fulfilled required etiquette, and the world shamelessly dived in. The soup was so good that we all were silent, inhaling it. I ate so quickly, lost in a tunnel of sublime sensory annihilation, that when I came up for air, my bowl was empty but for a few dregs hugging the bottom of the bowl. I took a piece of bread and was about to commit a small rudeness by wiping up the remains when André suddenly grabbed my hand and yelped, "Heresy!" Then he smiled. And released my hand.

"There is a much better way!" Aidan, who sat to my other side, looked at him knowingly and nodded for the initiation to begin. "You, my American friend," he said, "are about to have your first *chabrol*." He rolled the "r" like a Scottish word, and the "l" came unfurling off his lips like an expert boule player releasing the ball into the air toward a perfect landing.

"*Chabrol?*" No answer, just raised eyebrows and a nod. We waited for André to finish the last spoonful of his bowl, and he then took a bottle of red and splashed a healthy dollop into my bowl and then into his and passed it on to Aidan to do the same with his. Following their example, I picked up my bowl and slowly swirled it to capture all the remaining soup essence and then placed it to my lips and pulled long drafts, until all had been drained in one held breath.

If someone had taken a picture then, it would have been an image of three synchronized monkeys in a row on a bench, bowls up to their ears, and happy as hell.

Le Chabrol, I learned, is an old Périgordin custom of finishing off one's soup dregs with a swish of red wine in the bowl. One only does it with red wine and with all soup varieties except fish soups. (Maybe bread wiping is allowed in that one exception?)

Less than a hundred years ago, *le chabrol* was permitted only among men. It was believed that a woman attempting the decadent sweeping slurp risked sprouting a beard; it was a very manly practice. Boys were initiated into manhood with their first *chabrol*. But today, thankfully, both genders practice it with pride as a thing you do if you are really from the Dordogne. Perhaps somewhere in recent years enough women performed it to prove the whole beard theory wrong. I simply loved how a nice comfort food habit was deemed tradition and therefore allowed us to set down our spoons and slurp from our bowls using a healthy dollop of wine. Tradition and group identity will always trump the proper (read, bourgeoisie) use of table settings.

I, too, like all those daring women before me, earned no beard, though I am sure I must have come up from my bowl with an orange-red mustache that my dining mates were too kind to point out. And what a fine tradition it is, beyond group identity and more from the foodie perspective. For now I knew that there really was no more intimate an experience of that ephemeral idea of terroir — the wine's taste of the land — than to mingle the molecules of the wine grown on the same land as the vegetables and herbs in the soup. The notes from the rosemary, thyme, and pumpkin sang more harmoniously as the splashed wine plucked at them, more so than any prior spoonful.

Once again, André stood up, kissed me on the top of my head, and proceeded to help the chef bring on the next course. As he sauntered toward the kitchen, he said over his shoulder what everyone had written on their faces. "We are all little kids here, having a good time."

We were a group of people gathered for the communal winter feast. The idea of a winter feast, let alone one every season, four times a year, was novel to me but rang true of something far older than my modern grocery-store-shopping self. It spoke of ancient human behavior that was far more normal than our present lives of rushed and long-distance transported foods with no thought to the season.

Here in this land of Neandertals and Cro-Magnons, truffles and troubadours, each season needed to be marked with a feast made from the locally grown foods of that season. It was simply normal to these people, these beneficiaries of Cro-Magnon's inheritance who still lived close to the river, forest, and earth. I looked at them, first to my left and then to my right, to take in the fullness of this event.

Oc. It was a long, narrow table, seating forty people. There were three other such long tables in the *salle des fêtes*, a simple but beautiful stone building with big windows in the middle of the forest somewhere just east of Saint-Cyprien and west of Sarlat. The *salle des fêtes'* sole purpose was to be permanent place in the forest to gather for seasonal celebrations, nearby but removed from village and town.

Further to my left on the other side of André was a man from Salamanca whose parents had relocated to Sarlat when he was a little boy. His wife was from the Antilles, and she spoke French, Spanish, and English as a matter of course and added that her parents were from India. Across from me sat Nadiya, next to André's wife. And beyond Aidan to my right sat close friends from this forest, this region, this land, a couple who lived off of their farm and raised sheep.

As we cleared our soup bowls, the husband sheepherder explained his self-employed version of retirement. "I have 250 sheep but it is too much work. Next year, I am reducing the herd to fifty. Then I can take it easy." His wife, petite, blond, pretty, and perky, nodded energetically. Her eyes sparkled with sizzling ideas of what to do with him when there were fewer sheep about.

Nadiya and Aidan had squeezed in a space for me at the last minute at the winter feast, feeling that it would introduce me to the real life of the people and the land. The last communal feast had been in the autumn. Since then, the pumpkins were ready to eat, the winter spinach was flourishing, the truffle season was about to climax, and occasionally someone sacked a deer or a wild boar and shared the meat with friends and family. People had married, children had been born, some people had died, while others retired, sheep or not, or found another job. For some, a house was going up, being restored, or left to its own devices. The cycle of life was noted and celebrated, once a season, swapping tales of its rises and falls while basking in the rekindled warmth of connectedness.

What struck me even more in all this beauty was how everyone listened to everyone, how they gave space to each other to share their stories, how a person took time when it was their turn to tell their story of time's passage in a manner that was interesting and worth listening to. It reminded me of summer lunches at my grandparents' in Tehran. Relatives and friends would unexpectedly drop by and an extra chair or table would be pulled up in the dining room and extra plates set. Sometimes my brother and I would be sent again to the baker at the bottom of the street to buy more flat bread, *nan-e-taftoon*, to accommodate the expanding, boisterous crowd. Iranian cooking always allowed for more people than expected, with its mounds of rice and big pots boiling with herb and saffron-rich stews.

I kept looking down the length of that long table, trying to absorb every moment of magical suspension it offered, as if I could see forever beyond it, where it connected to all the communal tables since the dawn of humanity, all the way back to when we humans first gathered and broke bread and laughed and got to know the nuances and quirks of our neighbors and deepened our bonds with each other over food and cheer.

Maybe I was also looking for a beloved relative I hadn't seen for over three decades, conjured out of the steam from the dishes that arrived next on the table. It seemed also in that moment that wine was a perfect liquid to represent blood, that perhaps wine was as thick as blood for the magic it could unleash in bringing us humans together. Like blood, it bonded us.

I also became more and more cognizant that my glass was never empty. Either André or Aidan seemed to make sure it was a magical chalice of abundance. I even came under the illusion that my French was improving by the sip. I lost track of how much I'd drunk. I sipped and ate, happily, without a care in the world.

While Aidan was the main bottle handler after André, he had maintained a moderate relationship with its contents while enjoying casting aspersions upon me for my reckless indulgence. This he did with a charming mix of English, Scots Gaelic, and Algerian Arabic, three languages few in the world can swing together. He particularly enjoyed picking on my American-ness, saying that only Americans and Aussies seemed to drink more in France than the Scots and the English. I told him I was normally quite moderate, but André was a bad example. André smiled, then laughed, filled my glass and then his. Add the chap from Toulouse to that list of hedonistic drinkers of English, Scots, Aussies, and Americans. His wife was the designated driver; I noticed she sipped one glass and did not allow it to be refilled.

The much-awaited main dish, one that everyone had whispered was a truly traditional winter specialty, arrived at the table with applause and fanfare. *La mique* is a classic rural Périgordine stew, a sort of *pot-au-feu* topped with bread dough that bakes as the stew cooks below.

La mique was originally cooked in a big, thick, black iron kettle hung over the fire, like the fireplace at Petrus and Jean's farmhouse. It conjured up images of witches' cauldrons bubbling over an open fire. It was filled with all the vegetables of the season, a huge chunk of meat (beef, lamb, or chicken), all manner of sausages, wine, herbs, salt and pepper to taste, and then covered to seal it with a lid made of kneaded bread dough. It was hung over the fire for hours until the bread fully baked and took on an outer golden hue while its underside sealed the pot and absorbed the simmering juices and rising aromatic vapors inside. Everything cooked, rose, and arrived together.

André again did the honors and guided me through selecting meat, carrots, potatoes, and pork sausages from the serving dish and then cut off a piece of the fragrant fire-baked bread and set it to the side of my *mique*. He added punctuation marks with a handful of cornichons and a dollop of mustard. And more wine, this time a fuller-bodied red from Pecharmant. Then he sat down and simply said, "*Attaque!*"

For several long, savory moments, we were simply four long tables of silence other than the sound of chewing, tearing, and sipping. We were like *la mique,* all covered with one great piece of dough, collectively cooking into a unified and well-seasoned communal stew. That I got to be a new member of this old family of belonging filled me even faster with total satisfaction than the rich and hearty winter dish.

Following *la mique* came a locally picked butter leaf salad with the perfect mustard-whisked-caper-crushed-shallot-minced-red-wine vinaigrette. A cheese plate followed with three local varieties from soft to medium to hard, and goat to sheep to cow's milk. And then dessert. A mango custard with a crushed pistachio crust and mango coulis on top.

Okay, while the mango and pistachio probably were the exception to the locally grown, seasonal meal, we all easily overlooked the fact for the pleasure of such an ingenious and aesthetically beautiful combination.

André and Aidan both felt the dessert called for more red wine, and again my glass was the magical chalice that ever replenished itself.

True to French form, even those who drank a lot stopped after the mango custard. We set aside wine bottles and glasses and replaced them with espressos and carafes of water while certain community members set up a special winter slide show on the region's patrimony. We then spent the next forty-five minutes digesting, getting sober, and learning about new hiking trails to historic sites all within our little corner of the Dordogne, *notre petit coin de paradis.*

After we all hugged and said *à la prochaine* and *à bientôt,* Nadiya, Aidan, and I made our way back to Sarlat via a grand tour of the heavily fortified and war-ready, cliff-looming-castle-towns flanking the two sides of the Dordogne River. The Hundred Years War fought during the mid-fourteenth to mid-fifteenth centuries came raging to life as Beynac and Castelnaud faced each other off and towered over us on the left and right banks. Then came Domme's fortified walls and the tower in which Templar Knights have been fabled (a contested history) to have been held in the first decade of the fourteenth century, all for an unfair trial and execution by a pope, Clement V, who was more in love with earthly power and politics than a spiritual path. It left its own whispers of a thick past. As legend goes, but some historians are beginning to question, Templars had left remarkable graffiti in that tower that spoke both of sublimely transcendent devotion to Mary and Jesus, maybe even of a holy grail, and of scathing opinions about the corrupt pope whose face is carved along with a sinuous serpent's tail emerging from his robe.

Even if it were not the Templars, that tower still had been used as a prison for criminal and counterculture elements alike, and those carvings had served as solace for those held within.

That sobered us up more than time and coffee.

Back in Sarlat, we had a digestive cup of herb tea together and planned how to get me to Lascaux before I returned to Galicia. Nadiya, as always, had a plan.

Two days later, Nadiya dropped me off on the same enchanted hill, making sure it was now open for visitors, as she and Maria, a woman from Oporto, Portugal, who helped Nadiya clean the apartments, zoomed off to Brive, each for her own errands. Nadiya liked to help as many people as she could and today it was me and Maria.

As they drove off, I held my breath. That humming energy, invisible but pleasingly electric, was still there. It was quiet and still early and no one else was on the hill but the tour guide with whom I would visit the cave in thirty minutes time. I could see him down the hill where he was having coffee in the ticket office. Before heading there myself, I sat on a rock in the parking lot, hoping against the odds that magic would strike twice. As if reading my thoughts, that little red-breasted bird careened down from a high branch, flew right across my line of vision a few feet away and then landed on my rock. He then hopped to my feet and did a loop about me as before.

You know what your heart feels like when it experiences magic — the sighting of dolphins near shore, the touch of your true love, the kiss of your grandmother on the top of your head? That is how it felt.

"You're back!" I exclaimed. Hop, hop, hop. I felt silly. I'm the one who was back. Addicted to magic. Clearly this little guy had staked out Lascaux as his territory. And rightly so. His ancestors had been here as long, or much longer, than mine. And we both had evidence engraved and painted on the stone wall below. Now I knew. There was a direct connection.

For thirty minutes we sat there, the *rouge-gorge* and me. He came and went from his tree to my rock, sometimes hopping a wee closer, then sitting as if we were in meditation retreat, and then flicking momentarily off again. At my appointed hour with the cave, I stood at last, reluctant to break this interspecies dance. He flew back into the thickness of the overhead oak as I went down the hill.

While I was about to see a modern replica of the original cave, which had been closed to protect it from further degradation from so many warm-bodied and bacteria-breathing visitors, I was giddy with excitement. This particular replica was famed as being true to the original experience. It took twenty artists and eleven years to execute, right there a few hundred meters from the original cave on the same hillside, right next door to the same feng shui and the mood and energy. I'd read that the walls of the replica, Lascaux II, had been painstakingly contoured, engraved, and painted to within slim millimeter differences of a perfect copy.

Still, as giddy as I was, I was expecting a modern experience of something ancient. I smugly did not think that time would have a chance to overwhelm me. But I still had to find out for myself. Come what may, I'd always have Lascaux Hill and that magical time with the *rouge-gorge*. My cup already flowed over.

I met my guide, a man in his late thirties, passionate about prehistory, fortified by strong coffee, and excited each day that he got to show people the magnificence of Paleolithic art. It was just the two of us today. Caves needed to be entered quietly and at one's own pace, and it looked like I was going to get to do just that.

He opened the gate. We entered. He flicked on the low lights intended to illuminate the paintings as they would be seen by fire light. Before I knew what was happening, my knees buckled and tears rushed to my eyes and spilled over and down my cheeks. I heard myself gasp, but it sounded as if it had come from someone else in a distant corner. In the great chamber, the size of an intimate Romanesque church, overhead and all along the sides, giant bison, horses, and deer galloped, looking as alive today as they did thousands of years ago. Often described as the Sistine Chapel of prehistory, I would now have to say we've got the order all wrong. The Sistine Chapel should be described as the Lascaux of the Renaissance.

"Is this really like the original? I asked in a soft, shaky voice.

"Exactly," he answered reverently.

My guide was patient and content to let me have as much time in this great chamber as I wished. He was used to the buckled knees and tears and saw it as normal. No one else had driven up and it remained just he and I and the great animals our ancestors deemed important to commit to stone in masterful strokes of form and color. My guide also warmed to the fact that he had an interested audience of one and began to tell me more about the cave than was in the ordinary tour. We lingered over the bodies of the animals drawn on natural sculpted contours on the cave wall. We were beginning to arrive at the narrowing portion in the back with horses, when two others arrived.

I smelled them before I heard or saw them. It gave me yet a new perspective on caves: they funneled and magnified odors. And sound. Click, click, scraaaaape, smooch, smooch, click, click. Cruuunch.

Soon, before us stood a newly married fifty-something couple from Argentina on a check-it-off-your-bucket-list honeymoon in France. The woman was in spiked three-inch heels and a tight black skirt and satin fuchsia top, and her perfume was everywhere, a heavy musk layer. I felt a splitting headache coming on.

To magnify matters, the man was equally doused in cologne, thankfully of a fresher note, but still overwhelming. He had on slick patent leather dress shoes and a formal suit. They looked as if they had just come from an all night disco in Bordeaux and had driven here for a little tête-à-tête, which they were having frequently with each other. Each explained in breathless half sentences finished by the other that they were trying to see as many famous sites in France as possible before returning to Buenos Aires. Smooch.

My guide was gracious but his tone and style shifted. No longer were we on a spontaneous and intimate tour of one of the world's most remarkable ancient sites. The couple kept nuzzling and kissing instead of looking at bison, so we were now on the official scripted tour that moved along quickly.

When we got back to the narrowing passage with the horses, we passed into a tight space where all the pigment was red, only red. The horses were pregnant horses. Prehistorians here discuss the idea of fertility but are cautious to say more. But standing there, it was hard not to think of being on the threshold of a birth canal in the earth's womb about to be pressed out. I thought fleetingly that if I were a pregnant woman about to give birth and I venerated a great divinity whose abode was often in caves and the deep places of the earth — likely a feminine divinity considering how much life and nourishment explicitly comes from mothers — I'd also want to go to where I thought I had been born, in her womb with the safety of walls all around me. It was protective and loaded with the comforting idea of Home. Yes, I would come here, to such a place, to birth a child from one womb into another womb, a beautiful transitional passage into the blinding light of life outside.

But all this was just my own visceral feeling, another one of my own unprovable, amateur theories. We'll never really know unless some piece of evidence is unearthed that gives us better insights into the prehistoric mind.

Outside, the Argentines planned a Michelin-starred lunch in Les Eyzies along the Vézère River before driving to Rocamadour and then on to Provence and the Côte d'Azur, then Burgundy and back to Paris. They'd already done the Loire before heading south via Bordeaux. Just listening to them made my hair fly back and I felt strong wind on my face. I also understood why they were continually groping and kissing in public, because their itinerary gave them very little time to be still in a private room. And even then, I imagined them collapsing from exhaustion into bed every night and falling asleep before anything more could happen.

As they whisked off and I thanked the guide, I still had four hours before meeting Nadiya and Marie. Mr. *Rouge-Gorge* had gone off to hunt for lunch and I decided to do the same. I walked down the hill along an enchanted path to the village of Montignac three kilometers away. It increased my appetite and cleared the perfume from my saturated head and nostrils.

My lunch was also on the Vézère but not at a Michelin-starred restaurant. Instead it was a locally loved Gallo-themed little café that sat right on the bridge overlooking the river and that deserved stars too. I ordered the dish of the day scribbled on the chalkboard set out on the foot passage on the bridge: an omelet with black truffle slices (not grated!) that came with fries and aioli (cave visits call for hot, greasy food), a green salad (good counterbalance), and a cold beer (cave visits call for cold frothy beer). I discovered that this combination worked better than a pain pill for a bad headache and overly-stimulated olfactory cells. Perhaps, also, because my nose had been so taxed, it offered the truffle a chance to be tasted differently by my palette. I was in perpetual motion, fork to mouth, fork to mouth, fork to mouth, without pause. This cycle served to keep the addictive omelet arriving where it delivered sublime pleasure, without pause. Maybe I had been wrong about the truffle. Maybe it was worth the high price. Maybe more research was needed. *Oc.*

As I ate, a local rat terrier wandered into the café and befriended me. Like the *rouge-gorge*, he did not seem to be mooching. He was simply there for camaraderie. Here is another reason I love France: dogs. They are allowed everywhere and are for the most part well-behaved and so have earned the right to be everywhere.

The terrier's human companion, a man in his eighties, eventually came around the corner and found him and said, "Ah, *c'est toi* who has now captured my dog's eye! Beware, he is a flirt but one with good taste." I laughed and enjoyed the compliment, knowing full well who the flirt was.

It was curious too that this was not the first time in recent days that I learned about French sexuality through their dogs. One evening in Sarlat, Nadiya invited me to an evening of champagne and appetizers with friends whose parents were visiting from the Loire. She suggested it as a nice chance to meet more locals and to practice French. We arrived right as Richard was uncorking the first bottle and his parents-in-laws' Jack Russell scrambled after the cork that went flying through the air, caught it, and began to chew it to bits, completely ignoring us. His name was Jack, in English, same as his breed name. He established his character from that moment. He was obsessed, focused, and intense.

Richard handed me a glass. We toasted and sipped, and then he asked, "How are you enjoying your time here?"

Feeling bold from the bubbly, I translated the English phrase, "I'm so happy, I'm walking on air." "*Je suis si heureuse que je m'envoyer en l'air.*"

Yes, I was pleased with myself that I was able to capture in French the extent of my intense happiness. I looked at my new friends anticipating enthusiastic delight, but instead the entire table had fallen dead silent. Everyone just stared. There was a flirty sparkle in Richard's eyes but his wife and in-laws just looked, trying to understand why I would say such a thing over canapé and champagne, *quoi?*

Nadiya thought for a moment and a light seemed to go off inside her, and she leaned over and whispered something into Agnes' ear, Richard's beautiful wife, who turned back to me and smiled kindly, as if I were a child who did not know better, which, now I realized, I did not. All the while, Jack had just finished destroying the champagne cork and was now circling under the table, weaving in and out of our legs. Nadiya at last explained my faux pas, first addressing the others.

"Beebe was translating a phrase that in English means she is just very happy." Suddenly everyone was smiling and a few ahs swept the table. I was coming back to life, having experienced only a brief near death. I felt a tug at my leg but ignored it for the moment of truth had arrived. Nadiya turned to me.

"In French, 'walking on air' has a more particular meaning, connected to the bedroom." I just looked blankly at her, missing any cues she may have been sending me. "You just said," she finally blurted, "that you were in that special and brief moment between orgasm and lighting up a cigarette."

Shazam. I felt a bolt hit me right between the brows. How had an English phrase changed so much over the Channel?

"The French actually have the act parsed out," I stuttered, "to blow-by-blow segments and designations?"

She just smiled and nodded. "French is a subtle language."

But Jack was not. The tugging on my leg continued and I looked down to see him begin to hump my leg in earnest. Agnes' father saw it at the same time and was torn between the finishing punch of Jack's timing and the need to discipline the ornery dog. We both pulled the dog away and for extra measure confiscated all other wayward champagne corks. The table then went on vigil for the rest of the evening for Jack had this double problem of infatuation both with corks and with legs. No one understood it for he was well-trained and went for lots of walks and received frequent attention otherwise. But in that moment, I saw him clearly. He was a solitary fellow in a sex-obsessed culture and he desperately wanted to achieve all the states of being humans considered worth dissecting and labeling. He sought this Nirvana by the act itself on any available leg, and symbolically, through any instrument that flew through the air.

Near Lascaux and the residence of flirty dogs and their humans, I finished my lunch on the banks of the Vézère. Following an after-lunch espresso, Nadiya and Marie rolled into town and back to Sarlat we went. When I told Nadiya that the bird had returned, she looked delightedly at me in the rearview mirror. "It's not everyday things like that happen," she said. She held my gaze long enough to make her point.

The day arrived all too soon when it was time to leave Sarlat. In Le Chardon, I listened to the church bells one more time as I stood by the open window, letting the vibrations hit me square on the crown and wash down like a refreshing waterfall. I then packed and had my last coffee and toast in the kitchen overlooking Philomena, Bernard, and Bernadette. I smiled at the Buddha on the mantle and touched his third eye and then my own, where I think it is — the Buddha has his well marked with a little bump on the sculpture. I whispered a prayer asking him to help me come back, promising me that I'd see him again in this building and this apartment that after a few weeks still smelled like the homes of my grandmothers.

I stripped the bed, cleaned the surfaces, and packed my lunch and dinner with my last market purchases from that morning to prepare for the three-train journey, planning on an overnight stop in Oviedo. The next morning I would board a final and fourth train for Galicia and San Roque's fishing village.

Nadiya took me to the train station, saving me the uphill walk in the rain. She hugged me goodbye and whispered, "You'll be back. See you soon." My heart filled. I almost cried but didn't. I think her Thai culture may be more stoic than the best of New England's stoics, so I didn't want to freak her out with my Iranian-American double set of emotional genes.

Like my trip to France, my return to Spain was also accompanied by strong winds, rain, hail, sleet, and this time, snow was thrown in by Zeus and Poseidon too, for good measure, so that we mortals knew it was still winter. It made for a beautiful crossing through both the Pyrenees and Cantabrian mountains of northern Spain where I could see the stirred up and raging ocean to my right and the snow and wind-whipped mountains to my left. It reminded me of why I love this whole region and see it as a unified corridor. It was especially beautiful given the firm foothold I'd found now at one end of it.

It was strange, too. It had been a passage in both directions begun and ended with news of death. When I had been heading toward France, having just arrived in the city of Oviedo, I received a message from my mother that a dear family friend, Fred, had died. He was among my earliest memories in Colorado. To me he was a favorite uncle who charmed me with his quirky Brooklyn Ashkenazi humor that was a perfect cultural match to my father's sharp wit and play with words. They considered each other brothers, and his loss hit hard. A huge anchor from my original spawning place, my salmon birth waters, had unmoored with a loud ping and flew out of the anchoring waters.

Then, arriving again in Oviedo on my way back to Galicia, I'd received another message from my mother, this time delivering the news that one of my favorite cousins, Sheri Khanoum, had passed away. She had been a strong, self-sufficient woman who had doted on me as a child and believed in me as an adult. She was also a rare last anchor remaining in Iran. I saw her smiling at me when I was twelve. We were in the mountain village of Ilika, hiking to a family tomb. We were at the Caspian Sea swimming and then drying out on her beachhouse terrace, planning what we would grill for dinner. I heard the other anchor pop up and fly out, leaving that world anchorless.

It was eerie first to hear of Fred on the trip going and then of Sheri Khanoum on the trip coming back. Chapters closed and bottoms fell out. These were the last of a long line of old friends and family in both America and Iran who in recent years had died. Old America and Old Iran were fading completely, and I was on new turf in many ways. I felt even more that my journey to Sarlat was significant, a new magical place and life wrapped between the parentheses of death.

Perhaps it was a rebirth into a world entirely of my own making, taking with me all I learned from those I loved and admired from both Colorado and Iran?

You may wonder, why weren't my parents anchors? They were in their own way but not geographically. They were the original nomads who uprooted and made a new home. Fred and others like him were our anchors in that new home, just like relatives in Iran were older anchors east.

As my old life, my old self, the people who knew the younger me were falling away, I realized I was blessed to be already on a new path where new people were welcoming me and inviting me in. I redrew that map of my life and planned my return. Nadiya was right. I sought that swinging anchor that had heaved up after Fred's death, and I grabbed it tightly, and it swung me east. Then I turned and found that other anchor released from its mooring upon Sheri Khanoum's passing and seized it on my eastward swing. Holding both anchors tightly, one swinging east and one swinging west, they eventually alighted into the middle and fell still. They reset into seabed, one Atlantic and one Mediterranean, and I let the ropes go and dropped and landed perfectly in Sarlat. Completely naked and safe. Both feet planted on the earth firm and steady.

Yes, I would be back, even if how and when eluded me. It all seemed an impossible dream that was happening before my eyes. I knew more was to come. The signs were there, the timing had been perfect, and the magic momentous. The *rouge-gorge*'s territorial song danced in my head as my song too, and like the shaman of Lascaux cave, my soul was already making its flight home. Now, to get the rest of me there. How was the big question. •

FIRST SPRING

This river, this country, belong to the poet, Rainer Maria Rilke. It is not French, not Austrian, not European even: it is the country of enchantment which the poets have staked out and which they alone may lay claim to. . . . I believe that this great peaceful region of France will always be a sacred spot for man and that when the cities have killed off the poets this will be the refuge and the cradle of the poets to come. . . . France may one day exist no more, but the Dordogne will live on just as dreams live on and nourish the souls of men.

— Henry Miller, *The Colossus of Maroussi*, 1941.

St. Sacerdos' Pear Tree in Spring

Chapter 8

RETURNING

I arrived in Sarlat on a Friday afternoon of a mild spring day. The landscape had narrowed into that intimate forested and limestone-cliffed world I loved. Red poppies and little purple wildflowers grew out of the crevices and waved as the train rushed by. The fields and trees were in a fresh green dress of multiple shades and the contours so easily seen in winter from bare trees were now covered in a thick rolling verdant blanket.

I WAS WALKING NORTH OUT OF SARLAT TO A LITTLE VILLAGE. It was all uphill and green with rolling fields and oak forest. I saw a church at the top, and in that moment I heard a whisper: *look for the dancing six-petal flower.* A pulsating image of an animated flower flashed in my mind and was gone.

What?

I woke suddenly to find myself in the thick, dark gray of coastal southern New Jersey in winter. It was wet, windy, and cold, but though the sun had not yet risen, I still felt the warmth of the soft sun and the cheer of that green hillside. It had been very real, even if now I knew it occupied a place in my dreamer's imagination, a place of fantasy, because in that first winter in southwestern France, I had never walked north of Sarlat, only south. To the north was unexplored territory, as was the aching longing in my heart each time I thought of Sarlat.

I lay in bed and stared at the ceiling, wide awake now while those whispered words reverberated in my ears. Look for the dancing six-petal flower. Who had said them? My subconscious dreaming mind? Why would it say that?

I delayed getting out from under the warm covers and did the math. It was now just over a year since my winter in Sarlat, but Sarlat and that feeling of homecoming had never left me. It haunted me from the moment I departed. Back in Spain, then back in New Jersey, the pull was still there when awake and then again in my dreams. But this dream was the most vivid and the least understandable. I was beginning to take these vivid dreams more seriously ever since the one of Cédric. They were rare occurrences but were clearly different from the usual night inventories that organize our subconscious mind.

This dream beckoned me to take action: to explore north of town and look for an animated flower. Six petals. Was there a village there with a church on the hill? It was time to find out. I threw off the covers, shielded from the rush of cold air by the warm cloak of hope and return.

Since that magical winter in Sarlat, the year had unfurled into spring, summer, fall, and winter again. I had traveled some more for writing work but was resettled back in the remote, offseason, gray shore of southern New Jersey seeking to increase my writing revenues and looking for editorial and consulting gigs. The semi-nomadic temperament had been of necessity dormant but still tossed and turned in its sleep.

As a solitary writer, southern New Jersey is a good place to get a lot of work done, with its quiet and stunningly beautiful — in a dark, moody manner — slate blue winter ocean and dramatic, beach-pummeling northeastern storms. That quiet winter also delivered a barrage of sunny letters from friends in Sarlat who remembered me from the prior winter. They all signed off with: *when are you coming back?* It wasn't just the letters, but they sealed the deal. The cathedral, Saint Sacerdos, would beckon me in my imagination with her Tibetan bowl bells. The little red-breasted bird would sing from the other shore of the Atlantic, reminding me as he puffed out his orange belly and stuck his proud elegant beak into the air that he lived only in Europe, making special appearances at Lascaux. And the uncanny and deeply delicious sense of that perfect blend of my American and Iranian self when I was in Sarlat, fully using all my cultural sensibilities, rather than quieting one or another, whispered longingly in my ear. I knew I had to go back and soon.

Then. All the doubts. Tumbled. In. Could I direct my writing efforts, my pitches to editors, my vision of bigger works in that direction and successfully make it happen? And then what? How would Miles and I work this out? Where would we live? Then back to the original nagging question: how could I make this work with my work? How could I pay for it?

As I sipped my coffee at the kitchen table that morning of the dancing-flower dream, my mind spun in circles like a dog trying to find his comfort spot on a lumpy cushion. It might have been my silence and the out-to-lunch expression on my face that prompted Miles when he walked into the kitchen to closely study me and, astute surfer that he is, read the surf report hovering over my head. He then did what he does best for me. He disengaged the overly analytical spinning in my head by saying the unexpected: "Why don't you plan a trip to Sarlat in the spring and just show up? You can see on the ground what to write about and then pitch from there. You have a laptop and Le Chardon has internet. Work from there. Just go. Find out. Take a chance."

My jaw dropped. How did he know I was thinking about Sarlat? And how splendid. Just go. Take a chance. What a remarkable man. As his own independent film and writing work kept him more stateside or took him to Berlin and Lisbon, he still supported my love for Sarlat, a place somewhere in between.

Miles' family has been in America for many, many generations. His background is mixed European, family members from the distant past having come from Wales, Scotland, England, and Germany. Unusual to that muttish tribe, he is also fluent in Farsi (Persian), my parents' language, among other languages. This was a quirk of personal history from when at school in California, having fallen in love with the Persian mystical poet Rumi, whose works in translation appeared in a book that sat on his landlady's coffee table in Carpenteria. He had decided then and there to learn the original language of the poet and to read the original music of the transcendent poems. When his parents asked why he was studying Persian, he said it was one of two of the most beautiful languages he'd ever heard. The other was French.

Indeed, French and Persian are related as members of the same Indo-European language family and have several cognates, as do English and Persian. While it is written with the Arabic script, and because of the advent of Islam and Arab influence in Persia, Persian absorbed a lot of Arabic words into its portfolio, but it is still an Indo-European language and one that English speakers would find familiar in grammatical structure and cognates. To me, it sounds like French and Polish pressed together.

Miles then added in response to his parents' question that he also wanted to study a language from a part of the world that would not show up on the cover of *Time* magazine.

He was serious. That was just before 1978, when all hell broke loose in the Persian-speaking worlds of Iran, Afghanistan, and the Persian-speaking Soviet satellites edging toward independence, like Tajikistan and Uzbekistan. He rose to the occasion anyhow, and he went and found out. After book studies in graduate school, he decided to take leave and volunteered for several months as the director and interpreter at a medical clinic for refugees in Chitral on the border of Afghanistan and northwestern Pakistan. He saw hundreds of thousands of Afghans fleeing the Soviet occupation of their home as he helped doctors from France and America administer to burns, bullets, shrapnel, trauma, and depression. He knows life is short, and we must seek our bliss when and where we can.

At our wedding in Colorado, he recited lines from Rumi's mystical poetry in Persian as a part of our wedding vows, and the Iranians in attendance sighed one collective, appreciative sigh. They hadn't seen that coming from the mouth of a north man.

So, with the dreams, the inner knowing, and the final push from Miles, I set to work and planned a return in the spring, a just-show-up-and-find-out first spring to follow my first winter fifteen months earlier.

By the end of April, I was off. I went with the thick and anxious hopes that I hadn't over-idealized that place and those people with whom I'd associated homecoming. I landed in Paris and took a train south through yellow mustard fields and red poppies in bloom. I was in a dreamy state; I was really going back.

A dapper elderly man sat across from me in the train car and delicately ate his lunch sandwich, lightly dabbing the corners of his mouth with his napkin. He ordered an espresso from the passing lunch cart. He sipped it with an extended pinky. He lulled me back into my idealization of splendid French culture where everything was done with grace. I was back, I was back, I was back. I wiggled my toes and ordered an espresso, too, because jetlag was beginning to fog the edges of my brain, and I also wanted to participate in his lunch culture.

A few minutes after we'd both finished our coffees, the elegant man delicately brushed sandwich crumbs from his lap and then proceeded to navigate the interior of his nose with his index finger for long drawn out minutes and flicked what he'd scored onto the floor.

Arrrrgh.

That popped me swiftly back to reality. I stopped wiggling my toes and pulled my feet back. I told myself to be prepared for the possibility of going back to Sarlat and discovering that it had all been a beautiful winter dream now overtaken by nose pickers. I braced myself. So much rode on this return: if successful, my whole life would change; if not, I'd plunge into a deep depression and float anchorless into outer space.

I arrived in Sarlat on a Friday afternoon of a mild spring day. The landscape had narrowed into that intimate forested and limestone-cliffed world I loved. Red poppies and little purple wildflowers grew out of the crevices and waved as the train rushed by. The fields and trees were in a fresh green dress of multiple shades, and the contours so easily seen in winter from bare trees were now covered in a thick rolling verdant blanket.

At last the train slowed and crossed over the high aqueduct-like bridge over Sarlat, linking the hard-to-nail-down hills together and offering a bird's eye view of the town tucked into so many crevasses and forests. She was a long and elegant yellow stone woman adorned in rubies and sapphires and wrapped in a velvet green cape. I sighed like the Iranians at our wedding.

Nadiya was on the train platform waiting for me. She had on a big grin. Le Chardon, she said, was all mine while I was there. "I knew you would come back. You dream, you do," she said, launching immediately into her skill of dropping loaded one-liners disguised as chitchat.

Before settling into Le Chardon, perhaps to intensify the sweetness of homecoming with delay, Nadiya treated me to coffee at her pink café, now decorated with more burgundy tones as if coming down to earth. Or had I remembered wrong? Was I coming more down to earth? The same kaleidoscope of sweets was offered and we snacked on dark-chocolate-covered ginger strips with our coffee as Nadiya told me that Aidan was in town for the month and that I'd dine with them tonight. She was going to prepare a traditional northern Thai meal. She then left me with the key and I walked to the cathedral square to open the door to Le Chardon and a new season in Sarlat.

That rush of seeing one's love after years apart swept toward me at the sight of Saint Sacerdos' bell tower and the pale blue shutters of my studio just half a stone's throw to the left. The reminder of the dancing six-petal flower leapt in my head. I made a mental note to buy a topographical map of the surrounding area. I inserted and turned the key to the blue door and pushed it open as the familiar ancient smells rushed to embrace me. It was so intense and unexpected, that rush of emotions when one's recall of the past collides with the magic of the present, that I caught my breath before realizing I needed to take a deep gulp and take it all in: the scent of both my grandmothers' immaculate stone and plaster walled homes; the smell of sour cherry jam stirred into hot black tea; the smell of my grandfather's workshop filled with tools, wood, and must; the fragrance of cooking rice and baking bread; and the distant melodies of rose and jasmine. That feeling was still there, rich in olfactory-photo-album-associations, and it spoke clearly of that knowing sensation of home, of coming home. And I was adding to that photo album, enhancing it, by being here.

I took several more deep, refreshing breaths in the coolness of the stone, wood, and stucco and then made my way up the flights of stairs. When I got to the top stair, I stood there for a while. Tears of gratitude streamed down my cheeks while disbelief permeated the air around me. I made an extra high lift of my foot, took the last step, and arrived at the door. My door, all mine while I was here.

I inserted the key. Click. And click. And entered.

It felt as if I'd never left.

The apartment seemed to know me well. The presence of other renters since my winter visit evaporated. I went into the kitchen and pushed open the windows over the sink, and my friends the church bells began to ring their five-in-the-afternoon chime. I felt the vibration penetrate my forehead and heart as I watched sparrows pecking at the cathedral's rooftop terracotta shingles for seeds. I noticed for the first time a gargoyle in the shape of a sea otter's head with his hands around his mouth as if making a proclamation. One of Miles' favorite animals is the sea otter. Just go and find out he shouted across the rooftop so I would hear. I have. I shall. Thank you. I replied.

Below the birds and the sea otter were Philomena, Bernard, and Bernadette, holding their holy trilogy of sacred stories. I waved. Even further below, a beautiful woman in seventeenth-century dress was performing an historical tour of the town. Fleur, La Belle Sarladaise. I'd read about her. She enacted historical dramas and pulled in tourists to play other parts as she took them along on a walking tour of the medieval town. Her petite body belied her booming bouncer's voice, and with the bells, her dramatic French ricocheted off the fifteenth-century walls, tumbled onto the modern counter, and bounced along the ancient floor. I followed it and turned toward the big room and to the Buddha on the mantle. Our eyes met. We smiled. I went over and touched his third eye, then mine. "Thank you," I whispered, "for fulfilling the promise and bringing me back."

All rituals of return but one fulfilled, I turned next to the big French windows in the room and pulled them open. Down below a solitary man sang a cappella in front of the cathedral's entrance as dazed visitors strolled about, stunned by the ethereal live music as much as by having wandered onto the natural set for over fifty historical films. Most of the visitors were holding hands and smiling silly smiles of total contentment knowing that their biggest next challenge was to find a café for a glass of local wine in the splendor of the medieval plaza.

I was stunned too. I went and looked into the mirror over the mantle where the Buddha sat. I needed to be sure I was really here, to confirm it with physical evidence. I stared back at myself. I went back to the big window and took it all in. Even with all these many people in town, many more than in winter, no one looked up, except for the occasional photographer who wanted me to oblige him with a French-woman-in-the-window shot for his slide show back home. I obliged. I liked being the token French woman in the window. It was the quickest way to becoming French and involved no paperwork.

I then went out and do the usual first things upon arrival: buy coffee, milk, and eggs for the morning, and see if Madame would remember me and still have that crazy canned elixir of wild mushrooms in truffle sauce. I grabbed a basket that Nadiya had left for that purpose and closed the door.

That rush of the scent of plaster, cherries, linen, and roses engulfed me. I skipped down the stairs. The top one I adjusted for without a thought. I might have been whistling. I knew with strange certainty, not nose-picker illusions, that I was home.

Madame indeed did have the elixir on her shelf. She even narrowed her eyes at me as I went to pay. I think it meant she was working out if she'd seen me before. I then took a slow stroll along the main drag that divided the medieval town of Sarlat, and wandered, window shopped, and tried to control the beaming smile that dominated my face into a closer composition of culturally accepted dignity and self-respect.

Americans abroad are known for being a little too friendly in how quickly we proffer smiles to perfect strangers. Cultural guides tell us that once we land in France, especially Paris, we should wipe the silly, even if democratic, smiles off our faces and take control of our jaw muscles. But, if they only knew, Iranians are even friendlier in their manner with perfect strangers. So, when the two cultures come together in one person, she has to work extra hard at controlling her face muscles in France. And both Americans and Iranians love France, adore the food, love the culture, and the lifestyle. (Iranians also love American culture. Just so you know.)

But in Sarlat, I was discovering that more locals than expected offered a slight smile as they passed along a matter-of-fact *bonjour*. This established a hopeful cultural baseline. It told me that just maybe, within reason, my goofy, friendly American-Iranian gene might get some exercise here. But I still had to reign it in.

That night at Nadiya's, I ate my first meal back in the Dordogne: local white asparagus with Thai chicken in coconut milk, lemon grass, and scallions on a bed of rice and yams. Dessert was fresh-picked strawberries. Nadiya had cycled to a nearby farm that afternoon and picked the asparagus and the strawberries. Sometimes, she added, she also liked to forage for extra ingredients in the forest, a skill she had learned as a child from her grandfather in northern Thailand.

As a night cap, seeing my eyes drooping from jetlag, Aidan got out a bottle simply labeled *liqueur inconnue*, unknown liquor.

"This is just the thing," he explained, as he set the bottle on the table, "to digest a rich meal and also to cure any future hangover headache you might have from all the wine. It's also good for jetlag," he added to complete his case.

I looked at the bottle's tag that hung around the neck. It noted a long list of ingredients and a history. I leaned in to read the fine print. It explained that since 1826, the Sarlat distillery of Tant Mïon had made this elixir. It originally had been made for and exported to French colonies in the tropics as a cure for numerous exotic ailments. Sometime after the colonial era ended, the exact recipe was lost.

But recently, the distillery found the original ingredients, if not the exact measurements, and began experimenting, working out the best proportions of each spice and herb infused into a brandy-like *eau de vie*. It included cloves, nutmeg, cinnamon, peppermint, lemon balm, angelica, calamus, cardamom, arnica flowers, and wormwood, many heavy hitters in the world of medicinal and aromatic plants. I was more game to try it after reading the list.

"I always drink it after a night of heavy drinking and eating," reasoned Aidan, "and I've never had a hangover." He uncorked the bottle and poured. The glass glistened with a pale yellow liquid. He handed it to me and looked at me hard and reminded me that we Americans had quite the reputation for drinking. I shot back that the Scots seemed to have quite the skill for pouring a libation at every turn and never leaving a glass empty. He laughed, raised his glass, and said in his Scottish accented Algerian Arabic, *bsmillah!* We clinked and he threw back his shot of *inconnue*.

It was thick, strong, and sweet like heavily fortified whiskey that had marinated everything from the plant kingdom. I could feel it kill everything that ailed me, except jetlag, to which it contributed. Before Aidan could cast aspersions on the American's inability to hold her unknown liquor, Nadiya got me home in time for me to fall hazily into my bed and a tomb-like sleep.

Five hours later a shovel scraped ice and metal. My eyes flew open. I flicked off any last vestiges of jetlag. The fishmonger. The fishmonger! I jumped out of bed and ran to the window and pushed open the shutters, shocking the vendors setting up below with my airborne vigor at such an early hour. Clearly, *l'inconnue* had worked. The rush of cool spring air was better than splashing water on my sleepy face. It was laced with perfume from the verdant hills and the thick yellow stone warmed by a gentle sun.

The bread baker looked up and smiled — a certain sale he knew — and so did the elderly man who sold herbs and lettuce from his garden, though it was not quite a smile that he proffered. Two winters back we'd had a hard time comprehending each other. It took five minutes of French, Occitan, Spanish, and finger pointing to walk away with a bundle of winter lettuce and parsley. He'd had a bewildered look on his face, perhaps wondering why I hadn't done what other non-fluent visitors do: revert to English while pointing fingers. But I'd wanted to try out the Occitan, the only language he seemed to speak or cared to understand, and I also wanted to have an exchange with him in a language as close to his as possible. He nodded his head toward me less with the baker's anticipation of a customer than with a hesitance that suggested I was going to torture him while making myself look silly. Encore.

I dressed and rushed downstairs. At least they remembered me. I pushed open the heavy blue door with anticipation, and instead of a gust of cold wind rushing in, sweet, succulent, pollen-laced air danced about. I walked directly into spring, rich in colors, fragrances, temperate earth, and many, many more people at the market. The gray and cold and wind of winter were a distant memory on that same square. I had opened a door to a warm and colorful festival that didn't die down as the day wore on, but simply changed clothes and shoes for the shifting times of day. It was a celebration of light. I soon learned that in spring nearly, every market day flowed into a festival and all the festivals centered on food, drink, music, and tradition.

Once out on the cobbled stone, I decided that bread and lettuce would have to wait. I turned right, went straight into the large square, crossed it, and bee-lined to the olive and spice stand. Jean was there. When he saw me, he gave me a huge grin and came around the table to give me a bear hug. Petrus, he said, was out in the market doing some shopping while he held down the stand. I'd likely see her if I went looking, so I did. It was like looking for a dragonfly in a riotous garden of flowers in bloom. Flit, flit, flit. But find her I did, amidst an overflowing garden stand of fruit trees and flowering bushes that had turned the major intersection in the heart of town into a plant nursery. She was closely studying a butterfly bush when I approached.

"*Dedans! C'est toi!*" She let the bush go, straightened up, and gave me an energetic hug. "We have to celebrate your return. Crêpes! On me!" And we were off, she at her tall, long-legged pace, and me double-timing it to keep up. We zigzagged past shoppers regarding shoes, Provençal tablecloths, women's sweaters, kitchen goods, leather works, underwear, fleece jackets for the whole family, workers' plaid shirts, and arrived at a small stand in the middle where a young woman turned out crepes on a round griddle offering a choice of a sprinkling of sugar, a hit of honey, or a chocolate-hazelnut spread. Once adorned, she folded the round crepe into quarters and handed us the triangles. We clinked our crepes like champagne flutes, bit in, and then Petrus was off again, munching, talking, and laughing.

By the time we finished celebrating, Petrus had piled me up with market foods to take home and enjoy for lunch. She then insisted I join her at the olive and spice stand for a cup of ginseng-licorice tea and a slice of homemade walnut cake. I went and sat in a chair they'd set aside for stand visitors and sipped my tea and ate the nutty cake made with ground walnuts, whole walnuts, and walnut oil, and watched as French, English, and Dutch shoppers queued for Petrus' tapenade.

"I began making it this year," she said over her shoulder. "The processed stuff is horrible and expensive. This is the real thing." At that moment, two little girls of five and six arrived with their grandmother and requested a taste. Petrus handed each child a small tasting spoon glistening with ground olives and peppers. They both first nibbled the tip like angels and then clobbered the rest of the spoon like demons. Their eyes lit up with delight. The grandmother swiftly ordered 200 grams.

I added my order for tapenade and also picked three *petites poches* of olives and paid up just before their market stand swelled with even more customers clamoring for tapenade, olives, dried fruits, nuts, and spices. I then slipped away toward the market throng and Petrus called to me a promise that we'd have a hike and a farmhouse lunch soon. As I walked away, I basked in a warm glow, one akin to the glow in the eyes of those two little girls tasting Petrus' tapenade, that affirmed that I had been immediately folded back into the lives of those long ago winter friends without skipping a beat or having to ease into getting to know each other again. It was as if I'd never left. I now felt more fortified to face the Oc gardener.

Back in the cathedral square, the Place du Peyrou, I warmed up my French by purchasing bread from the baker. I then stepped a few steps to the side and placed myself across the table from Monsieur Oc. He had vibrant lettuces, radishes, and herbs arrayed in spring's best just-picked splendor. Having no idea what the correct words were in Occitan, I placed my request in the best French I could muster for two kinds of lettuce — the red leaf and the curly green leaf — and a bunch of red and white radishes. He looked at me with reticence.

As he delayed, I looked to the nearby stand of a woman who sold strawberries, a fruit now fully in season and arriving in over five different varieties. Today she had two kinds: *les fraises charlottes* and *les fraises gariguettes*. She explained that both were fragrant, but that the *gariguettes* were a bit more delicate. *Charlottes* were best for strawberry tarts and *gariguettes* for eating with fresh cream, she guided poetically. *J'ai eau à la bouche,* I would have told Philippe le Taxi if he were standing next to me. I smiled. I momentarily forgot Mr. Oc and that he made me wait. No, beg.

The *charlottes* looked a lot like the strawberries we see in the States, only their fragrance was so strong it was hitting me in the nose from several feet away. The *gariguettes* were a whole new creature with longer, more elegant bodies and long, white necks that reached up to the leaves, which fanned about like a queen's crown, while those of the *charlottes* lay flat like a prince's collar. My mood lightened. Come what may with lettuces, I would be sure to buy a pint of each of the strawberries.

At last, we surmounted the impasse, the lettuce gardener stopped ignoring me and gave me my greens and radishes, and this time with even more: he explained to me how to order them, next time, in Occitan. "Listen," he began like a grandfather deciding to patiently pass on his wisdom to a young child, "lettuce, *laitue,* in Occitan is *lachuga,* and radish, *radis,* is *rafe.*" I nodded. We both managed a smile. To him it might have been a minor concession, to me, a victory. I thanked him and tenderly set the beloved *lachuga* and *rafe* into my *pannier.* Food grown with that much awareness and love not only tasted better but was richer in nutrients. I was sure of it, which was why I subjected myself to his test. That, and I got to learn Occitan, a language of romance and dreams.

I next purchased *charlottes* and *gariguettes* and then went on to cheeses. First, a stop at Our Lady's soft cheeses for hockey pucks of blessed goat, and then the Dutch lady's semi-hard truffle cheese, plus one washed in walnut liquor and made by a monastery nearby. Near her, a man sold homemade dried salamis, and I walked away with three varieties: olive, pepper, and porcini.

Nearby, the wine man was offering tastes of the whites, the reds, and the rosés. I set my swelling basket down and tasted all of them.

Well stocked with locally grown and made food and drink, I took the remaining steps in the square to my front door, that beautiful French blue door, and hauled my market purchases up to Le Chardon. I took pleasure in putting foods away, on the counter, in the refrigerator, on the shelf. I glanced at the Buddha and smiled and went back out to soak up the animated market day. The market in spring was proving to be five times larger and with ten times more visitors than I recalled in winter. It took longer to amble between stands and passageways.

On my second round of the market, *pannier* empty again and along for the ride, I made a wider circle toward the craft, clothing, and household goods stands set up along the main drag, the Rue de la République, *la traverse*. On the way, I stopped quickly at the tourist office and picked up any pamphlets on events unfolding in the spring, briskly slipped them into my *pannier* without close study, and left.

Walking along *la traverse*, I smelled the sweet scent of lilies of the valley, flowers that appeared back home a little later than here, soon after snowdrops and then grape hyacinths pushed their way through winter slumber into the growing light of spring. Their fragrance reminded me of Miles, who loved to grow them in his mother's back yard in southern New Jersey under the skirt of an eastern red cedar.

The smell opened my eyes to take in greater details, looking for the source. All along the street I suddenly saw that there were a lot of little kids with their mothers selling fragrant bundles of lilies of the valley at stands a lot like lemonade stands back home. The rich perfume from multiple bundles was so delightfully pervasive that before long I too was carrying two just-purchased bunches of the little white flowers that I had acquired from a little redheaded girl with a long, thick braid of curly hair. She made her sale by catching my attention and beginning a humorous litany of all the very good luck with which her lilies would grace me if I bought them from her, and her alone, and especially if I bought more than one bunch.

I stopped to listen to all the reasons her lilies offered luck and chanced to learn that lilies of the valley in the Périgord were considered a sign of well-being, a triumph over winter and its gray isolation. To buy them from kids, she told me matter-of-factly, was even better luck and assured me long life, *bien-être,* and abundance.

I spent the entire day wandering through the market, over and over again. It continued to reveal its layers and nuances, and I knew it always would, no matter how many times I passed through it along the same traverse.

I stopped at Vincent's books as he and a client discussed leylines and how to clear bad energy from living spaces. It was a next chapter to the winter's energy grids. This time it involved a pendulum and clearly-set intentions, not copper wires.

When I finally went home late in the afternoon, still not tired of the market but feeling the edge of jetlag returning, I carelessly set my pannier down, which tipped to its side. But I left it toppled. I still had my lilies, which had been wrapped by the little girl in a wet cloth and then foil. I wanted to get them into full water and set them in a small glass from the kitchen. Their soft perfume quickly filled the recesses of my studio and mingled with the plaster, stone, and wood smell and added a new note to the association I made with this old new home.

I placed the lilies on the table near the big French windows and concluded market day seated there, the windows thrown wide open, letting in the light, ion-filled spring air, and ate a very late but satisfying lunch of paella, Oc garden salad, and dry and chilled Bergerac rosé.

Long after eating, I remained seated at my window perch, mesmerized, half sleeping, half dreaming. Just as I wondered how it could get any better than this, the sun began to set on the square and the soft street lights came on, creating candlelit lighting on the café tables below and on the golden walls of the cathedral. I heard laughter and clinking glasses tumble up the stone walls onto my ledge as if I were a part of the dinnertime festivity at the outdoor tables of Le Bistro and La Crêperie down below. A few people continued to wander by and marvel at the cathedral. Its bells began to chime and my cranium absorbed the intoxicating vibration. I took the last sip of my late-lunch wine of the same color as the lowering sun.

When I finally got up to wash dishes and prepare for an early bedtime, I saw my forgotten and overturned pannier. I went to set it aright. Out slipped all the pamphlets I'd picked up from the tourist office. I dropped the pannier again. One pamphlet had made my heart stop. Its corner slipped out from between many others, a simple little piece of paper in pastel green with a simple little design: a six-petaled flower. I pulled the corner and took the pamphlet in my hand. It was a schedule of events for the *Centre Spiritualité de Notre Dame de Temniac*. Where had I heard that name before?

It came quickly crashing back, that article I'd found on the internet my first visit here in winter, the article that had helped me decide to make Sarlat my home base, sight unseen. In it, the authors had talked about the spirituality center founded by the Catholic diocese in the Périgord to invite interreligious and spiritual activities and conversations. But I had not yet found materials on the center itself.

Wide awake now, I sat at the table in the large room and turned on my computer. I typed in the web address listed on the pamphlet and hit return. A flower popped onto my screen. The flower was animated. It pulsed about, blinking like lights on a Christmas tree. My heart stopped again, and I forgot to breathe. It was the very image in my dream. The dancing six-petaled flower. Here it was. And it was as literal.

Dreams.

But what did this flower have to do with the *Centre Spiritualité de Notre Dame de Temniac*? How did it fit in? Was the hint with *Spiritualité*, with *Notre Dame*, with *Temniac*, with the *Centre*, or all together? Nothing on the website explained the flower, but it was clearly central. It was their logo and it appeared on every page, dancing away. Someone had wanted it to dance.

What do you do with uncanny stuff like this?

To me, my mission was clear. I had to just go and find out. I would walk to Temniac, look for the flower, find the Center. Find the center. I laughed at cosmic humor. As I read more deeply into the website, I learned that this Center was in tune with my own all-inclusive perspective on religion and spirituality. Everyone was welcome, and no one had a better god than the other. God was God, gods were gods, and humans were humans. All this was celebrated through programs on sacred Israeli dance, sacred Tantric dance, Buddhist meditation, Anglican services, Catholic prayer sessions, Muslim, Jewish, Buddhist, and Christian exchanges, and explorations of the pagan universe. Implied was that it was their duty, as the current inhabitants of this region with ancient caves and sacred sites occupied by humans for at least 400,000 years, to act as the spiritual stewards of this deep land's ancient legacy. I had to find this place.

I cut out the six-petaled flower logo on the pamphlet and set it at my bedside, a talisman directing the unfolding adventure. I slowly fell asleep. The last thing I recalled was the sound of clinking glasses and laughter from the plaza down below. Amen. •

White Horse of La Canéda

Chapter 9

TREKKING WITH EARLY MODERNS

I walked everywhere. Walking is the best way to see the subtle details of this intimate landscape with its deep ancestry of human occupation. I walked east and explored the hidden neighborhoods in Sarlat's undulating hills. Each homestead was in town but in its own little crook of a hill, with kitchen gardens, sometimes chickens, and often a dog or two because life without dogs here is inconceivable.

At seven in the morning, Saint Sacerdos' bells rang their habitual and riotous fifty-six chimes (I lay in bed and counted them) and woke me up. It was Sunday. While Saturday in Sarlat was market day and active from the moment the fishmonger arrived to the late diners in the square at midnight, Sunday was a veritable day of rest. The square below was dead but for one early rising bread patron coming back from the only open bakery on the traverse. His eyes were half shut but he had a baguette tucked under his arm, and in his hand, held out in front of him, he carried a small bag of croissants, a natural carrot at the end of a stick.

I made coffee and studied my new topographical map. I located Temniac, north of Sarlat, just as in my dream. A little red circle with a cross on it marked the holy site of the church in the heart of the little village. Somewhere near it was supposed to be the spirituality center. By the look of things, the village had maybe twenty homes at most.

By the time I donned my walking shoes to go out, Saint Sacerdos rang her half-an-hour-before-mass bells, a similar riotous clanging that would roust out anyone who had slept through the earlier bells. I stepped out and along the cobble stones to Saint Sacerdos' western door and entered, my cross trainers silently tapping on the heavy slabs of large flooring stones and my backpack promisingly provisioned with topographical map, water bottle, a bag full of almonds and raisins, and Miles' trusty old compass that I'd brought with me from New Jersey, just in case.

Sarlat is an ancient place, as is pretty much all of the Dordogne. It is certain that Neandertals and Cro-Magnons wandered across the area, several times, evidenced by the many prehistoric flint blades and scrapers that locals unearth habitually as they till the soil in their gardens and farms. Just a stone's throw outside Sarlat's west side is a surviving Neolithic dolmen, attesting to early farmers being in the area perhaps as early as 6,000 years ago. From records kept during restoration work on Saint Sacerdos cathedral during the seventeenth-century, we know that bronze statues of Venus and Minerva were unearthed under the medieval foundation, confirming that this heart center of Sarlat was a Gallo-Roman locale as well over 2,000 years ago. The Gallo-Roman presence is also reinforced by the occasional coins turned up during spring planting and autumn harvest seasons, reinforcing again that gardening here is a fertile enterprise for both growing food and connecting with the riches of the past.

But the first firm historical foundations of Sarlat proper as a human settlement date to the ninth century, when a group of monks, besieged by unrelenting Viking raids along the Dordogne River, moved upland and away from the great snake body of water. They wanted to re-establish their monastery in a place where it was less likely to get sacked but still promised good access to water and food. They scouted the location of today's Sarlat and discovered it to have both: a rich, subterranean supply of water that fed the lush forests and intimate hills, and a snug setting in a long valley where it would be easy to hide. That source of good food, water, and protection served them well; the town whose emblem features the salamander was reborn many times over many centuries.

Underground water still flows and feeds the town and also remains a beautiful mystery. It emerges at the Mary fountain in the heart of the medieval town and then again at fountains and streams north and south from that spot. It appears to flow right under the cathedral and the lanterne des morts, adding to locals' discussions of a telluric energy flow through town that peaks there. When I stood there, I felt engulfed in a warm, invisible force field that simply made me feel good.

The original chapel where Saint Sacerdos Cathedral now stands was ninth-century pre-Romanesque; it was later replaced by a twelfth-century Romanesque church. Even later, a larger Gothic church took its place, which was then refortified with late Gothic and Baroque fixtures. But a bit of the twelfth-century Romanesque remains, right as you enter. The bell tower with its Tibetan voice is one remnant, and the other is the archway at the entrance and the four ancient carved faces to your right, just before you pass through the main door.

I stopped to admire them. I recalled them from the winter, hidden just inside the entry arches. When I looked at them, they looked back. Their faces are like those of people from the region today. Three of the carved faces are men. One is clean shaven, one has a magnificent mustache — thick and full — and one has an equally exquisite beard and mustache. Together they look like a masculine rendering of the Celtic trinity of Maid, Mother, and Crone. The fourth face is a young but majestically-mature-in-carriage woman with a flowing head wrap, a lady who doubtlessly inspired the half-dozen twelvth-century troubadours for whom streets throughout Sarlat were named. She especially held my gaze and seemed to be trying to tell me something.

These four stare at each visitor as they pass, both welcoming and challenging them to go deeper, not to be a mere visitor. *How deep do you want to go?* They appeared to ask. *Deep*, I replied swiftly. Really deep, as far back as Neandertals, if possible.

I turned back toward the door and entered. I first went over to the back chapel on the left to give my respects to the three ladies represented there: Our Lady of Lourdes, Bernadette at her feet, and Our Lady of Fatima off to the side observing the two. There too was a sturdy woman in her seventies wearing a no-nonsense blue heather pantsuit, orthopedic shoes in black with laces, and a certain and solid bowl cut hairdo that accentuated her thick, straight gray hair. She held court with the other ladies while lighting a candle and seemingly studying the exact placement of it on the stand. I decided not to bother her ritual and walked on and found myself a pew midway up the nave. I turned back around in time to see the pantsuit woman leaving the church. I grew more curious about her. She clearly was not staying for mass, but her ritual was intimate.

I hesitantly set my pack on the floor and looked around to see that many others were coming to mass in jeans, walking shoes, and comfortable warm sweaters. I relaxed in the easy and welcoming atmosphere. Mass began.

Two little girls joined two little boys in the ritual honors at the altar. As the mass progressed and many members of the community were involved, of all ages and genders, I felt for the first time the true alchemy of wine and bread transforming into Godly matter. It surprised me. Real magic was at work. A universal message of love was delivered, and just as the noon bell rang, the priest leading the Eucharist boomed lustily, "*Bon dimanche et bon appétit!*" I picked up my pack, slipped it on, and began walking.

I set Miles' compass north, first passing through the sinuous medieval spaces of Sarlat, past the Mary fountain set deep in its cavern, and then following the main road out of town. Everyone was sitting down to a large Sunday lunch, and traffic was reduced to the one person late for it who had just zoomed past me over the speed limit as I left Sarlat. I walked into open fields framed by forest and steeper and steeper hills. After several turns of the road, I saw a sign to my right for Temniac. I checked the compass: it read due north. I took it.

That road led me onto a single lane road and deeper into the rolling hills and countryside. It was identical to my dream image. Except that each time I reached the peak of the next hill, and I hoped to gain a view of Temniac, I instead saw vineyards alternating with wheat fields but no village. I also met up with some very inquisitive goats who ran over to see me. I waved to two farmers who were finished with lunch and setting stakes above just-planted tomato plants and undoing bugs and weeds. A herd dog, temporarily without his sheep, herded me. I walked past an aperitif distillery that sadly was closed as my thirst mounted. I savored the green hills that exploded with the full spectrum of colors from spring's wild flowers.

When I thought it couldn't possibly get more beautiful, a red-breasted European robin, the *rouge-gorge*, a relative of the bird who came so close to me at Lascaux that first winter, flew by and landed on a fence next to me and sang his colorful territory-marking song. He did that three times, flying to the next fence I passed and belting out his music. Just beyond him, cherry trees and lilacs were in bloom, and all around them, daisies and the full flush of wisteria. The air was awash with an orchestral perfume of numerous harmonious notes. In all this magic, I still did not encounter the spirituality center, nor any sign of a church, nor any inkling of a six-petaled flower, let alone a dancing one, and yet even with the distillery firmly closed, I was intoxicated.

The wind shifted, the sun was lower in the sky. My bag of almonds and raisins was now empty, and I was hungry. I turned back toward Sarlat and retraced my footsteps. The topographical map and the ground were not lining up. I passed the same goats who just looked at me that way only goats can, from the side and with mischief, and maybe even with a little bit of telepathy. But none offered any aid in directing me to elusive Temniac.

How could I have missed it? There was clearly a village with a church just north of Sarlat, which was exactly where I was. I checked, tapped my compass, and double-checked. North. Exactly. But somehow, the roads did not match up from theory into practice. I resigned myself to the fact that the mists separating dream and waking reality would not part for me today, that my quest for the six-petal flower had only just begun, and that like Perceval I was left to wander the forest until I could revise the questions that I asked. Such as: Why had I had such a weird dream to begin with, and why on earth was I now following it? To what purpose? The eerie recall of the pamphlets falling out of my pannier and of finding the animated flower on the website rushed back.

By the time I got to Sarlat, dark clouds had gathered. A sudden spring thunderstorm erupted fifteen minutes after I arrived inside Le Chardon. I looked out my window to see a flood of new tourists walking for their first time into the medieval heart of Sarlat, utterly undeterred by the weather. Magic is magic, and this place seemed to have a big serving of it. Umbrellas huddled and bobbed along and their bearers' faces said everything that was written in my heart. This place was simply amazing and unbelievable. I vowed to find Temniac soon. As I made myself a late lunch, I also vowed to walk more into that intoxicating countryside, in every direction, my starting point always Sarlat. Maybe the point of the dream had simply been that. Maybe I was the dancing flower, and I had the six directions of the compass to explore, to animate, to dance?

Indeed, the next days were a glorious dance. All I did was walk, go to the weekly markets in Sarlat and nearby St-Cyprien, and then join Nadiya for coffee or wine to meet yet new people whom she introduced me to in order to feed my interests in the community and region and to give me a chance to practice and improve my French.

For example, there was the lady who taught Occitan at a school in Sarlat. She grew up with bilingual parents who were fully fluent in Occitan and used it all the time. Her older brother, she explained further, still spoke the two languages, separately, but she grew up *entre les deux cultures*. "So I spoke a patois of Occitan and French as a child. I mixed them, unlike my brother. Purists turn their noses up at patois and say that it's not Occitan." She was just happy that at least she spoke it. "It wasn't until I went to school that I learned to separate the two languages."

Then there was the septuagenarian builder and flirt who saw every woman as beautiful and game and who invited me to go with him on a road trip to northern Portugal. (I declined.) Then there were people at Nadiya and Aidan's dinner parties, such as the mayor of a nearby village, who spoke of his family farm's occupation by Nazis when he was a boy of seven and how his family thinly survived. And, an incredibly talented watercolor artist with a handsome grin, who was just getting divorced a second time but had the warmth of an innocent young boy and the sex appeal of a peaking truffle, without knowing it. (Which added to it.) Or, the usual suspects from that winter communal feast in Castels, especially the calm shepherd and his kind and perky wife. (The reduction of the number of sheep in his flock as his form of retirement had done them both good; the sparkle in her eye was stronger and the sparkle in his had fully returned.)

These were chances I was given to learn from locals how one existed closely with the land: how to heal it and be stewards of it, how to see it, flirt with it, paint it, and how to work with it through rocks, plants, and animals, and create symbiosis with it.

Then, there were a few misfires, such as the quiet and stern accountant, a woman who wanted to improve her English but whom I could not get to speak in either French or English, her lips as tight as a fresh oyster. We sat over coffee one afternoon in silence as my coffee went cold and until it was time for me to politely excuse myself from our "conversation."

I walked everywhere. Walking is the best way to see the subtle details of this intimate landscape with its deep ancestry of human occupation. I walked east and explored the hidden neighborhoods in Sarlat's undulating hills. Each homestead was in town but in its own little crook of a hill, with kitchen gardens, sometimes chickens, and often a dog or two because life without dogs here is inconceivable.

I walked west and found the cemetery full of stories of several generations of people. There were the names I saw in town on storefronts and in the local newspaper, names of long-time Périgordines families born and raised here. There were the names of Muslim and North African citizens, some coming as early as the 1920s through the French colonial presence in Morocco, Algeria, and Tunisia. Many were honored as war heroes for fighting for Mother France. There were many Portuguese names, reinforcing my awareness of how many people from Portugal had come to France to work and had not gone back. My favorite waiter in town was from a Portuguese family, had been born here, and exhibited ease and fluidity between the two cultures.

At the southern end of the cemetery was a tall stone honoring the Jews from Alsace-Lorraine who, during World War II, were evacuated to Sarlat and nearby as Nazis were occupying their northern province. Many went on to live and die here after the war, but those who returned to Alsace-Lorraine after the war were listed on the stone as well, to honor that they once wove their spirit with this place and that this place did not forget them.

That stone was the capstone to all the rest, and together they knocked my sense of belonging one notch deeper. Here was poetic evidence of a place that loved its entire people. Walking west, I also found more hidden villages and nooks and cranny homesteads where donkeys and goats resided and tomatoes were staked to grow high on the vine near rows of spring lettuce, onions, and kale.

I walked north again and mysteriously missed Temniac, again. Maybe I'd missed it because in a land where every inch is ancient, fascinating, and full of mystery, I was easily distracted. Such as at the stream that ran north-south through Sarlat and went underground in town and re-emerged in the heart of the medieval center at the Mary fountain in a limestone cave. That stream was a whole world unto itself. On its north end it had a whole community of frogs who hopped like popcorn as soon as my shadow passed near their bank. Near the frog society was a grand kitchen garden and its old farmer contemplating his next planting as he stood in the middle of his teepees of green beans and rows of onions with his house making a nice backdrop on the hill above us.

In my ecstasy, I told Nadiya all about the frogs on our next coffee meeting, which happened to be with the stern accountant who said not a word. So, it was not she, but Nadiya, who gifted me with my new word of the day, *la grenouille*, frog, sweet little frog. As bio-indicators, those little *grenouilles* told me that the earth and water were healthy here, that the appearance of the good life was truly beyond skin deep.

That northern path also introduced me to two dogs who became my buddies and came to know me as I passed: a miniscule Yorkie and a gargantuan Saint Bernard. The two lived in a yard full of ochre-colored chickens, white doves, and black-and-white rabbits. Sometimes when I went by, I saw the Yorkie curled up in the neck of the Saint Bernard, who was passed out on the ground. His little yelps and rush to the gate to greet me rousted his giant friend who slowly lumbered over to slobber liberally on my extended hand, while the little guy leaped up and down for height and attention.

But it was my walks south, toward the Dordogne river, that made me forget all about the dream and the flower of Temniac. There, I kept finding myself in a world of Occitan farmers and vocal *rouge-gorges*, those little red-breasted messenger birds. There, I learned that what we think of as modern France is a far more beautiful and charming place but thoroughly unknown.

I walked south on the path that swept up the hill to the train station, the path I had walked when I first came to Sarlat in winter. In spring, it had both tame and wild flowers lining the road along the steep hill. On it, I would pass an octogenarian lady seated at her kitchen table, reading glasses on and scanning the newspaper with her windows wide open and her laundry drying on a line tied between two hefty plane trees across the street. The laundry line too was of great interest, for on it hung sexy lacy lingerie — undies, push up bras — which I learned over time and cautious investigation belonged to the same woman with her newspaper, not to a daughter or granddaughter. I realized that it was I with limitations, not she, to assume they belonged to a younger woman. When I occasionally saw her husband, either seated at the kitchen table across from her or gazing out across the street (usually at the laundry line) from their door stoop, he had on a perennial broad and content smile.

Next, on that same southern train station path, I also often passed a woman who was always in her blue-and-white apron and habitually attacking falling leaves with her broom. She was nearly always out there the moment one leaf interloped on her well-groomed walk. It would be in mid-fall when she came out her front door and allowed it to kiss the ground before shooing it off.

I also knew that somewhere along this stretch lived a man in a cream sweater with a sense of love for the world in general and a cheerful *bonjour*, who would open his door in a winter tempest just to welcome the stranger new in town and affirm to her that she was arriving home. I had not yet seen him again but kept my eyes open. I knew the door, dark wood with frosted glass.

And at the very top of that train station's road was a woman in her seventies who regularly greeted me in Occitan. Looking back, it seemed that the line between French and Occitan in town was drawn there. The farther south I went, the more Occitan was offered to me in greeting, sometimes trumping French.

Soon after crossing the Occitan line, going further south from Sarlat on foot had two options in order to avoid the narrow winding road that most drivers took too fast. There was the old railway-turned-bike-path to Carsac that I'd walked in the winter with its patches of dark and light, and there were the small roads to the village of La Canéda with its old Templar church.

One day I took the little roads to La Canéda to visit its twelfth-century church. Tucked into its own set of gently rolling hills that play hide-and-seek with the walker, I walked past farms, stables, fallow fields, and the occasional vineyard. A white stallion ran up to greet me, but then was miffed that I had no carrot. Red poppies blushed in a field green with swaying spring wheat, and in the distance, walnut trees posed with their witch-like figures, knobby arms raised, fingers praising the heavens. An occasional donkey held up his grazing head as I passed and then dropped it back into the grass and ignored me (word got out I had no carrots), and the *rouge-gorges* were everywhere. I passed an elderly man weeding his garden and heard overhead the familiar territorial orchestration of the *rouge-gorge*. I stopped to spy the bird in the tree, which was when the man saw me and got up and came over to the fence where I stood.

"He's my friend, that one," he said in Occitan, clearly and slowly so I would understand. Delivered that way, I did understand but could only respond in my faulty French. He didn't seem to mind and continued in slow Romance. "When I garden, that little *rouge-gorge* comes to visit. Now, I have a little bowl of water for him," he pointed to a little ceramic bowl near where he was weeding, "and he'll just fly over, sit there, drink a little, and we talk. He's wonderful." So are you, I wanted to say, for being such a lover of this world.

I continued down along the same road as the man and bird's and onward to La Canéda. Soon, maybe three hundred meters later, I felt a strange pull from just over a small rise. I climbed it and, as I did, looked to my right, the direction from which the pull had come. There, a homestead came into view, and when it did, it was its vineyard that arrested me in my tracks. The feeling had come dead center from there. It was on a small slope with seven rows of vines that went along for some sixty meters per row. Beyond them was a dilapidated wooden tool shed and to its right, a simple old home built of local stone. Between vines and home were varied fruit trees and beneath them sheep and geese mingled and grazed.

Nothing marked the home as any more exceptional than the places around it, yet I felt something intangible. It was as if I had entered a place that was deeply loved and more closely attended to than other places, and for no one other than the occupant, for his or her own solitary pleasure. I looked for the person but found only the sheep and the geese. I walked on but carried the vineyard inside me. So much so that two days later I returned, hoping to meet whoever lived there. I was in luck. There stood a man of around eighty, planted like his vines between rows five and six of the small vineyard, dressed in a t-shirt that had "Sarlat" embroidered on the left pectoral and the signature French blue overalls of men who labored with their hands. He was just standing there, eyes closed, taking in the air, palms to his side, open and slightly upward, a Buddha-like smile on his face.

The sound of my wooden walking stick against the paved road alerted him to my presence and he opened his eyes. He cheerily barked "*Bonjorn!*" and proceeded to speak a mélange of French and Occitan. I returned his greeting and seized the chance to ask him about his vineyard.

"I'm curious, what grape variety are you growing here?"

"An old and venerable one," he beamed. "*Le raisin inconnu.* The unknown grape. It's one that has been grown here locally, forever it seems, but no one has given it a name or a designation."

I was hungry to learn more. I wanted to ask about what he was doing, palms up, eyes closed, silent whispers on his lips, but kept to concrete conversation. "Are you growing it for your own pleasure or to sell to the public?" I wanted to buy a bottle. Taste the whispered magic.

"Ah, no!" he laughed. "I make it just for my own pleasure! I worked in Sarlat for thirty-two years and am now retired." Her patted his chest over the embroidered Sarlat. He explained that he had worked in the decades following the Malraux Law passed in the 1960s that prioritized preservation of France's historic patrimony. Sarlat was to become one of the most spectacular examples of that preservation effort, resurrecting the town from sleepy decay to the top-choice film set for anything medieval to Renaissance. That the restoration was done carefully and authentically, applying old stone craft, added to its enduring beauty. I felt a special respect for this man who worked with his hands stone by stone to rebirth the town, giving its emblematic town symbol, its salamander stepping out from the fire, its next resurrection and life. It also made me wonder what magic he worked on his own land.

"I enjoy making and drinking my own wine." He returned from recounting his rich history to answer my original question, then added, "That's what life is about, enjoying the everyday."

I started to ask what his wine tasted like, but he grew a bit nervous, looked side to side, and interrupted my question midway. "Listen," he said carefully, "there's an old legend — you understand *légende*?" I nodded my head. Yes, legend. He continued, "There's an old legend around here that says if you speak too much about the wine, especially in front of the vines, you could ruin it."

His expression was serious and edged with worry, which made me feel distressed that I had ruined his peace. We quickly shifted topics and chatted about the weather, leaving the vines in peace.

After a few more moments I said goodbye to let him get back to his grape communion. Further down the road, I turned back and there he was, eyes closed, standing still in the vineyard with palms up and his lips forming silent magical incantations. Was that why I felt such a good vibe from that vineyard? It seemed that this elderly man treated his vines as individual spirits, precious children, and communed with them every day. What would it be like if I treated the life around me like that, with that level of awakeness and reverence?

I stored that thought inside and pushed on, returning as the day before to the twelfth-century Templar church in La Canéda. I found it closed again but was still intrigued by its incredibly tall and narrow stature and thick walls. No windows allowed a peek inside. It had been built for defense during a time when the village must have retreated into these impenetrable walls when a threat rose over the hills. I then turned back toward Sarlat. I passed the old man's vineyard again, but he had gone. I passed the other old man, who was in his garden with the *rouge-gorge* by his side drinking at the water bowl.

And as I entered Sarlat's town limit, crossing that invisible Occitan line, I thought of the vine whisperer's comment about the old legend. It made me see him as a fair-handed father who didn't want to put too much pressure on his children to achieve but just enough to thrive. He had also helped make Sarlat thrive like a good wine, perhaps with the application of the same brand of patience, love, and stone-whispering.

I realized that thriving was far more livable and present than achieving. I recalled what the doctor told Miles and me when I asked him for Miles' mother's prognosis when she had made a turn for the worse.

"She's failing to thrive," he'd said. I inquired into his use of that word. "That's how doctors are taught to detect when a person is preparing to die," he offered. "She's crossed a final line in that direction. She is past the point of thriving."

That doctor and that old man taught me something profound about where to place one's quality of life. I decided then and there to learn from them, to make thriving a priority over achieving. And to savor every sip.

One day, I went to St-Cyprien by train from Sarlat, and then began walking from the long distance trail that began behind St-Cyprien's hilltop church and disappeared behind the town into a vast native evergreen oak forest and limestone hills and cliffs. Often the trees hid the cliffs so I stuck carefully to the trail.

It grew strangely quiet. I began to pass caves with signs of longtime human habitation. I stopped to check my compass because the trail markers had disappeared. An eerie sound cut the silence. It was a long, continuous slicing sound over leaves to my right. I turned to see a five-foot serpent of black leathery skin slowly slip into sun along the trail and then disappear again into the forest floor's undergrowth. I still heard his continuous slide over leaves for drawn out moments since he'd become invisible again.

After my chills subsided, I realized I had not seen a single person during the two hours since when I'd left St-Cyprien. It was a strange sensation, given that now in the fullness of spring the Dordogne region was swelling with visitors in the same manner the river was swelling with spring rains. People were everywhere. But here there was no one but a long, thick, black snake and me. I felt my brain recalibrate to a different time in this ancient place, maybe move a little teeny tiny bit closer to how Cro-Magnon or Neandertal would have walked here and slightly less like that of a modern human's mind acclimated to grocery stores and cafés.

My goal was to arrive in the heart of the prehistoric Dordogne, Les-Eyzies-de-Tayac, where the National Prehistory Museum resides in the center of several stunning world heritage cave sites. The Vézère River passes through Les Eyzies, and it is this river, up and down stream from the village, that is home to more prehistoric Paleolithic sites than anywhere else in the world. I wanted to arrive there on foot, the old way. My trail connected St-Cyprien via those forest and cliff-side passes to Les Eyzies due north. It was a path that lyrically connected the Dordogne River, on whose bank St-Cyprien sits, to its water cousin, the Vézère. My trail map said it would take two-and-a-half hours to arrive, but it neglected to mention the extra two hours I would need to find the way after I got lost due to faulty trail markers, or the absence of them, at sensitive turns.

Four and a half hours later, after several double backs and uphill climbs, I staggered into Les Eyzies and made a direct path to the Café de la Mairie over which stood the famous limestone sculpture of Neandertal Man gazing over the valley from a nearby rock shelf. I did what he would do under the circumstances and ordered a cold, frothy blond beer. As I sat savoring my well-earned brew, I reflected on where I had just been.

I had wandered through thick oak forest that wove in and out of caves and rock shelves that were perfect shelters for our ancestors. My brain had become more alert, present, and calm. It took in greater details all at once: different plants in the undergrowth, animals' movements along the forest floor, unique turns in the landscape, the shift of wind, a bird call that seemed to silence all the others, a particular tree that seemed to bear promise of autumn nuts, and was that a stand of porcini under those decaying leaves from winter?

In those four and a half hours, I had time-traveled as deeply as I had foot-traveled. I had heard birdsong without the sound of car motors or a distant thresher from a farmer's field. I had encountered a surprising winemaker, tying his vines in the southern sun in a clearing in the forest on a slope perfect for his vintage. I had stopped and talked to a farmer harvesting the hay in his field with an old-fashioned scythe, the clarity of sunlight and physical work shining in his eyes. Twice, local dogs had appeared from the forest and walked along as if we had known each other all our lives. Chestnut flowers swelled with the promise of plump meaty nuts later in the year. Of necessity, when the trail markers failed, I'd trespassed across a farmer's field and passed black-and-white dairy cows and someone working hard at making lunch who glimpsed at me from their kitchen window and seemed to understand my predicament. When I'd finally arrived in the Vézère valley, limestone cliffs emerged like a dramatic stage set, telling me I was on the right path. A sign next appeared, telling me I could buy wine just fifty meters to the left. A café appeared selling frothy cold beer. I sat. I sipped. I savored. I had returned to civilization.

I finished my brew, smacked my lips, and wandered a few meters down the road to the Abri Pataud, a limestone protective shelf that was occupied for thousands of years, starting around 35,000 years ago. When I took in the overhead engraving of an ancient goat from 22,000 years ago, I think I understood better the reality of the person who had made it, who had carefully studied the animal and then patiently and alchemically rendered its body and spirit into the stone. I also enjoyed getting to know our guide to the rock shelf site, a young woman with thick red hair and shining clear eyes that spoke of her passion for her region's prehistory. She took us through all the layers and thousands of years of early modern human occupation at Abri Pataud as if it were an adventure film.

An old farmer had used the rock shelf to shelter his animals in the first half of the twentieth century. When he decided to expand it, he discovered remains that have now been dated to 22,000 years ago, including a young woman's grave and her jewelry. Archaeologists excavated the site in the 1960s and discovered that other humans occupied it from 35,000 to 20,000 years ago. They mapped every stratum and discovered that 34,000 years ago there was one central fire around which everyone gathered, but that by 22,000 years ago, the cave had sections, each with its own fire, seeming to indicate that people went from a more egalitarian and shared culture, to a more segregated and possibly hierarchical one.

When the tour was over, the guide turned to me and asked, "Where in the USA are you from?"

"I now live in New Jersey," I said, "but was born and raised in Colorado."

She brightened. "You know, many of the remains found in the Périgord are contemporary with the Clovis Culture of Colorado in the United States. So much so that some people from the Dordogne say that the ancient Americans of Colorado are their long lost Périgordins relatives." Though I knew that not everyone agreed with this, I liked that and told her that maybe this was why I felt an affinity for this region. She smiled and said, "Why not?"

Not too much later, I read in the news from my hometown in Colorado that landscapers, while digging in a client's backyard, hit something hard a few feet down that gave off a pleasing ping, that sound of air slicing and chiming at once that only flint can make. They immediately stopped the work and called in a Paleolithic archaeologist who confirmed the pit was full of beautifully crafted flint tools from the Clovis people who may have stockpiled them there during a hunt some 13,000 years ago. I knew that geography well. From the accompanying picture I knew the hillside, a place where as a child my brother and I used to play. It had been very close to our old house. When I was there, I used to imagine time-traveling to other realms and times, apparently an old habit of mine. Many times I would just wander and gather plant seeds or multicolored sandstone or mica, falling into that old mental cadence of deep presence and awareness of the environment. I often tried to imagine myself back to the first people's who traversed these hills. It was similar to what I experienced often here in the Dordogne.

My subjective worlds were coming full circle, connecting pathways across the earth that had been laid out long before I ever existed, offering a map to my soul. •

The Wedding Tree

Chapter 10

NEANDERTAL FIRE, TROUBADOUR LOVE

> Let's see, I thought rapidly. I hardly knew him and even for the more relaxed French who invite people into their homes more readily than the Spanish, this is a bit too quick. I also recalled that it was unusual for a man one hardly knew to visit one on a Sunday morning with strawberries and ask to come up, a man who had a family, a wife, and kids. I said, *"Non."*

WEDNESDAY EARLY MORNING AS USUAL I POPPED OUT of bed with the fishmonger and her ice sounds, always with that same excitement of a kid on Christmas morning, that ripe potential joy of adventure in the air that never seems to get old. And as usual, I made my first stop at Petrus and Jean's stand, which on Wednesdays went up near my two favorite market cafés in the heart of the main square, the Place de la Liberté.

This particular Wednesday, town workers were setting up for a weekend festival when all the flavors of the land were on display and for sale in Sarlat's two main squares. Special four-legged and feathered visitors would be here too, to advance the magical mood of wine, food, and more food. They were building a temporary farm and barnyard around the cathedral to accommodate the visiting geese, pigs, cows, rabbits, goats, sheep, and donkeys who would attend as special guests, in more ways than one, with the throng of visiting gourmands for the weekend.

I stepped around bales of hay and temporary wooden fencing, and I went deeper into the market. After tea and homemade nut cake with Jean and Petrus, I went out to gather my food for the next few days from the various vendors who were becoming more and more familiar: two pints of local strawberries and a bundle of fresh radishes with long red-white bodies and green edible tops from the organic farmer; a head of red leaf lettuce from the Occitan gardener and his wife who both kept the exchange to *lachuga* and money; a long, leaner version of baguette I learned was called *ficelle* from the baker next door; and a bunch of shallots bundled together at the stems with a braided piece of twine from the next vendor. He had arrayed beautiful, woven gold shallots and white and purple garlic bulbs across his stand. I was just enjoying standing under his umbrella, taking it all in as I waited for my change for the shallots and already setting my sniffer in pursuit of that dry-cured, thinly-sliced duck breast to which I was becoming heavily addicted, when out of the corner of my eye I saw something incongruous. I suddenly felt an odd sensation, a ripple in time's fabric, a temporary disorientation.

It had been a passing whirlwind carrying with it the distinctively robust and hairy form of Paleolithic archaeology professor Harold Dibble, with whom I'd studied years back in Philadelphia. The silhouette of full-yet-sprightly girth, thick reddish-blond beard, and longish blond-red hair flew past and disappeared. *Non. Pas possible*. But it was hard to shake off. That figure, that beard, and that hair were hard ones to replicate. I quickly took my change for the shallots, dropped the duck hunt, and stalked that flitting illusion of another time and place.

In that brief eye-corner glimpse I thought maybe another, thinner man walked briskly with him, moving his arms in animated conversation. The two had whisked past garden stands, olive sellers, foie gras tables, jarred and preserved black truffles, and walnut liquors. They then passed into the narrowing of the northern end of the square and disappeared beyond the Mary fountain. I rushed there, and I saw no one. By then I had convinced myself that they had been nothing but my imagination.

But that form was emblazoned on my eyelids ever since two decades back when I had been a first-year anthropology doctoral student. I hadn't seen him in years.

I rushed to Le Chardon, searched for Harold's university email on the internet, and quickly sent him a message, asking if he were indeed in Sarlat or if someone else were masquerading about town as he.

Not much later I received his surprised response affirming that he was in the Dordogne, not too far from Sarlat, and that he and his colleague, fellow Paleolithic archaeologist Dennis Sandgathe, had come to Sarlat to meet another associate for lunch. This was his usual dig area and he came here every year. But me, what the heck was I doing here? I wrote back about my current writing and research in the Dordogne, explaining that my interest stemmed from the same reasons his favorite research subjects — Neandertals and Cro-Magnons — had made this region home. Past and present, we were all drawn to the great experience here of cuisine, culture, climate, and immense beauty.

We arranged to meet for lunch the next day in Carsac, just south of Sarlat, at the Hotel-Restaurant Delpeyrat, run by the family of one of my kind badminton partners that first winter here.

Dennis was joining us too, and I quickly learned that like Harold he also had a taste for bad jokes and that this congenial team flew from North America to France nearly every spring or early summer and opened up their dig house in the Dordogne to prepare for the summer season and the arrival of the rest of the excavation crew. That's what they were doing now. The prior year they had wrapped up several years of digging at the Neandertal site of Roc de Marsal, best known for the discovery, during earlier excavations in the twentieth century, of the skeleton of a three-year-old Neandertal child. This year they were commencing a new excavation at another famous site, La Ferrassie, known for seven Neandertal skeletons unearthed, also in prior digs in the twentieth century. Issues of burial and whether Neandertals intentionally buried their dead were among the heated issues they were investigating at both sites.

Another heartily debated issue these two and their team had taken on was whether Neandertals made fire or only controlled it after gathering it in the wild, such as from lightening strikes. We were welcome to join the heat if we wished. Nadiya and I were invited to visit Roc de Marsal in two weeks time, when Harold and Dennis returned from Morocco. There, with their French colleagues, they would be conducting a day of formal site visits for the *Societé Préhistorique Française*, the French Prehistory Society, a group of around three hundred professional archaeologists and amateur archaeology buffs. Once a year they made visits to archaeological sites that for a weekend were opened to the public. Nadiya already wanted to go out and buy herself an Indiana Jones hat for the occasion.

Harold and Dennis had included Nadiya when they learned that she had been excited over the prospect of lunch with archaeologists ever since I'd mentioned to her what had transpired at the Wednesday market. I think, like me, she also secretly loved Neandertals, but in her proper Thai manner, unlike me, did not come out and blurt it. Quite so often.

The next day we four sat down to lunch. The restaurant owners, Philippe and Aline, and their grown children, Aurelie and Sabastien, came out to greet us and to joust with Harold and Dennis. Philippe proudly stated that he had known Harold for over thirty-two years. He added that the two archaeologists pulled a practical joke on them each year. Aurelie smiled and went to the back and returned with a menu the family had saved from two years prior. Opening to the house specialties, she pointed at a menu item Harold and Dennis had secretly slipped into the regular menu. They'd replicated the whole page in its letter font, spacing, and even paper, and slipped it into the menu sleeve, replacing the original page.

"Here it is," she said, "*Beans à la Dibble.*" Its English translation described it as, "white beans simmered in secret base." The day of the menu heist, Harold and Dennis had stationed themselves at a table for two along the back wall and watched the lunchtime drama unfold as people inquired as to what exactly was Beans à la Dibble. The family was in stitches when they realized their menu had been hijacked. Philippe and Aline decided to improvise, asking Harold how to make the dish because some patrons were seriously thinking of ordering it. When pressed, he said, "It's really a cassoulet with white beans, tomato paste, onions, sausage, stuff, you know, a basic cassoulet, with a secret base sauce." Harold, I also learned, had a lot of secret sauces, from salad vinaigrettes to pasta dishes. He never divulged so that was left to the family to concoct, which they did as deliciously as everything they cooked.

"This year," Aurelie confided, "we know something is going to happen, but we have no idea what it might be." Both Harold and Dennis looked innocently on as if they couldn't fathom what she meant.

We all selected the four-course menu of the day for which the restaurant was famous. It was designed each day around the freshest ingredients plucked from their own garden. Our first course of comforting homemade vegetable soup arrived soon after and as we slurped it up I began to see the ease between these two talented archaeologists. Dennis smiled a lot at Harold's humor, and Harold chortled at a joke well told, often his own, but almost as often from Dennis, who could lob one back far better than I had hit that birdie with Aurelie. I simply enjoyed being there, being a part of it. I had loved Harold's class when I was a graduate student, both because of the engaging and humorous way that he taught the material, and also because the material — human evolution and prehistory — was, and remained, one of my most favorite topics and a big reason I was here.

I could also tell from the relaxed contentment washing across Nadiya's face that she too was enjoying the company. And the food. She was lost in reverie with the broth as the other two savored it over puns. I learned from Dennis that Harold not only loved to eat, as his figure attested, but also loved to cook really good, full meals for the dig team. He knew that the best way to keep a crew happy after long hard days at a dig site was to give them something to look forward to: good food and wine.

Harold listened to this, chuckled, and stated simply, "Dennis just likes to eat."

And both liked selecting and serving the wine. Dennis refilled my glass, a nice local red served in a pitcher, as Aurelie set before us each a slice of homemade pork terrine and Sabastien made sure we had more thickly sliced rustic bread. This was followed by a generous serving of thinly sliced tender roast beef with green beans and a dish of peas, potatoes, and asparagus simmered in olive oil, garlic, and white wine. The table was quiet for some moments, other than the occasional recall of something one or the other archaeologist had to do: contact local colleagues, buy more provisions, make sure all the tools were in place, repair a door or plank, call so-and-so — and whether Nadiya or I wanted more wine.

Dennis poured. Nadiya, the designated driver, declined. I happily acquiesced, knowing full well word would get back to Aidan and I needed to be ready to defend my American ways. Next came dessert: homemade raspberry crème brulée. Followed by espressos for all.

We said *bon voyage au Maroc* and *à bientôt* until two weeks later when I would call and get directions to Roc de Marsal. Soon after that lunch, I pitched and got a gig to write a feature story for a magazine back home on Harold and his work. I smiled when I wrote to Miles about the just-go-and-find-out-strategy. It was a good one. Had I not just showed up, I never would have run into my old archaeology professor in Sarlat's weekly market.

That afternoon I paid a visit to Saint Sacerdos, a daily pilgrimage where I liked to walk down the nave and then take a seat in one of the pews near the spiral-engraved pillars and with a good view of the Mary-standing-on-crescent-moon scene, a stunning and emotionally charged cobalt glass creation in the center of the apse. I stopped briefly at the four stone faces to see if there was anything more they wished to impart. It was the woman who smiled. I had asked to go as deeply as possible, and she said I would indeed be going deeply, as deep down as Neandertals and maybe even deeper, to the very soul of this place.

Before visiting Neandertals, a few other market days came and went, each with its own original festive air that helped temper the anticipation of seeing Roc de Marsal and Harold and Dennis again.

At one Saturday market, the Occitan festival called La Ringueta was picking up steam and would peak that night with traditional music and dance on a parking-lot-turned-outdoor-dance-floor on the edge of the medieval town. More people were in town than before and more friends and friends of friends also appeared. With my food shopping done, I stopped to join the pulse of friends who were gathering at one of the market cafés in the Place de la Liberté. Some of them I knew from badminton, such as Aurelie and Cédric, and others from dinners with Nadiya and her friends outside of the sports club. People came and went, the table expanded and contracted. I enjoyed my market-day café crème with the conviviality of acquaintances.

As I sat down near Nadiya, a man walked by behind me; I felt him before I saw him. There was an invisible pull, a force field. I turned and there stood a very handsome man, and very funny, it turned out, because rather than walk by, he stopped and began joking with one of the people at our table. His friend introduced him to us all and he went around the table shaking hands with the men and proffering cheek kisses to the women. When he and I were introduced, I felt sparks as his lips kissed my cheeks and electricity rushed through my body. Merde.

That night I had a small dinner party *chez moi*, Le Chardon. It was in part to thank Nadiya for all she had done for me and in part to test my new skills as a person desiring to live in France. I reasoned that to live in France, one must master food, from its production to its purchase to its preparation and the ritual of presenting that preparation over a four-course meal.

Could I actually pull off a dinner party for French friends and do it well? In all my time in Spain, no one ever invited anyone to their home until they were deep, close friends. Sometimes that took well over two decades to earn. In Spain, home was for the most intimate of connections, and an outsider could spend years and decades and not be invited to someone's home. Since my time as a student in Seville, living with a host family, I'd rarely stepped into a Spaniard's home. We always met in cafés, as was the custom with friends, even friends of many years. These were warm, jovial, and cheerful times, but they never resulted in entering that innermost circle of intimates.

What I longed for were friendships in both the winter and the summer pastures that lasted beyond my presence in a café. I wanted friends who wrote to each other when we were apart and picked up where we'd left off when we were back together. That simply had not transpired as much as I had hoped it would in Spain, whether it was the subtly *sospechoso* world of Galicia, or the more gregarious and vocal one of Andalucía. But in France, people had invited me into their homes almost as quickly as Americans did. While this did not imply intimacy, the way it would in Spain, it was a first step. People had written to me, too, when I was away. We'd already picked up where we'd left off from that distant winter.

Over coffee that day at market, after the rest of the group of friends departed, including Market Man — I could now think clearly and was happy for a rational focus — Nadiya gave me the final guest list, which I had left entirely to her. It would be Nadiya, her architect friend, Dominique, whom she wanted to invite to thank him for all that he was doing for her house improvement and building projects, and our mutual friend Cédric from badminton who was charming and made everyone laugh. For reasons inexplicable, maybe that first night of pun-filled badminton or the recall of the dream in which he'd featured, I felt an ease with him that was rare with someone I still barely knew. And all three were unapologetic gourmands. Nadiya was a master Thai chef in her own right, and both Cédric and Dominique loved to eat and drink excellent wine and discuss ingredients and vintages the way American football fans like to discuss plays. The pressure was on.

I had set dinner for Saturday night because I knew I could shop at the market and get the freshest and most local ingredients of the day, a first lesson in cooking for the French.

My menu would both cater to and challenge the French palate — and hence, delight the Thai one, more accustomed to spices and heat. I devised and wrote out a menu and set it on the counter to guide my path.

First, a simple appetizer of locally made dry salami, with cornichons and radishes. My friends, I'd learned, liked starting a dinner party with a glass of dry and cheerful champagne, a pre-dinner appetite opener with a few light nibbles to equally stimulate the juices.

Next, we'd sit down to a course of cross-section slices of *tomate noire*, a dark red and green striped tomato I discovered at the organic farmer's stand, layered with smoked Aquitaine trout and a vinaigrette I made with balsamic vinegar, olive oil, and finely chopped parsley.

This was followed by the main course, a tajine I'd learned from Berbers in the Sahara one very cold night in December when two professors and I, as the third adult there to teach travel writing and anthropology, and a gaggle of twenty students were camping out under the stars as a part of the cultural immersion program to Morocco. Because some of the students were vegetarians, the Berber chefs devised a traditional dish without meat. It consisted of caramelized onions in olive oil with chick peas, green olives, carrots, copious amounts of chopped parsley, ginger, garlic, saffron, lemon juice, more olive oil, and harissa, a North African hot chili sauce that would give a lot of Louisiana hot sauces a run for their money. They had served it up with good rice instead of bread. The tajine was Nadiya's request.

Then followed a salad and cheese plate. The salad was the coveted Oc farmer's red curly leaf lettuce tossed with little green mache leaves I'd acquired from another farmer, and a vinaigrette of minced shallots, apple cider vinegar, mustard, crushed capers, and olive oil. The cheeses were the walnut liquor cheese from the Dutch lady and her golden retriever, disks of *cabécou* from Our Lady, and St-Nectaire from Petrus and Jean's cheese-selling neighbor at the Saturday market.

For dessert, I'd decided on simplicity and picked up *gariguette* strawberries, the variety that was the sweetest and most fragrant, and sliced them to serve with dollops of crème fraiche into which I'd whipped a bit of local honey from Nicolas the bee-keeper with his handsome grin and thick beard. When I asked him to thank the bees for me, he'd said, "I thank them everyday for what they do for us."

For after dinner, I had ginger and lemon verbena herbal infusions and Armagnac. The bread I would serve throughout the meal was a rustic disk of traditional whole grain bread I'd picked up from none other than the baker beneath my window.

Throughout the afternoon as I sliced, sautéed, and stirred, my three guests called one after the other to ask what I was preparing. I was at first surprised by this, but I soon learned that it was done in the spirit of collaboration. They each had agreed to bring a bottle of wine to pair with each course, to lighten my load in the wine department and to be a part of the festivity of the meal. As I hung the phone up a third time, I smiled. I liked this level of engagement where everything mattered so much; it promised a great evening. I put the jolt of meeting Market Man entirely out of my mind, somewhere behind the now entirely forgotten dancing, six-petaled flower of Temniac.

At seven-thirty in the evening, my guests arrived, each with a bottle in hand, except Nadiya, who had two, one of champagne for the appetizer and one of Pouilly Fumé for the first course. Dominique had a Saint Émilion red for the tajine and the salad and cheese plate to follow. Cédric brought a white sweet Coteaux de Layon for the strawberries and honeyed cream.

We all sat down to an engaging evening of rich conversation, much of it revolving around food and wine, and by the main course my head began to spin from the rapid fire and animated French that I both relished but that was also like taking a spin class while needing to keep dinner on course.

Each dish demanded an explanation: its origin, its inspiration, and why had I picked it for tonight. Each bottle of wine demanded a deep discussion of the region it came from, the terroir, and the best foods from that region for the wine. Everyone complimented the meal and admired the order, the presentation, and the harmony of flavors. They even investigated each spice, from my usage to its origins.

By the time we had contemplated the deep origins of ginger, pepper, and saffron, we arrived at dessert where a hearty new discussion took over about the many varieties of strawberries and an insistent game of no-don't-tell-us-let-us-guess which variety you picked for us tonight.

I sat back and marveled as my three guests discussed for five minutes what strawberries I might have used and from whom I had purchased them, as if the strawberries were grape varietals and we were discussing wine.

From other conversations with locals, I also began to see a pattern: people didn't speak of seasons here as spring, summer, fall, and winter, but as truffle, asparagus, strawberry, chestnut, walnut, cherry, acacia, lilac, plum, and wine.

Like the wine-whisperer and his vines, we thrived. As diners ate on the square below, we felt as if we were a part of the communal feast below but in the best seat in the world. Each hour around our private table higher up, Saint Sacerdos rang her resonant bells, and we gazed at her tower at eye level.

As if this weren't already heavenly, the musical husband and wife duo, Paris-Londres, set up on the square in front of the cathedral just below. Their violin, guitar, and voices gave our dinner and dessert ethereal, trance-like, and deeply melodious music as the dark, blue light of night deepened until the medieval stones outside reflected the same warmth as the Armagnac swirling in our glasses.

As my guests prepared to leave, I noticed that all four bottles were only half empty — or half full. They really truly drank only to enjoy the taste of wine with food, not to get buzzed. Nadiya was the last out the door and whispered, "I give you one star for tonight." Smiling impishly with her self-appointed Michelin star power, I matched her gesture with a raised and disappointed eyebrow.

"I thought Chez Le Chardon deserved at least two, considering that the best view in all Sarlat is from its window."

She smiled. "Yes, I thought of awarding you two stars, but I don't want it to go to your head on your first dinner." She kissed me on the cheeks, and as she walked away added over her shoulder, "I want to inspire you to practice some more and test the recipes out on me." Her star power was self-serving but in a delightful way. "You're on," I called after her into the night.

I went back upstairs, high already from the pleasure of the evening and the success of making my friends happy with food. Too wide awake to sleep, I slowly set to cleaning up, leaving the windows open as I washed dishes. Paris-Londres had packed up and gone home, but a new music was wafting in from La Ringueta's music and dance festival a few hundred meters away. A lone flutist played a gorgeous and melancholy melody. It reminded me of the mystical poetry of my childhood, a legacy from my mother who loved the Persian poets Rumi, Hafez, and Sa'di. They wrote about the natural allusions to our soul nature as seen in the world around us, hints left to us by God, if we were willing to decipher the messages of our divine origins left in broad daylight.

One of Rumi's strongest images was of the human soul as a flute that had been made from a reed cut from the riverside, its roots and origins at the source of water. Ever since that separation, and even if for the beautiful purpose of singing the beauty of creation, the reed-soul has lamented its distance from the creator. This flute sounded like that soul, and I had to go and meet it. I left my dishwashing, threw on a sweater, and went out into the pleasantly cool night, following the plaintive sound.

As I drew near the large parking lot cleared of cars and with its canopy from towering plane trees that had been decorated with festive lights, I saw soft spotlights around a platform where sat musicians with drum, guitars, violin, and the flute. They performed one song after the next without stop, a continuous flow of traditional Occitan dance music from southern France. I knew from their mood that these melodies had been played, heard, and danced to since time immemorial, certainly since the troubadours began fiddling with them.

That solo flute alone carried waltzing couples deeply along a sultry and soothing melody and then stopped to let the rest of the band come back in and erupt into a rowdy dance tune. Couples separated and others stepped in, and people began dancing as a big group. After a few minutes I felt inspired and encouraged and also stepped into the circle. We went around and around and people near me offered cheerful fine-tuning to my effort to mimic my neighbors' dance steps. Round and round we went.

Rumi speaks of the importance of the circle. We are all in it, all included, none excluded, no one better or worse than the other because the nature of the circle is fair and just and mimes the nature of the universe, of the divine, and of our souls. Sweating and winded, we all took a break, and again the flute player returned, playing another doleful melody that suspended time and made the air thicken and movement slow.

I walked around the gathering of people toward large plane trees on the far side strung with colorful lights. As I approached, I noticed an elderly couple seated on two chairs set together like a makeshift love seat. They may have been in their late eighties, and both had a sweater on and a scarf against the evening air. Both leaned into the other, shoulder touching shoulder, and each had canes, using them as adjustable armrests. They leaned a little closer even and whispered to each other and gazed dreamily at the dancers, and in their eyes I saw the universe. I could tell with utter certainty that they saw themselves in the younger dancers, many years ago, dancing in the steps of the ancestors as these dancers danced now in their steps, carrying on traditions that were so rooted in this land that they were as vital and eternal as the strawberries, truffles, walnuts, and wine.

I drank in their eyes. It was one of those fleeting mystical moments when the veil of illusions was drawn back and I got to see how marvelous, how painfully gorgeous we are, as well as this life and this earth on which we have ever so briefly incarnated. I thought of Miles. I thought of Market Man. I wondered what I would look like, be like, when I was this old. Today, the answer to that question felt precarious. But I knew that deep, satisfying companionship looked far better than the fleeting rush of passion. Who would lean against my shoulder and whisper in my ear meaningful, interesting, and intimate things when I turned eighty?

The next morning my doorbell rang early for a Sunday. In spite of my late night, I had been up early and had already been two hours into my writing work and still in my nightgown over which I'd wrapped a warm, oversized wool sweater. Against the cold of the thick, fifteenth-century stone interior and an unusually cool summer, I'd also pulled on heavy wool socks. Near my laptop sat an almost finished bowl of coffee with milk, a new way for me to drink my coffee, which I'd come to love, because each time I picked up the bowl to sip it made me feel more French.

I saved my work and assumed, given the hour and that it was a Sunday, that it was Nadiya — who else would ring me anyhow? I went downstairs, unbolted, and drew back the big blue door.

"Bonjour Nadi . . . ," I began, but stopped as I registered that a handsome man stood there and extended to me a box of just-picked strawberries fresh off the plant.

"I thought you might like these with your breakfast."

Market Man.

I just stared at him. How did he know I lived here? Ah, we'd talked about it at the market café. True to the first time, he was still very charming and terribly handsome.

"Ah . . ." Was all that came out of my mouth.

"May I come up, have a cup of coffee?" He peered around my shoulder toward the vestibule and then around the street as if looking to see if we were being watched.

"Ah . . ."

Let's see, I thought rapidly. I hardly knew him and even for the more relaxed French who invite people into their homes more readily than the Spanish, this is a bit too quick. I also recalled that it was unusual for a man one hardly knew to visit one on a Sunday morning with strawberries and ask to come up, a man who had a family, a wife, and kids. I said, "*Non.*"

"*Non?*"

"*Oui, non.*"

His face was crestfallen. Handsome, terribly handsome, and crestfallen, but however I looked at the situation, each angle said, *non*.

But I liked him. I actually knew I could trust him, which was the weird thing. And I knew that there was some reason bigger than midlife-fidelity-testing at work, but right now wasn't the time to find out what that was.

"No, but listen, I'm happy to meet you in an hour for coffee in a café," I stressed the last three words.

Market Man handed me the strawberries. "No, I have to pick up my kids in an hour, but keep the strawberries. Enjoy them alone." He too stressed the last three words. But then he brightened. "I was at La Ringueta last night. I looked for you. Were you there?"

"I was." Gulp. "It was enchanting." Now it was confirmed, not my imagination.

"Yes, it was. Well . . . ," he looked as if about to say, "but it's cold outside, can't I come in," but instead took the high road, "See you at the next market."

"Yes," I brightened, "that would be nice."

Before he turned to go he gave me that classic French body scan, taking in my wool sweater wrapped over nightgown and my wool socks bunching at the ankle, none of the colors matching. "*Très chic,*" he said with a somber grin, then more cheerfully, "*à bientôt,*" and turned and climbed up rue Montaigne.

I looked at my feet. Yes, very fetching, I thought. No wonder it was so easy to walk away. This was hardly the image of those seductive French women's sleeping attire ads. *Tant mieux.*

I watched him go. As he walked away, some people crossed the square and began to enter Saint Sacerdos a little before mass. I looked up at Bernadette, rolled my eyes and closed the door. But I didn't go up the stairs right away. I leaned my back against the sturdy wooden door for firm support from the old building that had seen it all, standing in one place for over six centuries, and asked myself what had just happened. I looked at the strawberries, cupped in my hands as if in church asking for grace, big bucketfuls of grace. And clarity.

Was this simply strawberries or a gesture of strawberries for other fruit?

I went back upstairs and set all these matters aside and forced myself to focus and get back to working on the piece I was writing before the doorbell had rung. It was a blessing, a much needed change of topic. And I did enjoy the strawberries. Alone. *Charlottes*. Nice choice.

In early June, Nadiya and I drove to an unmarked, Dibble-directed (via cell phone) road, then trail, then narrow rocky passage, to a place only a Neandertal today would find without a cell phone, and thus arrived at Roc de Marsal, where Harold and Dennis were offering day-long discourse and presentation of the Neandertal site.

We knew we were in the right forest clearing and hung up the phone when we saw a very professorial character come out from the trees and speak to us in midwestern American English, directing us to a small, narrow foot trail that was our last leg before getting to Neandertal central. We thanked him, learned that he was a visiting American archaeologist, and then followed the path up the rise to the rock shelf and cave that had been occupied around 80,000 to 40,000 years ago. It was prime real estate in any epoch, with its Tuscan-like-rolling-hills-view of the valley below. The valley was full of life.

As we'd begun the ascent, I'd seen a small red deer in the woods, its light brown fur and white speckles playing with the forest's dapple shade. Soon after, just before approaching the cave near the top, I heard and then saw the telltale slide of the *couleuvre*, that harmless but big, thick, and black snake of these forests whose French name I'd learned since the day of my hike to Les Eyzies. Though reasonably harmless — they still could bite if threatened — I shivered. He had just slipped off the path when a hawk took flight from a branch just overhead. Between these emissaries of earth and sky, I felt time shift, and just in time. We looked up and there was the cave mouth of Roc de Marsal. The forest had helped us time travel back to the more ancient reality we would soon encounter.

Harold stood at the cave mouth, donning an Indiana Jones style Fedora. Nadiya saw it first and just looked at me with a slightly accusing stare. I had disabused her of the idea that archaeologists in real life wore Indie's hat, explaining that the science-bound reality was different from the irreverent fiction. Thus outfitted, Harold was chatting, or more accurately joking, with his colleagues, Guillaume Guerin, from the University of Bordeaux, and Alain Turq, a chief curator at the Musée National de Préhistoire des Eyzies, the National Prehistory Museum in Les Eyzies. Dennis stood deeper inside the cave and was speaking French to a visiting couple from the Loire who were local archaeology aficionados. He was just explaining that during the recent dig seasons, the team had located thirty distinct fire hearths, indicating fire use during certain periods of its occupancy by Neandertals.

Nadiya and I joined the couple just as Dennis detailed a curiosity about those hearths. They corresponded only to strata that were related to periods of warm climate, not cold.

This hearth-strata alignment carried over to their findings from another nearby Paleolithic Neandertal site that they had excavated a few years back, Pech de l'Azé IV, very close to their current dig house in Carsac. There they also found evidence for fire use, controlling it and using it in discrete spaces, along with the accompanying burnt bone and flint in the hearths, but again, "There was no evidence," Dennis said, "for fire when it was really cold. The fire strata at Roc de Marsal was during warm periods. The same is true at Pech de l'Azé. Warm periods had more lightening strikes."

At the coldest periods during the European Middle Paleolithic, which occurred around 120,000 years ago and again around 60,000 to 70,000 years ago, prime periods of Neandertal occupation, the temperatures could drop to around ten degrees Fahrenheit colder than today. If someone had the ability to make fire, wouldn't they? But they didn't.

In the world of Paleolithic archaeology, this was a revolutionary statement. But they weren't finished. In their re-examination of all the excavation data, from prior digs and from their own, they uncovered yet another controversy.

Roc de Marsal had been famous since the 1960s for possessing evidence of what looked like an intentional burial of a Neandertal infant. Dennis took us over to the hole where the skeleton had been found decades back and explained how in the 1960s amateur French archaeologist, Jean Lafille, excavated the site and came across the fossilized remains of a Neandertal child buried face down in what looked like a pit.

The infant and the sediment around which it had been found were carefully removed and taken to a lab in Paris for further analysis. The find was viewed as evidence for intentional burial among Neandertals. But when Harold and team reopened the site, they discovered that in the cave were ancient subterranean water channels running through the rock, creating holes and grooves.

"We went back to the original descriptions," described Dennis, "looking at field notes and very basic information. But when you do look at the description, there's something that contradicts this, like digging a hole. The skeleton hole was continuous with the sediment layer." As if it had been covered up naturally by the slow layering of sediment that had also filled the rest of the channel.

The evidence showed that the Neandertal infant had been found in one of the water channels, and it appeared that a hole had not been dug for him. That he was face down added to the sense that maybe this was an accidental burial. Perhaps the infant had fallen into the channel and drowned, or was placed in a natural grave and left there.

"Thinking that Neandertals buried their dead," continued Dennis, "makes them more human, more like us, so we like this idea. But there's not enough evidence to prove it. It's a case of emotion overriding science and, however warm and fuzzy the feelings, one must remain neutral and stick to the facts."

We learned that as far as we can read the evidence, both hominids — Neandertals and Cro-Magnons — were capable of symbolic thought, such as language, art, rituals and the like, but that unlike us, Neandertals didn't seem to use it as much as we did, so perhaps they just didn't cultivate it as we did. But we and our immediate ancestors ran with symbolic thought and engaged the potential to communicate ideas not only spatially to each other but also across different groups and different generations, thus allowing for a creative idea to last long enough to be modified and perhaps even perfected to a strong adaptation that enhanced our ability to survive.

While I was fascinated by this revelation, I also couldn't help but wonder if Neandertals, even if now extinct, perhaps for this very reason, weren't really the smarter of the two. Maybe they could see down the road that the capacity for more and more symbolic thought would mire us down. They certainly avoided the complication of over-adapting that our cultures and technologies eventually brought about, leading to a very different sort of threat to our survival because this time it involved the entire planet and would take all other life with it.

Nadiya and I filled up on Neandertals as much as we could. When we finally left the cave and thanked out hosts, we stepped out to the edge of the cave's ridge for one final look out on the forest below and the horizon beyond. That was when we both heard it before Nadiya saw it, about ten yards to our right. Sliiiiiide. That invisible, leaf-slipping sound only snakes, big ones, can make. It disappeared before I could glimpse it, but Nadiya said it was four feet long and had pale gray-green rings along its body. It wasn't the black *couleuvre* this time, though from the related subfamily. (I later looked it up and discovered our human name for it was Aesculapian snake and considered among Europe's largest serpents, thankfully, nonvenomous.) Unlike with the deer or hawk, its long silvery form appeared and disappeared smoothly, the sound remaining long after the image left us shivering on the warm day. At the same time, we felt the awe and beauty of this strange creature with no arms and legs. He couldn't control fire, let alone make it, but he sure could set off a strike of electricity in my spine every time he appeared.

On our return drive to Sarlat and not far from Roc de Marsal, Nadiya shared with me two of her favorite local places. The first was a holy shrine, Redon-Espic, an old shepherd's keep in the middle of deep forest where in the nineteenth century a young woman received a vision and messages from Mary. It was at the bottom of a hill and downstream from an underground water source coming from the site of an eleventh-century Romanesque church on the hill. The shepherd's keep was surrounded by small trees on whose branches someone had recently tied little white crepe paper flowers.

"Someone is getting married today," Nadiya said. "Local couples like to come here to gather good luck from the shrine for the start of their married life."

The church of Redon-Espic had once also been a monastery and the spot had been selected for its forest wealth, hilltop location, and pure and abundant underground water source. We walked up to it, and it felt as if the ground were alive with electric energy that pushed from the earth into the air. The church was solid, small, and perfectly harmonious in its rectangular base but arched and towering ceiling. I said something to Nadiya, and my words rose effortlessly like liquid and flowed all along the walls, emitting perfect acoustics all around us. Sung prayer here and an inspirational sermon would elevate the words to something more immediate, more emotional, given their musical transformation by these walls.

The second place Nadiya took me was where a natural underground hot mineral spring rose to the surface. It was near the Dordogne River on an expansive farmer's field of walnut orchards and corn. A huddle of epic trees stood in the center of a cornfield and marked the source's spot. Their roots fed deeper down on the mineral rich water, and these trees felt as if they were living spirits, guardians of the source, dancing and watching in turn.

We passed beneath their outstretched arms and edged toward the bank of the mineral pool. We crouched down and sat on our heels and watched. The clear water was ethereal, otherworldly in its light and movement. I fell into a trance as I watched thermal bubbles that formed on the silt and then rose from the underwater earth and traveled to the surface through almost blue-silver water to pop and disappear in the air. I could smell the wealth in minerals, and I could see that the sediment around it was silky fine and reflected glistening, rainbow trout-like colors that contrasted with the dark brown earth of the surrounding field.

A soft wind picked up, and the trees whispered a peacefulness back. This was a place, I thought to myself, where a person could have heavenly visions, too. Maybe it was only a matter of time before a young farm girl or boy would come forward and speak up about visions that transpired here while tending sheep or gazing at the stars on a dark, cloudless night.

In both these places we thought of the richness of the land and the presence of the ancestors. We also looked cautiously for more of those coming-out-of-hibernation snakes. While that day we didn't see anymore, we felt them all along our spines, moving up and down in a mixed tingle of awe and respect for the earth upon which we stood.

We returned to Sarlat in satisfied silence, each lost in her own thoughts. It was only as Nadiya dropped me off near the center of town that it dawned on me. "We saw a deer, a hawk, and each of us a snake. That's seeing an animal of the earth, an animal of the sky, and an animal of the subterranean world in one afternoon. Maybe we are becoming whole, maybe the message is to be complete, to see all as one, to weave it all together."

Iranians, like Thais, like traditional Europeans, like North Americans who still enjoy reading and telling those tales, know that fairytales always deliver their messages in threes if the hero of the story looks for the signs and the messengers. We'd just traveled in a magical realm, so I was willing to make it a fairytale as well.

Nadiya smiled. She and Aidan were having issues, big enough that they seemed to be challenging the foundations of their partnership and it had shaken her to her core. This bit of old magic seemed to help as did the enchanted day. "Yes," was all she needed to say.

And me? I was looking for and had found home but had no idea how I was going to be able to fully claim it. Life was asking of both of us to trust ourselves and our abilities. It was inviting us to make ourselves complete, weave ourselves and the world together, be fully in it, trust that it was all interconnected.

"Yes," I said. I didn't need to say more.

I was perusing Vincent's book stand during Sarlat's next Saturday market and had just picked up a used copy of Rabelais' famously hedonistic novel about Pantagruel and Gargantua, two giants who go about sixteenth-century France eating, drinking, and indulging all their senses without limit. It is a French classic about the full-out enjoyment of life's pleasures. As I turned its pages, a man came up to my right. I felt that electric snake shimmy up my spine.

Market Man.

He smiled and approved of my reading material and asked if I'd enjoyed the strawberries. "Would you like to go for that coffee?" I nodded. As we turned to leave, he picked up a book not far away from Rabelais', on the poetry of the troubadours in the twelfth century, and tapped the cover.

"Maybe attraction can be like that of a troubadour's," he said, "heated, enjoyed, but from a distance and innocent at once?"

That was forward, bold, and somehow actually appropriate at once. Its message delivered, punctuated by the intensity with which he regarded me, he waited for my answer. I nodded again.

"Maybe," I smiled at last. "*Oui*. That sounds promising." •

The Tower in Spring

Chapter 11

THE SEASON

He did not ask to come in, only to be remembered through the sweetness of the fruit. He knew my season, like strawberries, was coming to an end in Sarlat. I was touched by this gesture but also saddened. Even when immersed in immense beauty, from baby birds to troubadour berries, life could be a bittersweet and complicated affair.

AFTER SEVERAL DAYS OF COLD, WET, AND GRAY, THE warmth of spring returned and that intoxicating air of new life poured into the atmosphere of Sarlat. It was again market day, and I pushed open the large French windows in Le Chardon and let the ionic air and the market chatter float in as I worked.

By mid-morning, the gentle and entrancing sounds of Paris-Londres flowed in, adding to the sweet spring air and market burble. Rather than distract, it took me deeper into my writing. There was a trance-like quality to their music, an originality that connected one to spirit and creative energy. How I would love to know more about that duo, thought I as I continued to type and fall deeper into sweet reverie.

My doorbell rang, and I flew out of my pages and back into the room. Before throwing open the blue door, this time I used the intercom in the apartment.

"*Ooooouuui?*"

"Beebe. *C'est* Nadiya. Can you come down for a minute?"

Still in my fetching morning attire, sans socks, but no longer worried of charmingly delivered sarcastic comments from handsome French men, I hopped down the stairs and opened the door. Standing with her was Sophie of Paris-Londres. Oops. I should have worn something a little more, ah, chic.

"I want you two to meet," she said matter-of-factly in French. "I have the feeling that you'll enjoy talking to each other." How on earth does she do that?

"*Mais, l'ecrivain, elle est toi?*" exclaimed Sophie. "Nadiya kept telling me about an American writer I must meet." She turned to Nadiya to explain as I just smiled on. "We've already met, but we talked about music, not writing." She then broke into her native London English, Sophie being the Londres part of Paris-Londres, on violin and backup vocals. Bruno, her husband, was the Paris half of the band, on guitar and lead vocals. She and Bruno began to perform together after they met in a metro in Paris where Bruno was busking. Their music melded perfectly as did their chemistry.

How had Paris-Londres landed in Sarlat? I learned that some time after their meeting in Paris, they began traveling from town to town, performing on the streets and squares of market towns across France. They were in Bergerac and planning to head to Nice when someone told them about Sarlat. They decided to add it to a stop on their way to the Mediterranean, but Sarlat had different plans. That night, just as they drove into town, their car ran out of gas. They managed to push it into the nearby public parking square of La Rigaudie. They had just enough money for two coffees and a half a baguette at a nearby café. They slept in their car, hungry and tired.

Early the next morning, they were awakened by sounds all around them and discovered the market setting up on all sides of their car. This was from a time when Sarlat's market used to set up on La Rigaudie, before it moved a few hundred meters into the two medieval squares nearby. Among the many skills of street performers is their ability to adapt.

"After we pushed our car off to a side street near the square," Sophie recollected, "we took our instruments and returned and began to play. By the end of the market day, we'd made enough money to stay in a hotel that night."

Sarlat was already showing its grace as a town that supported its artists. This is rare in most of the world, and so for the next week, they stayed on, sleeping at times in a hotel and at times in their car, which by now they had pushed downhill to a gas station and filled up. Car full of gas, pockets full of enough earnings to move on, they instead felt the pull to stay, to give their nomadic ways a rest. The next week they rented an apartment to see how things would go. That was years ago, and they've never left. Sarlat had called them, and they answered.

This sounded familiar. It was becoming my story and was that of many others who had come here under similar magical circumstances and found the place supported them and wanted them to stay. Sarlat, I realized, was herself a being with a strong and loving will who spoke to us, and we trusted her enough to listen.

Since then, Paris-Londres has become a defining icon of Sarlat, like Fleur Moulin (La Belle Sarladais), the annual truffle market, Boétie's house, and the great bullet-shaped tower of the lanterne des morts. The market without them and their lyrical music wafting over walnut and truffle oils, cheeses, sausages, strawberries, breads, and lettuce would no longer be Sarlat's market. Some locals had already told me that Paris-Londres is the true musical expression of Sarlat, giving their town her lyrical singing voice. Each time Sophie and Bruno played on the square, I would swear that Saint Sacerdos sang backup harmony.

But Sophie was not only a talented musician, Nadiya informed me. She was also a gifted writer and storyteller, which was why she wanted us to meet. A spark set off in me. Another writer. Someone to talk to. Sophie and I agreed to meet later in the week over a beer at a favorite café to talk craft.

I felt myself go another layer deeper.

I looked up from my increasing depth. From Neandertal encounters to new friends, strawberries, and stone faces in ancient churches, I had gone deep enough that I was now in the earth, the surface was above me, and greater unknown depths waited below.

I also had on a big grin thinking about this as Sophie returned to her stand, and she and Bruno began another music set on the square with Saint Sacerdos harmonizing. Nadiya looked at me, clearly pleased with herself. If she'd had a pen and that famous first map she'd given me two winters ago, she probably would have exuberantly placed an "x" right on the spot in front of the cathedral. (I still had that map like a treasure map, tucked into the back page of my writer's journal.) One of her missions in life seemed to be to bring people together who ought to know each other. I was feeling as if everything here felt so right, so good, as if I really was home, and I said so to the satisfied Nadiya before me.

"I keep having this weird feeling as if I'm coming back to this place from a past life."

She got that lighting-crew look on her face. "Other people who are sensitive and drawn to deep places have said that here. It might be a past life or it might be that you are tuning deeply into one of the most ancient places on earth, and it speaks to you."

A few days later, the Wednesday market morning unfolded under the threat of a tempest, but the building thunder and lightening held off dropping heavy rain until the afternoon. Under the building squall, our several days of intoxicatingly pleasant and sunny spring days were cut like a light switch going off.

As I watched from my window, merchants still set up on the square without missing a beat. The bread baker, the cheese seller, the sausage man, and the walnut oil vendor were all at the baker's sharing their traditional breakfast of champions: red wine, sausage, cheese, and bread. The Oc lettuce seller had yet to arrive, but his stand took less time to set up, and he often arrived after the communal breakfast.

Once he and his wife arrived, I too went down to the square. Under the darkening sky, I bought a two-euro bouquet of vibrant orange ranunculus from the wife who had harvested them from her kitchen garden right next to her husband's lettuces. Like him, she also had spoken Occitan before she spoke French. It was an unstated sturdy reality that this was the land of *oc*; *oui* people were administrative newcomers. And don't get them started on Parisians.

As I gathered the staple of spring's radishes, asparagus, and strawberries, whose season was nearing its end, I discovered that the first of the season's ripe cherries were arriving, these from the Tarn-en-Garonne just south of us. Summer, the cherry farmer told me, was inching north as strawberry season segued into cherry. Summer would be here soon and, along with strawberries, I would be absent too.

I'd received word from Miles that his music and film work was taking him to Berlin. Could I join him there? As much as I hated to leave Sarlat, it was going to be a terrific adventure to see him in his element and share it with him. I arranged a flight from Paris to Berlin that would connect to my return flight to the States from Paris and left it at that. Life was a delicious mystery unfolding like strawberry season into cherry. Deep down though, I knew I would pine for this delicious strawberry season in Sarlat.

Petrus and I held up our glasses filled with golden dry Fino sherry from southern Spain and toasted the sunset from the ridge at the edge of her and Jean's property. The sun behind us to the west, we faced east to see her palette cast upon the entire Massif Central. It tumbled before us with its infinite layers of mountains, hills, and plains in backlit hues of dark purple, blue, green, pink, orange, and yellow. Petrus explained that all she had to do was look at that eastern landscape to know what the weather forecast would be because nearly all weather fronts come from over the Massif.

We finished our sherry and went inside to prepare a dinner of salmon grilled in the fireplace with leeks and had discussions of mystical poetry and art with Jean. This time I stayed the night, sharing my bed with Ferdinand and Marcelito, a new feline addition to the family; Minicat was out roaming, enjoying the romantic summer eve. Marcelito (pronounced March-eh-leet-o) had sleek and solid black fur and was very acrobatic and handsome, as one named Marcelito would be. When he wasn't helping Ferdinand hog the bed by pushing me onto the edge, he stalked me in the garden as I plucked herbs for dinner and leapt onto my shoulder and rode there for the rest of my harvesting.

Early the next morning, Petrus and I took off into the forests further north and east because the forecast from the Massif Central the night before had indicated an overcast but dry day, a perfect day for her to show me one of the secret splendors of the Dordogne in spring: wild orchids.

These prehistoric flowers that once cohabited with dinosaurs are found nearly everywhere in the world. Here they were beginning to push through the warming spring earth and bloom in dozens of varieties and colors, from flesh-tone to bright pinks and purples. Some grew in clusters on stalks like foxglove and formed strange mouth shapes with their pouch openings. Others bloomed in single flowers and demurely hid under ground covering, only allowing the most astute to spy them out in their frilly skirts.

We trailed all day through thick oak forest, through villages, and along truffle and wheat fields, ever searching for orchids.

By late afternoon it was time for me to return to Sarlat. As Petrus drove me back, she suddenly put on the brakes and pulled to the side of the road and excitedly jumped out. I thought she'd seen something to rescue or salvage — not unusual with her — but next I saw that she was cutting a few small branches from a flowering tree. When she returned to the car, she thrust them onto my lap and announced, "Acacia! A local specialty!" The air filled with a pleasant, dewy honeysuckle-jasmine smell.

"Acacia?" I asked as I pressed my face deeply into their dewy snap-dragon-like faces.

"Acacia! It is only in bloom for a short time in spring," she explained. "It's a local delicacy. People pick the flowers, dip them in a light batter of flour, eggs, milk, and water, deep fry them, and eat them with a sprinkling of powdered sugar." My mouth watered. She went on to tell me that this culinary delicacy is called *beignets de fleurs d'acacia*. She insisted I write down the recipe and make this one-week-a-year fried floral treat when I got home. "You won't find it in the restaurants, I assure you. This is only something locals make at home. Then, you'll be a true local."

Of course those were the magical last words. I did just that when I got home. What another world that was. Try to imagine the classic beignet but lighten it a lot and add the taste of sugar snap peas and nasturtiums. Something told me to join it with a Bergerac rosé, perhaps because of the scent of honeysuckle and freshly hulled peas that this dry rosé held in its Cyrano nose. I was learning to be more adventurous with partnering wine to food, learning that similar notes, or complementary ones, like on a color wheel, often played out well. The plenitude of excellent and affordable local wines, ones whose price tag was far higher once exported, made this experimentation possible.

I held back enough flowers from frying to make a bouquet that sat on my writing table as I gazed out on the square below, the rose-colored setting sun pouring in and my rose-filled glass in hand pouring out. I thought of the magic of the prior night's sunset at Petrus and Jean's. I crunched softly on floral beignets. I sipped. Pure honest magic. The notes harmonized, all from the same land. As my every sense was intoxicated, I wondered what the forecast was coming from the Massif Central tonight as witnessed from Petrus and Jean's ridge. The acacia filled all the corners of the room with the delicate scent of fresh spring dew. I was exhausted and happy and finished my spring flower dinner and went to bed very early that night. I missed

Ferdinand, even though he liked to steal as much space on the bed as possible.

A few days later, as a pre-departure ritual, Nadiya and I went to Lascaux together, for old time's sake. Aidan was not with us this time, and he seemed to be slipping out of the picture more and more. This weighed heavily on Nadiya, and while it wasn't her practice to speak about these sorts of intimate issues, over my weeks there I felt a heavy and growing sadness around her.

In our unspoken understanding, we hoped to find that same magical *rouge-gorge*, the little red-breasted bird of Lascaux, from our winter two years prior. Somehow we felt that if he showed up, all would be well, and life could go back to normal for her and Aidan. For me, I added superstitiously, it would be a sign that I would return to Sarlat.

But the *rouge-gorge* did not show himself — if he were still alive since it had been a year and a half — but his relatives were in full birdsong in the forest around and above Lascaux. I took that as sign enough for both of us and, hearts lightened, we followed the flight of two *rouge-gorge* overhead as they flew through the forest toward the 70,000-year-old Neandertal site of Le Regourdou. We went deeper into the forest and were now both wishing we'd bought ourselves an Indiana Jones hat to look as dashing and ready for adventure as had Harold. But the site was closed and closed off, so we turned our prehistoric adventure toward a prehistoric rock shelter I'd been wanting to see all spring: the *Grotte du Sorcier*, the Cave of the Magician.

It was a very small cave but held numerous 19,000-year-old engravings made by Cro-Magnons. There were mostly animals but quite unusually, there were two human forms. The original cave was low and narrow but was deepened in the 1950s by the owner who wanted to make a wine cellar near his home next door. As he began clearing debris, he discovered an engraved bison just above eye level at the cave's entrance. Pressing deeper, midway into the narrow cavern, excavators discovered a rare prehistoric image of a man, very likely a shaman, fluttering as if with wings overhead and with a large head and an equally large erect penis, which curiously, if the viewer followed its point, was aiming right toward a triangle. That was believed, according to our guide, to be the prehistoric mind's way of representing a woman.

If Nadiya could grow quieter in her demure Thai manner, she did by several notches while standing there, staring. But I could hear her brain working, and I think we were both thinking the same things: What did it all mean? It was bald, bold, and graphic, but what did it really mean? Was it some form of fertility magic or just an old story of men acting like men? Or were we all missing the point because it all seemed so obvious? Or were we limited by the constructs of our modern minds? Why was the man all embodied and the woman just a triangle, abstracted? Was it mere target practice or was the abstract representing the greater feminine, the Great Mother, who like our Trinity God, represented also with a triangle, was ineffable? Was this the origin of the trinity, the triangle of the vulva? A return to the original cave from whence we came?

Before we had a chance to digest this graphic art further, our guide directed our gaze to another rock surface where an engraved human head with no body was looking directly into the eyes of a horse who stood before him in full body and was looking just as pointedly back. Both seemed to have a smile just beginning to break out on their profiled faces. Both also shared a kinetic energy with the other, as if they were reading each other's thoughts, communing, connecting in some intangible, deep way, an interspecies morphic resonance.

The name of the cave pointed in the direction of the most popular theories about a virile shaman-magician capable of both fertility magic and communing with animals. That these two human forms engaged types of earth magic seemed certain. For our modern minds and bodies, so far removed from the natural world, we can't easily theorize about what an erect penis or gazing into a horse's face with a smile could really mean.

We moderns have so compartmentalized sex from other forms of creativity, an unnatural division, that we are handicapped to understand human creation, including sex and the sex act, from a time when we were more holistically in touch with our bodies and less disconnected from the facts of life. And even if we can get the general gist of things, it seems we still miss the fine details, the ones only an Upper Paleolithic person knew intimately of their world, their culture, their bodies and spirits, and their relationship with other life, let alone their relationships with each other.

The next morning I was thinking of the bird of Lascaux and of the engraved images I'd seen in the old magician's cave when I threw open my windows in Sarlat to let in the sweet spring air. At that moment a little blue-and-yellow baby bird flew into my studio and landed on the drawer handle of a nearby table and clung to it for dear life. He was so still that he seemed shocked, and I wondered if he was hurt and that by my opening my window when I did, he had a chance to escape from some unknown threat outside.

I rushed and got a little basket, wrapped my hands in paper towel since I didn't have gloves, and placed more paper towels in the basket. I then set the basket near him to let him hop into it if he wished and also to see if he could unfreeze and move without hindrance. He released his grip on the handle and went to the basket. But just as I withdrew one wrapped hand from the basket to carry it near the window, he turned and hopped and quickly grasped it like a frightened child on a mother's skirt. And he would not let go. I felt his little feet firmly holding, but gentle enough to be endearing.

I was in love. I held my hand still and the basket underneath, walked to the table near the open window and set the basket upon it, my hand hovering just a few inches above it. I waited and hovered. I wanted him to make the next move. After a few minutes, he relaxed his grip and turned and hopped back into the basket. I left him alone to make his own choices about when to leave and in what direction. I went and opened the kitchen window as well, and filled a little bowl with water and set it near the basket.

And we sat, me staring at him in wonder, he, who knows? I thought of the engraved image of the man facing the horse in the Grotte du Sorcier. Here was a magical creature of blue and yellow with delicate lines of black and white, a perfectly painted creature of sweetness and elegance, our eyes meeting and connecting in some intangible place. I later learned he was a titmouse, in French, *une mésange bleue*, native to a great swath of territory across Eurasia.

After ten minutes of sitting still with me utterly enchanted and giving him space, the little fellow visited the water bowl, sipped a few drops, and then turned and flew out the window. I followed his flight and saw that he landed on the rooftop of the building across the narrow street below. He flew gracefully and was even something of an acrobat. He sat there for a few seconds and then he flew off toward the cathedral and disappeared. His flight was strong. My eyes followed his trajectory, a swoop down and then off and away to the left. As my eyes flew with him, there on that little street below, I saw a man looking up at me. He waved and smiled, a stunning troubadour's smile. In his hands were strawberries. *L'homme du marché*. How long had he been watching? He indicated he would stand and wait, not risk coming to the door.

I went down and found him near the cathedral's north wall, directly under the stained glass window of Saint Bernard giving out handfuls of his miracle bread. As I approached and we greeted each other, just as his lips puffed the air above my cheek in that traditional French cheek kiss everyone offered in innocent greeting, lightening-like electricity jolted through me from my face to my feet. Nailed as I was to the ground and temporarily unable to speak, he handed me the strawberries, this time *gariguette*, the last of the season.

He did not ask to come in, only to be remembered through the sweetness of the fruit. He knew my season, like strawberries, was coming to an end in Sarlat. I was touched by this gesture but also saddened. Even when immersed in immense beauty, from baby birds to troubadour berries, life could be a bittersweet and complicated affair. I slowly unnailed my feet. We talked for a few minutes and agreed to meet for coffee with friends on my last market day, the day I was departing, three days away.

As I returned to my blue wooden door and went up the stairs, the scent of *ma grand-mère* hit me yet again, and an old pain rose to the surface. The end of those summers as a child visiting relatives in Iran always hit like death. Two weeks before having to pack up and leave for the States, I would become a somber, teary child as I visited older relatives one last time to say goodbye, feeling that it might be the final time. After my last visit in 1976, it was indeed. Forever thereafter, I would live with the knowledge that whether they were alive or dead, I would never see them again.

That same feeling of mourning began to hit me on my last days in Sarlat. I reprimanded myself, telling myself to savor these last days with a light heart and with joy over the luck and good fortune that I was here and could be here. I promised myself I would come back. I practiced allowing hope to flood my being. Strong desire began to offer a balance to the sharp edge of old sadness. I felt the tinges of healing the past begin again, this time in new depths, as when I'd lost my armor in this very place and initiated the process. It was possible now because at last I'd found that place that once and for all would be my place in the world.

Here.

Even as I turned my direction to Berlin, I left my spirit's promissory note in Sarlat, under Bernadette's watch in Saint Sacerdos cathedral with the *rouge-gorge* in the nearby forest. I said I would be back and that my spirit would visit as often as it liked. If I could master bilocation like Padre Pio, that would be swell, but until then, I would visit in my heart and soul and eventually, somehow-who-knows-how, return.

My last evening, I had a Stella with Sophie of Paris-Londres and we launched our writers' group with its first gathering. We met in one of the market cafés on the main square. People passed by and greeted us and we swapped writer's tales, from what it took to walk this life to stories we were working on. We spoke of how we nourished and sustained our creative work, of learning other languages and how that affected our writing, of growing up bi- and tri-culturally, and of living in a place like Sarlat when not born to the place or culture.

The next morning arrived my last market day. I nostalgically savored the five-thirty wake up call from the fish seller's ice. I dreamily watched the merchants set up and then enjoy their breakfast of champions as I sipped coffee and ate the few leftovers in my refrigerator for breakfast. I felt a pull that today I would do no food shopping, no kitchen stocking in this grandmotherly kitchen. I then packed.

When I went to close the big window and head down to meet friends for that last coffee, a Japanese tourist below quickly snapped a shot of me framed in the tall window with pale French blue shutters. It warmed my heart. I knew then that when I left, that somewhere in Japan, somewhere in Korea, somewhere in Argentina, somewhere in China, somewhere in Holland, somewhere in England, somewhere in Germany, and somewhere in America, there would be photos in many homes, shown to many friends, of the "French" woman in the window in Sarlat. I loved the feel of permanence of that. I latched the window more cheerfully than when I had unlatched it and skipped down my uneven stairs and out for one last market gathering on the square and for one more jolt of lightening laced with poetry.

The train pulled out from Sarlat's station. I sat at a window seat, gazing out at Saint Sacerdos as her yellow stone disappeared behind the deepening folds of green rolling hills, and reflected on all that I had learned by coming here. In my first winter, I had learned how to pick and eat a truffle, how to sauté fresh spinach with lardóns, how to make pumpkin soup with shallots, herbs, and fresh cream (and then clean the bowl with a swish of red wine), how to spin a leg of lamb on a string over an open fire and let it roast, as greedy but patient cats watched, how to return a birdie in badminton, how to pay attention to one's dreams, and how to pick a good robust red Pecharmant for a winter meal.

I next reflected that this season I'd learned how to deep fry flowers Petrus picked off of trees at the roadside, how to distinguish five varieties of strawberries, how to turn sudden flashes of spring lightening strikes into succulent troubadour song, how to plan a four-course dinner and let guests partner each dish with the wine, how to soften the Occitan lettuce grower into saving a bunch for me, and how to knap and dine with Neandertals.

I also thought about the long, thin red-and-white radishes that were just coming in, as were cherries and tomatoes. I was sorry to miss this new wave in the market but comforted myself with that promissory note with Bernadette and the *rouge-gorge* and the hopeful knowing that I would be back somehow and would ride more market waves.

I noted all these personal wonders in my journal as the train left the hills of Sarlat and wended its way toward Bordeaux and the straighter, vineyard covered landscapes of Bergerac, then St-Émilion, then Graves de Vayres. Before closing my book, I wrote one more note for my return: Seek out and really find that six-petaled flower of Temniac.

In the airport in Paris, about to board my plane to Berlin, Aidan called as I was handing my boarding pass to the attendant, so his call went to voicemail. Before I had to turn off my phone for take off, I remembered to dial in and pick up his message.

There was the familiar Scottish cadence. "Beeee-be," it began. "While it is a sadness to see you go," he paused and unsuccessfully held back a chuckle, "the wine in the carafe now does more plentifully flow." He guffawed and crackled into the phone and then added in full-lilt, "Don't worrrryyy, you'll be back sooner than you knooow." Hahahaha. Click.

Ah, Robert Burns would be proud. There, Le Chardon, the Thistle, was in its perfect rhyming essence, the metaphoric tough and tender flower of Aidan's homeland that gave my studio its name. It was a perfect message, one that kept me from dropping big wet tears and feeling all weepy over departing. Instead, I laughed. I knew I had been very lucky to live where I'd lived and meet the folks I'd met and that it wasn't over, that there was no reason I wouldn't be back. It even seemed that half the adventure was not knowing how or when. And while it all seemed out of my control, there was one thing I could control at that moment.

I hit reply and texted Aidan. "The wine may last longer now, but somehow, it won't taste as good. I'll be back." I pressed send and turned off the phone, putting to sleep that French number for who-knew-how-many months. I knew that while I thought I had gotten in the last word, a Scotsman never forgets. I'd be the butt of some clever joke upon my return.

I couldn't wait. •

FIRST SUMMER

[Josephine Baker] judged the Dordogne to be "civilized and wild by turn . . . God did his work well here," she exclaimed.

— James Bentley, *A Guide to the Dordogne*, 1986

July Sunflowers

Chapter 12

THE MAGIC FLUTE

Mozart perfectly picked the flute as his mystical instrument borrowed from birds, natural flute messengers from the heavens. Rumi picked the flute for his reed-bed-plucking poetry, a symbol of our souls and bodies being plucked from the riverbank of the Source. He likened us — body and soul — as fashioned like a flute, by God's hand, filled with God's breath, playing our individual music and longing all the while to return to the certainty of the riverbank and our place of origins.

A Pied Piper, wide of girth, nimble of finger, and with sparkling blue eyes peering over his tiny narrow-bodied wooden flute, stood in the Place du Peyrou. He'd positioned himself on the path between Saint Sacerdos Cathedral and Le Chardon, and he was enchanting children and adults alike, adjusting his rendition of the Bach partita he played to the rhythm of people's walking.

If a person or group sauntered by slowly, he slowed his tempo to their footfall. It would catch their attention and weave them into the fabric of the square. And if someone managed to walk by quickly — a rarity, considering that the square was thick with the mass of August visitors in a vacation daze with whole families and baby strollers clogging the medieval passageways of Sarlat — the Pied Piper played faster. He also somehow wove into his tune the mood he read in the same people whose feet he measured in music. Sometimes joy and wonder came out of his flute, sometimes stress and impatience.

I'd been there watching him and listening for a few minutes as I rested on a large stone planter just beneath the great window of Le Chardon three stories up. Every few seconds I looked up to see that the interlopers were still there, those two portly, meaty-palmed, lobster-faced vacationers who'd booked my studio for the month of August. Happily paying the premium August prices, they had their chubby digits wrapped around yet another helping of Bergerac rosé in my wine glasses and continued to rest their elbows on my iron window railing, looking out my window.

Yes, okay, I knew that Le Chardon officially wasn't mine, and perhaps more reasonably, Nadiya and Aidan, who really owned it, had to make the most of their rental income during the months of July and August. But still, those two felt like nothing other than inconsiderate squatters. I looked back to the flute player and reprimanded myself. For goodness sake, I was back, sooner than expected, and in Sarlat. Celebrate, woman, and stop sniveling. But then I wondered, did those two rosy people up above in my window also hear the whisper, also detect the fragrance of home, the perfume of *la maison de mes grand-mères?*

Apparently, I had a visible thought-bubble hovering over my head because the flute player suddenly turned his efforts onto me as I sat still — and invisible, I thought — in the partial leaf cover of a plant. He looked right at me and walked over to where I sat and played an allegro, a happy but edgy interpretation: *Happy to be back. Joyous. Home. But, what, a little discord?* He landed his deft fingers and played a disharmony so jarring to balanced Bach that several people on the square turned to look. I'd been sniffed out.

The flute player stopped right in front of me and held his flute to his side. He looked up quickly at the renters and then back at me, waiting for an explanation with one eyebrow raised. Suddenly, bless his soul, a little boy wandered past, walking right between us, and the flutist whipped the hollow wooden instrument back to his lips and resumed his sound-track interpretations of the Place du Peyrou in summer. The boy stopped, clapped his hands, and squealed with delight as his *maman* dropped a coin in the hat. I took that moment to quickly drop a coin as well in the loudmouth flutist's *chapeau* and made my escape before his music penetrated my soul writ large for the holiday renters above and the French on street level to see. Damn he was good. And damn, I needed to focus, be here, on these different terms, and see if it was still for me.

Only weeks earlier, it had been the flute again, forging a theme in spring and now summer, like strawberries and cherries. Over a month earlier, I had been looking deeply into the large soulful eye sockets of Mr. Moustier, a 45,000-year-old Neandertal adolescent. He was found in 1908 in a cave in the village of Le Moustier in the Dordogne, which then gave its name, Mousterian, to the entire Neandertal Middle Paleolithic stone tool-making tradition that is around 300,000 to 30,000 years old. I had gazed upon his cave during my first winter in the Dordogne from along the bank of the Vézère River, a hauntingly inviting place with a rectangular mouth opening at the high point of the hill, the actual Neandertal cave just below it, and both just underneath a plateau that led to a modern Buddhist retreat.

The whole beauty and placement of one human occupation after another spoke of a place of magic, of great attraction to us as well as to them.

Ironically, the day I'd gazed into the old young man's eye sockets with his hefty row ridges, I had been in Berlin, and our meeting had been entirely by accident, no less so than if I had walked right into him in the street to be greeted by his big toothy grin at an intersection.

Le jeune Moustier arrived in Berlin two years after his discovery by Swiss amateur archaeologist Otto Hauser. The Neandertal was purchased in 1910 by the Berlin Royal Museum of Ethnology for a very large sum of gold marks. He was such a heralded guest that at the beginning of WWII, locals packed him up for safekeeping. At the end of the war, with Berlin in the hands of the Soviets, the skeleton traveled to the USSR and was eventually returned to Berlin in 1958. No one knew he had returned until 2001 when someone identified him in his crate.

I'd found Mr. Moustier shortly after joining Miles in Berlin. I loved our neighborhood in the southern center of the city where Miles had rented a small apartment with a Bohemian nineteenth-century Parisian interior decor, a legacy of the owner's passion for France. I wondered if Miles did this on purpose but learned it was a coincidence, a happy coincidence. I loved how Miles was alive and so engaged by his work there, how his film and music writing seemed to fly, and how he savored deepening his skills in German. I wondered how we would meld our passions for different geographies. Then, I'd discovered Neandertals from the Dordogne in Berlin and knew somehow it would be possible. Somehow.

I even discovered that by coming farther north in Europe, strawberry season was just beginning and cherries were a couple months away. The berries arrived in the weekly Saturday organic market that unfolded half a block away in our neighborhood. The organic farmer selling them took me on as his linguistic project, seeing how I was struggling to formulate German phrases from my very basic skills in the language and with my head freshly front-stuffed with French and more anciently back-stuffed with Spanish and Persian. He gave me the word for strawberry, *erdbeeren*. These *erdbeeren* looked like charlottes and smelled like them. They were the only variety I found in this northern clime, but I was happy that strawberry season had persisted even if only in one varietal.

But try as I did to be fully in Berlin, I also realized that the world I existed in, even beyond our Parisian-styled apartment, still revolved around Sarlat.

In an effort to fully inhabit Berlin, one day I walked across town to visit the archaeology museum to see what I could learn about the original locals of this land, the people who first decided to hunt and gather and then settle along the banks of the River Spree. I loved the name, Spree. It sounded like an adventurous river and I wanted to learn more about its human origins. So off I went, seeking original locals and not expecting to come face-to-face with Mr. Moustier from the Dordogne.

I wandered in the museum from the Moustier Neandertal's case to a nearby case on early modern humans and the earliest known human art. It gave particular focus to carvings and engravings and made special note of several remarkable prehistoric flutes. Several bone flutes had recently been uncovered in southwestern Germany, near the city of Ulm. Archaeologists dated these delicate hollow bodied instruments to around 42,000 years old. One was lithely carved from a swan's breastbone, bringing stories rushing to my mind from the Brother's Grimm where wandering minstrels carved instruments from a swan's breastbone that had magical qualities.

They were considered the human world's first musical instruments. I stood still, blowing a stunned and silent whistle through puckered lips.

So, as far as we know of to date, the flute is our oldest instrument, outside of the human voice or percussive instruments such as striking natural surfaces of stone, wood, and bone. But the voice and percussion don't require the same level of conscious crafting for sound. The flute is more complex; it had to be formed with the focused intention to bring about sound. Sweet, birdsong sound.

Rumi, Cro-Magnon, and Mozart danced around my head like Papageno as I contemplated that for at least 42,000 years we've been musical beings. That cast a different light on the ancestors, made their fireside gatherings all the more enchanting, adding melody and trance to our collection of how to communicate with each other and the world around us.

Mozart perfectly picked the flute as his mystical instrument borrowed from birds, natural flute messengers from the heavens. Rumi picked the flute for his reed-bed-plucking poetry, a symbol of our souls and bodies being plucked from the riverbank of the Source. He likened us — body and soul — as fashioned like a flute, by God's hand, filled with God's breath, playing our individual music and longing all the while to return to the certainty of the riverbank and our place of origins. It was hard now not to think that both Rumi and Mozart inherited this idea from the first humans who created these bone flutes.

I walked home that afternoon humming Papageno and the Queen of the Night's famous melodies from Mozart's *The Magic Flute*, happy to be here, happy to have found out more about the ancestors, both from here and from the Dordogne. I knew that my love for Sarlat was intense and unique for me, a rare, once-in-a-lifetime love, but it was important to explore more widely.

I had no idea how evident my pining for Sarlat was to Miles. That he too is semi-nomadic in temperament might also explain how he can feel another semi-nomad's energy when she is restless, ready to pull up tent pegs and move.

One day in Berlin he brought it up. "What do you think if we were to give up our apartment in New Jersey, say, by the end of September, and tried living in Europe for a few months?"

"Where in Europe are you thinking?" I asked, wondering how he'd known I was thinking just what he proposed.

"Well, I love Berlin and Lisbon but I can't help but see how much you love Sarlat. And your writing has more to do with France than mine does with Germany or Portugal. So . . . "

"Sarlat?"

"Sure. You can even go ahead early and I'll join you later."

"So, we'll need to give our landlady notice soon. Are you sure? This is a lot of uprooting after a lot of changes in our life already." I was thinking of his mother's death, still fresh.

"Sure. Let's email our landlady today." Miles assured and went over to his computer and switched it on. After a few moments of silence, he came back into the sitting room where we'd had our conversation, smiling and laughing. "You won't believe this."

"What?"

"Check your email." There, in the inbox, timed at exactly the moment Miles and I had decided to pull up our tent pins in New Jersey, was an email from our landlady. Her daughter, she explained, was getting married, and she and her future husband would best begin their new married life in our apartment, so how did we feel about giving it up? If we were open to searching for a new home, could we aim to be out by the first of October?

Within twenty-four hours, we reconfigured the shape of our lives and Miles also suggested that I head back to Sarlat in August and look for long-term accommodations, maybe even something to buy, a little *pied de terre* that was affordable and offered a real foothold. "Besides," he'd added, "you still have to find the six-petaled flower of Temniac."

Almost as soon as Miles and I returned to New Jersey we began the upheaval of ridding ourselves of earthly holdings that were too cumbersome and putting the rest into boxes destined for a modest storage unit. While Miles carried that on, I boarded a plane destined for Toulouse via Brussels and then a train to Souillac and a bus to Sarlat. I landed in the heat of summer at the peak of tourism with no place to stay.

The sense of homelessness had never been stronger. I'd just closed one home and given up the lease, and the other was unknown, especially because of those two holiday renters in Le Chardon. I wished they would throw me a lifesaver and let me sleep on the fold-out cot.

Nomads aren't any less attached to places simply because they move all the time. Sometimes they are more attached to places because they are constantly leaving and arriving, parting and reuniting, and letting go, letting go, and letting go. They may see certain features in the landscape as sacred, as signs of home, both of the body and of the spirit, and when they arrive at a place designated as their summer or their winter pasture, it is loaded with all the sentiments and deep attachments anyone has of home.

I was unprepared for how gorged and changed Sarlat was in August compared even to the swells of June. My first days back, thanks to the kindness of Nadiya, I stayed with her in a spare room in her house outside of Sarlat. She had visitors who were also taking refuge in her kindness, so we were a full house. And Jean and Petrus, who offered me a tent in their yard, had so many visitors that their home already resembled a campsite without me needing to pitch an additional yurt.

After a lot of digging, I finally found a studio to rent for the rest of my stay in August, and I was able to give Nadiya her room back. Its rent was unusually reasonable, but it was in the center of the medieval town and I took it site unseen. I knew I wouldn't get lucky twice and that there had to be a reason it was still open, but I gambled just for the luxury of being back in the heart of things.

The studio was at the other end of the Place de la Liberté from Le Chardon. Though in a thick stone medieval building of beauty and grace, I soon understood why it had not been rented. It looked out onto other people's inner windows, and the permanent resident next door had a maladjusted adolescent son who screamed half the day and half the night, out of the blue. His violent eruptions disturbed any peace the thick stone walls could otherwise bestow. Instead, it felt like being in a dark stone dungeon where someone nearby was being tortured. But there was a far worse torture awaiting me.

The landlady of the little rental studio had none of the rural chic we associate with French countryside style outside of Paris. No embroidered bedspreads in linen white, no soft French blue shutters and window frames, no calming lemon and lavender patterns on a cotton tablecloth on the kitchen table. Instead, I entered a Hieronymus Bosch painting in tight spaces with curtains and wallpaper that were an opium addict's idea of what matches — a strange black-and-white orchid pattern wallpaper with silver streaks outlining each placemat-sized flower throughout the kitchen and bedroom walls. Against this, the curtains, in both the kitchen and bedroom, were a puke-green-and-yellow plaid. The beds were covered in English-garden-style floral bouquets of rainbow colors, and along with the black-and-white orchid wallpaper and puke-toned curtains, it all made me so dizzy I kept the lights off at night and practiced tunnel vision by day. Oh, but there's more. Turning the corner was a bathroom, tossed off in a Victorian pink-and-pale-green floral and leaf-patterned wallpaper.

When the neighbor boy screamed, I wanted to join him. I realized that he too might be living in an atmosphere of aesthetic disharmony, and I grew compassionate for him, but hoped never to run into him in the stairway.

But. I was. In. Sarlat. My beloved Sarlat. It was this or nothing. And it was temporary. Like everything. Moreover, with my two-pronged reason for being there, I was almost never in the studio except to sleep or to put market purchases away for picnics later. I took on my double mission with zeal — find a good place to live, and find that flower.

As I successfully slipped away from the Pied Piper in the Place du Peyrou, I made a point not to look up again at that beloved window of my first winter and my first spring. Instead, I marched over to the offices of the two real estate agents whose windows I'd studied earlier in the day to introduce myself and express my interests. We set up appointments to explore both rentals and modest places for sale.

The first realtor was a warm, mild Dutchman who had made his life here. We spoke only French even though I knew his English was better than my French. It seemed an unspoken code, that if I wanted local prices, it was best to operate in the local language. Or, as close to the local language as possible since neither of us spoke Occitan.

The second agent was an odd bird who could not get past the luck of me being American, and even though the only language we could speak was French, it did nothing to disabuse him from the very tasty but erroneous idea that I must be *une Américaine riche*.

He made me nervous, so for good measure, I called a third agent and offered the same explanations to her over the phone. She sounded pleasant and we agreed to meet during the afternoon a few days later, after I finished a morning round of visits with the Dutchman. I hung up and slowly wove my way back into the medieval town center and into the Place de la Liberté. There I found the one last unoccupied table at one of my two favorite market cafés, sat, and ordered a glass of rosé.

Life was good and I was back on course. And, on my foray earlier that day into the market, Petrus and Jean had invited Nadiya and me to a dinner gathering at their farmhouse the next evening. Things were aligning. I was home. I raised my glass and uttered a quiet *merci* on the square and enjoyed how the setting August sun created a riotous sorbet sunset in my rosy glass. It was more than half full, thanks to a little inside adjustment. •

La Vie Normale

Chapter 13

THE SOURCE OF SARLAT

"I knew when I got here that this town has a special energy running through it. It is powerful and feels good. Why else is the cathedral so fresh and dry inside when it sits on a sacred water source? Most other churches like that feel damp, like they are just stones without a spirit. But this one, it refreshes itself and anyone in it."

Though it was August, the interior of Petrus and Jean's medieval stone farmhouse was cool enough to warrant a fire for cooking as much as for cozy warmth. Nadiya and I arrived just before sunset, and the fire was going strong in the walk-in fireplace. Several guests were already there and gathered near it. There was a local couple from Sarlat, an American-Israeli couple who had a house in the Dordogne but lived most of the year in London, and two more guests who were due to arrive any moment. Petrus was excited about them and wouldn't tell us who they were, just that they'd get there as soon as they finished working that evening.

I rolled up my sleeves and did what I loved best Chez Petrus et Jean: joined in the cooking. Petrus was setting several whole, gutted trout onto the fire, some encrusted with toasted almonds and some with crushed garlic and just-cut herbs from her garden. Minicat was curled up on the seat closest to the flames, leaving her feline relatives, Ferdinand and Marcelito, outside to fend for their dinner in the wild. Minicat had been deemed the most civilized cat with dinner company and so was allowed to wait politely for trout scraps while taking a nap in the coveted fireplace chair.

After the trout was securely grilling, Petrus joined me back in the kitchen where I arranged the salad plates with a scattering of arugula, also from the garden, and she finished them off with slices of her secret-recipe-perfect foie gras, which involved Jerez sherry instead of Armagnac. She then arranged a platter with saffron almond rice and directed me to arrange another with grilled peppers and zucchini.

On the open counter between the kitchen and dining area sat two desserts: a poppy seed chocolate torte and a fruit tart. Near those perched a thick, round wooden board weighed down with ten types of cheese. Guests hovered and resisted dragging a finger through the chocolate or pilfering golden grains of rice. It was no wonder the other two cats had been exiled outside; it was hard enough for the humans to behave themselves.

Soon the trout was nearly ready, and we were all urged *à table* to start the first course of foie gras and greens. Jean poured a local dry rosé and the long wooden table was a sea of quiet contentment as we shifted gears and stuffed our faces. Petrus and Jean cleared our salad plates and, with Nadiya's deft assistance, each guest had a crispy trout lying before them, mine with herbs and garlic. Jean refilled my glass. Somehow he managed to do it quietly, unlike Aidan who would liberally pour and liberally comment. Sadly, he was not in attendance this night.

Somewhere in the middle of deboning and savoring my Dordogne trout, with Minicat abandoning her slumber and now waiting attentively to my right, the two mystery guests arrived. As two musicians walked in through the heavy, wooden entrance door, and as Petrus used one foot to hold back Ferdinand and Marcelito from diving back inside, she said by way of introduction, "This is what I love about Sarlat in summer. You meet all sorts of creative people and can invite them to dinner!"

She then explained that these two had just wrapped up a good evening of busking, filling Sarlat's medieval squares with medieval music. The first was a Catalan man dressed in a monk-styled floor-length habit of Cappuccino brown. Under his arm he lugged a heavy accordion. He set the instrument to the side and turned to introduce his companion to the group.

"This is my friend, Étienne."

Petrus exuded excitement and turned to me, "Isn't this wonderful! He's a flutist. We just met over our olives. Of course, that is how we meet everyone."

Étienne smiled at everyone and then pointed at me. "I know this one. From sight. But have yet to be introduced because she ran way before I could get her name." He made exaggerated eye gestures, looking up at an imaginary third-floor studio, and laughed. Petrus raised an eyebrow, wondering what was going on, but he wasn't finished. "Now, I will find out what you were doing there on the Place du Peyrou, always looking up. I will have your story," he threatened cheerfully, "before the evening is done."

Everyone stared at me. I had but one reasonable response. "Sure," said I, "but I will have yours too." He extended his hand, faux spat into it, and we shook. He then stepped closer and proffered the mandatory air kiss on each cheek. I could feel the bounding energy of his cheeky smile ricocheting off my face without having to look to confirm it. Nadiya gave me a sideways glance, a polite Thai way of saying, "What the f---?"

The two musicians shook off their outer jackets, rolled up their sleeves, and took their seats at the table where Petrus plied them with foie gras and trout at once so that they could catch up with the meal's procession of courses.

The Pied Piper sat at the other end of the long table right across from me. We each had been given the end seats "of honor," me for my return visit in summer, and he for being the most recent friend Petrus and Jean had made over olives. He ate and stared. His razor sharp blue eyes were only one notch worse than the impish grin and laugh that burst frequently from his trout-stuffed mouth. And he stared. Petrus, seated near him, at last demanded to know how I had met the flutist.

"She was enjoying my music more than most on the Place du Peyrou," answered Étienne before I had a chance. "So much so that she sat and listened for a while." He then took an enthusiastic mouthful of foie gras followed by a gulp of rosé. It was clear that there was more to the story, but Petrus didn't probe and I didn't elaborate.

Everyone went back to their conversations. But not Nadiya. "You were wishing you were in Le Chardon, weren't you?" I looked at her sheepishly, pushed a flake of deboned trout into my mouth, took a sip of wine, and said nothing, having learned a new technique from the Piper.

After the main course of trout we moved on to the cheese. As the round board worked its way around the table, so did Étienne. Not only a flute player, he was a magician. He began to pull coins and cigarettes from behind people's ears and shuffle a deck of cards to play the usual street games on innocent bystanders. When he worked his way to Nadiya, she had such a dubious expression on her face that he pulled out all the stops and performed such a good card trick on her that she couldn't explain it in any way other than "magic," and she dropped her guard and laughed.

We next destroyed the two desserts and retired around the fire for coffee and a homemade plum *digestif*. Étienne and the Catalan took their instruments out and sat on each side of the fireplace where the Catalan started a pulsating meditation on his accordion that furthered the digestive efforts of the plum brandy. Minicat suddenly lost all interest in food scraps and went over to him and sat at his feet in a mesmerized trance, staring at him intently. She seemed high from the vibrations of his purring machine par excellence.

The Catalan paused, and Étienne began, carrying the meditative medieval tune into a lively dance. Curiously, Minicat went to him next and stood on her hind legs and rested her front paws on his thigh, holding her head up as close as she could get it to Étienne's fingers and flute. She almost seemed to sway, falling into a bipedal trance. She stood that way as long as Étienne played, and when he stopped, she leapt into his lap and would not leave him for the rest of the evening. I had never seen a cat, or any other creature, so mesmerized.

Taking a break and with Minicat close in tow, Étienne came and sat next to me.

"What were you doing the other day, always looking up?"

I matched his directness and dived head first into the whole history, of how I came to Sarlat, how I found Le Chardon and Nadiya, how I felt I had finally found home and rootedness. Nadiya sat not too far from us and kept smiling and nodding at Étienne every time he looked up for confirmation. I explained that August had thrown me for a loop because Le Chardon was rented, but that really, it was all of Sarlat and the Dordogne that called to me, not just a studio in the Place du Peyrou, but what a sublime one it was, nonetheless. And others presently occupied it. I finished.

"I have something to show you." He said. "I understand exactly what you are saying. I too have this feeling. The next time I see you in Sarlat, I will take you there."

Nadiya raised her eyebrows. Was this another Gallic maneuver for amorous intentions, she implied, or some other clever magic trick? But then one look at Minicat's head-over-tail devotion lowered her brows and raised her smile. Animals have good instincts.

It did not take long to run into Étienne. The next day he was at his usual spot in the Place du Peyrou and I at mine. The occupying holiday renters were still there, looking a bit more worn from too much foie gras and rosé, but content and unmovable. Today, having completed my day of work and preliminary real estate research, my remaining mission was to just be there, enjoy the square, and at some point head into Saint Sacerdos to meditate. I eventually got up to do that, and Étienne nodded at me as he played his flute, adjusting Bach to the cheery tempo of my relaxed footfall and chipper mood. In Étienne's nod I also understood that when I came out from the cathedral he'd take a break and show me the mystery he'd promised.

Saint Sacerdos usually has a soft, sweet energy, as if year round a mystic sits perpetually in the corner praying and sending out warm waves of goodness. I can't explain it, but I feel a throb of earth energy there, one that makes me feel good, that balances out imbalances. But in this month, the August throngs seemed to have made that mystic sink below the surface and go deep into retreat. There were so many tourists coming to see the historic monument that it felt more like a large city's train station than a church. I made an effort at meditating, but after several cries from a child that ripped like daggers through the grand acoustic-magnifying chamber, I gave up and went back out onto the square.

Étienne was shadowing a family of four, focusing his flute on the father's firm and directed feet, making his five-year-old daughter laugh with delight that someone had singled out the stern patriarch of the family. The Piper saw me and winked. I went over to his hat to drop in a euro but he quickly swooped it up before I could.

"Buy me a cup of coffee instead." He slipped the flute into an inner pocket in his vest and emptied the hat of coins and stuffed them into a trouser pocket. "Then, I will take you to see *la source de Sarlat.*"

"*J'accepte*," said I, "on the condition that you also tell me how you landed in Sarlat. After all, you got my story, now I'll have yours."

"*D'accord.*" He bowed and flopped the emptied chapeau onto his head. Off we went to a café he knew on the other side of the medieval town. For some reason, he explained, tourists didn't visit that side as much as this one, even though it was as beautiful as all the other parts of the old town. But that was exactly why he liked that café; even in August it was peaceful. It likely had something to do with being slightly off the beaten track and void of surrounding shops selling medieval plastic trinkets, foie gras, oils, and wine. We sat at one of the four small round tables set in the narrow passage, and the owner came out and greeted Étienne, clasping his hand warmly.

"*La bas?*" Asked the owner.

"*La bas.*" answered Étienne smiling broadly. "*Wa inta, la bas?*"

"*Oui, oui, la bas, shukran.*"

My year in Morocco rushed back. These two were speaking Moroccan Arabic and saying *Ca va? Ca va. Et toi, ca va? Oui, oui, ca va, merci.* Now I knew Étienne had a good story to tell, one worth waiting for.

Our host, a Berber from Morocco transplanted for numerous years here "because it's a special town," he explained, then went back to make our espressos. I sat forward. "*Alors, ton histoire maintenant.* No more waiting." He smiled brightly. People rarely asked him about his story it turned out. The life of a performer was often one of engaging others and their histories. Our coffees came, and as he poured and stirred sugar into his, he began to pour out his tale.

A talented musician who enchanted children, cats, parents, and Nadiya, I soon learned he was also an energy healer. Half the year, during the hard, gray winters, he lived with Berbers in southern Morocco, and half the year he lived here in a little house above the cathedral. His street was my street. His square was my square. It had been so for four years, which was when he first came to Sarlat. The town mesmerized him the way he mesmerized Minicat.

"I was born in the Cote d'Ivoire, in Abidjan. My parents moved back to France when I was two. We moved to the north, near Belgium. As a young man, I moved to Brittany because I wanted to live near the ocean and I wanted to experience that magical land. It is profound and holds its spiritual energy to this day, but," he bore his eyes into mine, "when you are a nomad, you need a second home, and you find it by feel. I knew I had to keep looking. Morocco was one home, and here at last is the other. I think you know this." I nodded and set my cup down to hide the shaking in my hand. If energy healers read energy, then he was reading me like an open book.

"So what happened?" I asked as casually as possible.

"I kept traveling. Going to towns where I could perform my music live from the street. It was when I arrived in Sarlat that I knew, I felt it, I had found *mon chemin spirituel.*" He stared at me, "*comme vous.*" He leaned back, gave an impish grin, and threw back the rest of his coffee.

"*En plus,*" he went on, "I knew when I got here that this town has a special energy running through it. It is powerful and feels good. Why else is the cathedral so fresh and dry inside when it sits on a sacred water source? Most other churches like that feel damp, like they are just stones without a spirit. But this one, it refreshes itself and anyone in it."

I would have never explained it that way, but yes, exactly. I was drawn to the church for that intangible refreshing quality and visited at least once a day to light a candle and sit and meditate. I liked quietly greeting the four carved stone faces to the right upon entering the vestibule and then stepping through the doorway into what felt like a luminous energy shower. More accurately, it was like a swirl, a double helix of energy and light from the deep earth soaring to the sky. But did I tell anyone this? No. It sounded a bit kooky when you tried to put words to something intangible but viscerally felt nonetheless.

But here and now, I felt safe. I confessed to Étienne my feeling for the church and more. I added that I felt in my feet that "the energy" extended beyond the church, like a corridor that ran through the medieval town. It was non-rational, I knew, but when I walked from a small square, the Cour des Fontaines, to the cathedral, and then from there to the Place de la Liberté, and onward toward the Mary fountain, I felt as if I were walking on an ancient path, one filled with a channel of energy that the other paths in town, equally ancient and medieval, did not have.

He smiled again. "This is the perfect time to finish our coffee and visit the source." I paid quickly. To Middle Earth we swiftly went. We simultaneously thanked the owner in Moroccan Arabic, making him beam, and walked to Rivendell to meet the elves.

We went back to the other side of the old town and walked through the Place de la Liberté where a number of Étienne's street performer friends were setting up for their early evening performances. One was dressed as a court jester and preparing to commence his mixed performance for the gathering dinner crowd on the square. He did acrobatics, fire-eating, operatic singing, and ambitious juggling feats all at once.

Another was a beautiful Swedish woman with a voice of angels making her way across all of Europe far more nomadically than Étienne or I, with only a rucksack, her voice, and her guitar. We turned into a smaller side square and ran into a third friend, a man with bulging muscles dressed in rough cloth and leather, a cross between a medieval minstrel and mercenary, who sat strumming a lute and singing fifteenth-century Catalan poetry in the most extraordinary castrato alto. The high feminine voice was both stunning and unsettling, yet we were certain that if we could lift his tunic, he would be in full ownership of his manhood. This was confirmed when he stopped strumming and hailed the growing crowd in a burly bodyguard's baritone.

Sarlat was doing what it did every August, turning its evenings into a month-long Renaissance Fair, each square slated for a different performer.

We pressed through thickening crowds and narrowing passages. I soon saw that we were heading straight to the Mary fountain. I had thought all along, I said, that this was *la source de Sarlat*, but Étienne said yes and no, that it was more hidden than that. He went right past the Mary fountain and pulled open the door of the restaurant that was built into the rock shelf that shared its wall with the fountain next door.

"Bonsoir!" he boomed unapologetically to the room packed with diners. He sought out the owner in back and made eye contact. The other simply nodded and indicated with his chin that it was okay to pass deeper into the restaurant even when we were not paying diners. Apparently Étienne visited this spot enough for his ritual to be understood and accepted.

We walked through, every table filled to capacity with patrons masticating grilled duck, poached foie gras, omelets sautéed with cepes, and rinsing these delicacies down with copious local wines, their own personal supply of subterranean stream.

We wended our way past the culinary orgy all around us toward the back wall, which was not cut stone but the natural rock of an old cave. Right when I thought we could go no deeper, a tunnel appeared that led to a narrowing cavern. Étienne walked in, and I lurked hesitantly behind. The sound of diners disappeared. He stopped midway in the narrow limestone passage, his six-foot height meeting the top of the cave with a brush of hair that tumbled bits of stone dust onto his head.

Only a few feet in from the last dining table, all I heard were water drops and water swirls. He turned around to face me. "Before we visit the real underground source of water that feeds into the Mary fountain next door and then flows exactly underground as you described it, to the Place de la Liberté, to the Cathedral, to the Cour des Fontaines, and onward south through Sarlat, I want to show you something. Can you chant this note?" He gave me a comfortable G, within my voice's range.

"Sure, *d'accord*," I replied but gave him a dubious look. "I'm not a singer, and why . . . "

"Humor me."

"Okay, *d'accord*." I chanted my note, hoping that if I could no longer hear the patrons outside, then they would also not hear my singing. As I grew less self-conscious of the world behind me devouring dead duck, Étienne layered on a harmonious baritone note. And held. He indicated that I should do the same, to just keep chanting my note. Dubiousness melted away and enchantment spread all around and about.

Within a few seconds like this in that small passage, the slightly concave roof overhead began to vibrate. It echoed back a perfect acoustic resonance, a third voice to our two, and scattered more dust on Étienne's head. Our two notes danced not only in harmony but also with a dense presence as if sound was becoming matter. The air thickened. My head vibrated and, instead of feeling befuddled, it cleared as if I'd slept a deep sleep unbroken for eight hours. When we stopped our chanting, I had tears of joy running down my cheek and the resonance continued to pulse through my body. Étienne smiled.

"*Bienvenue à la Sarlat profonde,*" he whispered. He then led me all the way to the back where the tunnel, carved by surfacing water, first emerged into the small cavern, all of it carved out by that ancient run of water. I could just see an underground stream emerging from the rock wall, spilling gently into a pool, and then continuing on to re-enter the wall on the opposite end and slip its way underground toward the Mary fountain on the other side of where we stood.

When Étienne and I retraced our steps and returned to the restaurant's dining area, the shock of chatter and clanking silverware was jarring and louder on the heels of that cosmic sound experience. We meandered back out onto the Place de la Liberté, where we bid each other a good night. Both of us were done for the night — our nervous systems entirely rewired and ready for calm and solitude. I prolonged the magic by taking the upper medieval passageways that removed me from the spectacles on the square and led to the quiet upper reaches of the medieval town, and quietly entered my enchanted twelfth-century home, but kept the lights off as I entered my unenchanted, potentially haunted, psychedelic studio. I leaned against the closed door. I longed to smell the perfume of my grandmother's entryway, to inhale the aroma of my grandmother's kitchen. Maybe tomorrow, when no one was looking, I would steal a sniff from the mail flap set in the great blue door. But I was at peace, a deep knowing peace derived from profound earth vibrations delivered from the source center of Sarlat that told me my roots here were deeper than a studio three stories up.

The next week I took a map of Sarlat and drew on it where I felt the underground water flowed, marking like Nadiya's Xs the spots it appeared above ground at historic fountains throughout the town and on the town's outskirts. There were the fountains at Cour des Fontaines and the Mary fountain, which together were the oldest sources of water for the Sarladais ever since the monks settled here in the ninth century. These natural places where fresh water surfaced probably hydrated earlier inhabitants, too, perhaps back deeper into prehistory. Water was, and remains, key to so many important human settlements, a reason why a place became home and holy.

But then I began discovering fountains set in neighborhoods, fountains only the people of that quarter in Sarlat knew about, that were also old and venerable and flowing with good water and good energy. Each fountain had folklore attached, stories meaningful only to that group of residents, liquid histories that burbled and refreshed as sure as the water did.

Seeing my map and enthusiasm for subterranean flow, a friend over market-day coffee suggested I learn the local knowledge and lore from a dowser. I'd already heard about such people in Sarlat's market. They were gardeners, bakers, and brewers who were also attuned to the land and skilled with dowsing rods or a pendulum. It conjured images of an older Europe, one that still existed, real fairytale characters hidden just under the surface of a vegetable display on market day. I knew if I could go into this world, I would also tap a root as deep as the Occitan or Cro-Magnon one, a root that defined a vibrant and persisting traditional reality here in this corner of modern-day France.

I set about seeking a douser, a patient soul, who would willingly show me their talents and teach me about earth magic in the Dordogne. I added it to my list, just after real estate and that elusive dancing flower. Maybe it would happen this summer or maybe its timing was for another, quieter season? I was patient. If a person has a list concerning how to inhabit a place and its stories, that list will never end.

During the rest of my few remaining summer days in Sarlat, I saw Étienne almost every day, playing his magic flute and delivering his infectious smile on the Place du Peyrou, but the only conversation we had, or needed to have, was eye contact and a nod. After sharing the source of Sarlat, words were unnecessary. We'd gone to the center of the Earth and back, and that was more than enough.

Our lives also grew busier, he eliciting the music in people's feet and souls while earning his day's bread and me on the hunt for home.

In that I was better anchored thanks to the earth magic I'd discovered. I looked up at Le Chardon, at peace with the renters, and crossed the square to meet the first agent. As I did, I was beginning to understand that real estate would never capture what home was and was becoming. This was not going to be a story of buying a dilapidated farmhouse and fixing it up, noting the nuances of carpenters and neighbors. It was going to be about owning and inhabiting home, *mon chemin spirituel*, and noting the nuances of locals, friends, and neighbors and the signs they delivered along the way. But little did I know how deep down the rabbit hole that searching would take me. •

Mr. Stripes

Chapter 14

RECASTING HOME

Now, I knew in my heart that this really was home and that home really was not about owning something, it was about belonging and longing and being wanted somewhere so much that it worked. Floating. A very nomadic notion. Mr. Stripes did nothing but float all day and look at him.

THE NEXT MORNING I WAS OFF TO MY FIRST REAL ESTATE appointment when I crossed paths with Nadiya and told her my place-hunting schedule for the week. I was waxing poetic and idealistic about the beautiful and affordable old-style stone house with thick wooden ceiling beams I was going to find and buy. She gave me that sideways glance and said, "Remember? Stone walls perspire. They gather humidity. If you don't dehumidify constantly, it gets musty and then the integrity of the wall diminishes. It's like having a pet. You can't just leave home and close the door. Someone has to take care of it." She added casually that maybe Le Chardon could be free for me to rent if I came in the late autumn and stayed through the winter. Then for a reduced rent, I could be the one taking care of the stone walls while she visited her family in Thailand. I could learn to pet sit, as it were, and decide if I wanted to get one for myself.

"Would you ever consider selling Le Chardon?" I had wanted to broach this topic for weeks.

She shook her head.

"No. At least not yet. Maybe one day. But it is a part of the rest of the building. And don't forget what I said about sweaty stone walls. But rent. Fall and winter? Yes, very likely. Think about it," she concluded in her efficient Thai-French-English. "We can talk more, work out a rent." With that, she ran off to her next appointment.

It was a good chance encounter. I would have been eel bait if I had arrived at the real estate office with my prior idealism, buying the first cheap pile of stones I saw. I needed to ground myself and see what was possible.

I met the Dutchman. We made it an early start to maximize the morning and avoid the thicker crowds of summer as they woke up and wandered the medieval lanes looking for coffee and croissants. But August slowed us down elsewhere. We soon discovered that while many of his clients listed their places for sale in August, to maximize the freshness and mass of visitors, many of them left for their own vacations forgetting to leave their keys with the agent.

We spent the better half of our time calling and wrangling keys or rearranging visits to the properties when renters could let us in. By mid-morning we had several visits secured and were off, pushing through thick crowds. I had given a very clear description of what I wanted: an old building, even if it required a lot of fixing up, made of solid stone and wood and stucco, and not any modern construction. Yet, most of what he showed me were recently hammered-together shoeboxes. They were worse than my psychedelic studio because at least its hideousness was hidden in the heart of a gorgeous twelfth-century building. On the other hand, places that fit the old building description were gutted and in such a state of decay, with walls that didn't sweat but oozed, that renovations would have cost three times the purchase price. One charming eighteenth-century apartment was hovering right over the busiest street in town, and even double-paned windows were too thin to keep the merrymaking and car honking below at bay.

I wondered if it was my budget, my French, or the Dutchman's limited property listing that made for the disconnect between what I wanted and what I was seeing. I had also been spoiled. I knew that in Sarlat there was a splendid studio in a fifteenth-century thick stone building that had light, air, *avec l'esprit de mes grand-mères*. But it was not for sale.

The hunt was going to be harder than I had thought. Having seen the last shoebox on his list, we called it a day, and I went off to splash cold water on my face and prepare for my next real estate appointment that afternoon. I treated myself to a front row seat for lunch on the sidewalk in the main drag, the Rue de la République, and ordered a *salade chaude* (garden greens topped with tomatoes, lardóns, a perfectly poached egg, and two toasted disks of baguette with melting caramelized goat cheese on top), and a glass of Bergerac rosé. It made me feel abundant, satiated, refreshed, and ready for more.

Lunch over, I stepped to the other side of Sarlat's medieval town, the side less visited by tourists, where I had a rendezvous with the next agent. I followed her phoned directions, and after a few sinuous turns along several narrow cobblestone roads, I saw a woman about my age looking very official.

"*Bonjour!*" She shouted enthusiastically. "You must be Beebe." She stepped toward me and vigorously shook my hand. Her sharp features were softened by bright eyes and her welcoming manner. She held my hand for several moments, longer than the usual handshake, and looked at me as if scanning for something. She let go and gestured toward the door of a small stone townhouse. The stonework was pretty and recently repointed. The building, though small, had promise. It had a little terrace that had me imagining pretty terracotta pots planted with herbs and flowers for a small kitchen garden. Maybe even two patio chairs, for me and Miles. I was already moving in and planting when we stepped inside and my Thoreauvian fantasies came to a screeching halt. It was very tiny, far tinier than the outside implied. Each of its two stories was simply one room, a two-room house. My two imagined patio chairs would fill up most of the first floor.

"Where's the washroom?" I asked fearfully, looking around. Maybe there was none and I had to use a separate building in the back alley? She led me to an accordion door in the back of the first floor and pulled it open. Therein sat a refashioned water closet that seemed to have once been in an airplane, including its door. Where was the shower? I looked up. Correction. This was once the bathroom from a train's sleeper car; poised right over the toilet bowl hung the showerhead. A separate building in the back alley was looking good. My heart sank. I shook my head. "No, sorry. This isn't for me. I'm not feeling it." Even with a little imagination, such as installing a real washroom, the whole first floor would disappear to the gods of plumbing.

The sparkly-eyed agent stepped nearer me, if that were possible. "I have something to say. But let's go outside." Yes. Absolutely. As soon as we were through the door and a few feet away she said, "I think I can speak like this, because you used the word 'feeling.'" She paused, looking again at me as if scanning for something, found it, and went on. "I feel the spirit of people and places and we need to find a place whose spirit is harmonious to yours. If we don't, I would not be happy, nor would the house, *et alors*, neither would you."

The spiritually inclined part of me was intrigued. I recalled a friend who had been incredibly successful in buying and selling real estate. Her one secret was "sensing the spirit of a place." I wanted a place with spirit, like Le Chardon.

"Okay," I tried to sound positive. "Let's see if we can find that place."

She exuberantly guided me around the corner, and we walked a little farther along another sinuous street and stopped in front of a place with a for sale sign. All the windows were boarded up, completely blocking out the outside world, but from their frames and the glass, I could tell they were in good shape.

She unlocked the door but I hesitated. "Does someone live here?" I asked, "Or has it been boarded up until the next owner is found?"

"Well, it's complicated." She thought to say more but changed her mind. I noticed that she took a deep breath before pushing open the door.

Light poured in from behind us into a very black interior, one that sucked light like a dark hole in outer space. Someone lived here, sure enough, if the somewhat fresh loaf of bread and unwashed coffee bowl in the sort of kitchen that I sort of could see said anything. But whoever they were, light was their enemy, and maybe sound. Not only had they placed boards over all the splendid light-welcoming windows, but they had also hung heavy quilted cloth over those boards on the inside to be sure not even a sliver of luminosity or sound could pass in.

"Let's go." I said definitively, and the agent was happy to agree. I spun and exited as swiftly as possible. I'd seen enough. It was in fact a one-room house that occupied only one floor. No wonder the price was so splendid. I had no interest to know how this place had found a corner for the bathroom. I heard her move fast behind me and lock the door as if keeping the force on the other side from escaping. We both moved far down the lane before saying anything. All the while, though, I was thinking, why are these agents showing me the horror boxes of Sarlat, my beloved Sarlat, my town of troubadours, truffles, fairytales, and Cro-Magnon? Suddenly, nose-picker man along the Loire appeared idyllic.

When we were well out of earshot of neighbors who might listen in, I turned to her and said, "That was, *bien sûr*, less harmonious than the first place. Are there any other places, better than these, that we can see?" I might have been begging by that last sentence.

She kept her voice low and said, "I have a confession. I'm a medium, not only a real estate agent. Places tell me their history and people their present state of being. That place was dark and I was sure it wasn't for you, but these two are the only two places on our listings for homes in town."

"Really, this is it?"

"Unless you want a farmhouse about ten kilometers out of town."

Well, sure, I would love that. But it's a bit out of the budget and really, the image in my head was living in town, not needing a car, walking every day to do my food shopping. Just like I did from Le Chardon.

"So, right now, these are my two options?"

"So far. Be patient. Your place will find you as much as you will find your place." She pointed with the key in her hand back toward the abode we'd just left. "I actually was relieved you wanted to leave as soon as you did. It was overwhelming to stand there." She took another deep breath. "When you're sensitive to energies, you have to be careful not to pick them up and carry them; you have to protect yourself."

I momentarily forgot my disappointment in the housing market. "How do you do that?" I asked, building a toolkit for future house hunting visits.

"You pull light in from the crown of your head," she stated matter-of-factly, "and ground it through your feet." She closed her eyes and took another breath. "Then, let the earth take any energy you might carry from others that is heavy. Just give it to the earth, which is very good at cleansing and turning it to something healthy." I closed my eyes and decided to give it a try. It was calming, as if a weight lifted.

But then I thought about my quest for home and my brow must have creased because her eyes opened and she was scanning me again. "Don't worry," she said, "your place will find you. You may not even have to try. As soon as something opens up, I'll let you know. I feel so good when I find a good match, when people find their next home and the energies are complementary."

"Are you from the Dordogne?" I asked, wanting to know a little more about this psychic housing matchmaker.

"I'm originally from Paris. After a bad divorce, I had to get away. My parents had moved here and I came to visit. I really didn't feel good in Paris, but when I came here I felt this incredible ancient energy. It nurtured me and grounded me, and I have lived here ever since. I have good friends here, too, people who are light workers, *travailleurs de la lumière*, striving to bring higher energy and positive growth to others. I love being here. I feel supported and understood."

She certainly was not the first I'd heard this from, nor would she be the last. Hadn't Étienne just made a similar confession, as had so many others?

We walked to the real estate agent's car. "The next person to view this townhouse," she said, "is less sensitive. He sees it as an investment and will keep on the renter who is presently in it." Aha. "But you needed to see it for yourself."

Nadiya's warnings about seeping stone walls took on new dimensions.

A gentle rain began to fall. The medium realtor climbed into her car and rolled down the window. "Remember," she said, "your place will find you." She scanned me once more. This time the lighting crew that worked for Nadiya was there too. "Maybe it already has." With that she smiled mysteriously, added *au revoir*, and drove off.

I watched her go, nailed to the earth where I stood. The rain was as energy clearing as the breathing exercise, but the greatest power lay in those parting words. Maybe it already has.

The morning began with a beautiful fog hovering over Sarlat. It framed the medieval buildings to make them feel more immediate and intimate and saturated the earthy colors of the ochre stone into more vibrant, lit-from-within, amber tones. With the rain adding to the fog, the quieting mood about town calmed my nervous system further. I challenged myself to feel out what home here really could look like, to expand my options, which meant looking into rentals as well. What if Le Chardon was it? To know for certain, I needed to do more research, see other places for sale and for rent, and test, see, feel if one of them would speak to me in quite the same way.

My next real estate encounter came a day later. It was late morning, and I stood at the front window of the real estate agent's office waiting for him to arrive. As I did, I perused the window that was wallpapered with sale ads. One intrigued me: a luminous, white, high-ceilinged studio not far from Le Chardon. As I scanned the details I simultaneously felt someone scanning me from just behind, hovering. It made the hair on my neck stand up and I turned. It was a man attired in a crumpled tweed jacket and dress shirt who smiled and continued to scan me from head to toe as if I were one of the sale ads on the window. He was the realtor.

He extended a hand to shake mine. I hesitated but then began to extend my hand when he said, "So, you are the rich American." I let my hand drop. "What a good day for me," he continued without taking a breath, letting his hand hover a few more seconds

He walked to his agency door, oblivious to the fire alarms going off inside my head, and kept saying over and over, fanning the flames, "the rich American, the rich American. *Elle est ici, voilà.*" I looked around wondering where she was and when she would appear.

Ick.

I stepped into his office, hoping I had already endured the worst. Perhaps that one studio in the ad was worth pushing through this thick barrage of stereotyping. If I really wanted this studio, if its spirit wanted me, then Tweed Man was the only game in town. I glimpsed the asking price on one of the papers he flipped through. It was high, but I figured, as several locals had coached me, I was expected to make a lower offer to the asking price. At least I had a baseline from which to start. I tucked that information away, feeling hopeful.

I learned about the apartment's owner. She was a sad divorcée from Bordeaux. He used the word *triste* for her much as he used the word *riche* for me.

Alas, yes, she was a sad divorcée from Bordeaux in desperate need of the dough. Hence, as we walked to the studio, he explained further, that her asking price was the price. "*Donc*, there is no room for negotiating." Undiscovered as yet by Tweed Man, I was not *l'Américaine riche* of his dreams, and the Bordelaise's asking price was high for both the market and for me. But, I wondered, if the place's spirit wanted me, *peut être* the nice woman from Bordeaux would consider negotiating?

We entered the medieval neighborhood. We swept past the tourist office, then past the Place du Peyrou, where I glanced up at Le Chardon and saw that the windows were firmly closed. The current residents were either out touring or napping. Nadiya's words fluttered before my frontal cortex like that titmouse, the *mésange bleue*, who had careened this spring into my open window and landed. I carried it there as we made a turn deeper into the narrow street that connected the two squares. We next made a sharp sudden left into a very dim and slim alley. We stopped just where, overhead, dozens of pigeons roosted and defecated onto the entranceway below.

The front steps to the building, once golden, were now glimmering with caked white and gray excrement that violently pricked my nostrils with an edgy, acidic stench. A single fuzzy feather drifted down and hovered tauntingly at my nose level before finishing its languid zigzag to the ground.

"This is a rare and beautiful place," he said floridly. I watched the feather land and instinctively held a hand over my head. "Almost never," he waxed on, "will you see a place like this on the market, rich American." I winced. So far, I could agree. Never had my nose burned so much in an alleyway but now my spine stiffened at what appeared to be my new name. Yet rich in what exactly? Satire? Irony? Patience? Optimism? Overwhelmed olfactory bulbs?

The rich American in all this said nothing, but her sidekick, *moi*, deftly stepped to her left in time to miss a pigeon bomb that splattered onto the white-washed stone step. The realtor, blind to this, slowly opened the door as if illicitly unlocking the one forbidden door in Bluebeard's castle. I knew breadcrumbs would do no good in this fairytale, given the voracious bird inhabitants overhead. We all know how that story went.

Inside, it was splendid. It was clean, and before me was one of the signature old spiral stone staircases in vogue centuries ago in several of Sarlat's medieval homes. Just looking up at it was a pleasure of being viscerally swept skyward. It was stone in motion. The stairway was wide enough for one person at a time, and Monsieur Tweed invited me to go first, but I insisted that he should. Disappointed, he stepped up and spoke over his shoulder.

"The apartment is presently rented by a woman from Paris who knows that I am showing the apartment, and she is here to meet us." I relaxed as we climbed, and I feasted my eyes on the remarkable stonework of each step that had been shaped by hands and medieval mason's tools, each block shaped into a perfect pie. The narrow ends of the stones were overlaid and fitted, arranged into a spiraling fan pattern; it was as if we walked up a DNA strand.

We arrived at the door at the top. He knocked. The woman from Paris opened. I craned my head over his shoulder and before proper introductions were made, he pointed at me and said in one swift breath, "*Voici, madame, je vous presentez à l'Américaine riche!* She can buy this place, I am sure, with cash!" For God's sake. Give me a break. Where had that come from?

Madame's mouth hung open mirroring my own. "May we come in?" he asked, oblivious. She looked at me over his shoulder, and as I crossed the threshold and finally could get a word in, I thanked her for letting us see the place while she lived there and added, "*Je ne suis pas une Américaine riche. C'est une fantaisie de Monsieur. Je suis une personne . . . normale.*"

Mr. Tweed did not hear me. Madame gave me a compassionate look and nodded. It seemed she'd been through this a few times before. He was not much better in introducing her with her actual name. He called her *la locataire Parisienne*, the Parisian renter, and explained his many ideas about her, in front of her, that had little to do with her true biography.

I turned my attention instead to the studio and to whether the spirit of this place met mine harmoniously.

I took it in. I closed my eyes. I thought of the medium realtor. I missed her quirky honesty. I opened my eyes. The spirit of the place did not meet me, nor I it.

It was a stunningly charming little studio with high ceilings and a sweet kitchen set a step lower than the rest of the floor and done in natural woods. The bathroom was entirely new and had a swank shower and huge Belle Époque mirror before a generous porcelain washbasin with brass fittings that restored my faith in bathrooms. The whole place was elegantly and serenely decorated in white and tan to echo the stone walls. But standing near its two windows, I was reminded of the outside neighbors. The pigeons roosted on all the ledges, and I learned the Parisian never opened the windows on cool nights, though she longed to, because the smell was ammonia meets rotting fish.

My inner Thoreau imagined living here, each day passing that narrow entrance with fresh groceries, dodging pigeon bombs. I concluded the visit, thanked the renter, and after we descended back to street level, as deftly as possible thanked Tweed Man too, and bolted.

I first rushed toward the Place de la Liberté and took a deep gulp of fresh air. I then shot toward the Mary fountain to regain perspective and centering at the town's source. I connected to the spirit of this place, the real reason I was here, and felt that it connected with me; we were harmonious. *Your place will find you,* said I. *Maybe it already has,* whispered someone disembodied.

After a few moments, refreshed and centered, I returned to the large square and ran right into Cédric. "How is your house hunt going?" he asked.

I told him about my three agents and the inharmonious places I'd seen so far. He found it so very amusing — perhaps it was that thrill of an insider getting the local scoop on insiders from an outsider — that he suggested we grab a café table and have something to drink. When I finally got to the rich American comments he said, "That was rude." But then moments later, stopped calling me Beebe and instead *l'Américaine riche.* As a true gentleman, he smoothed the jibe and soft chortles escaping his lips by paying for our drinks. But drinks were not enough in hindsight. I would suffer for the rest of my summer visit from him finding ways to slip *l'Américaine riche* into conversation whenever he saw me. He'd chuckle with delight. I'd roll my eyes. Onlookers would look confused. I made him pay for drinks.

Mr. Tweed had nothing more to show me, I decided. The Dutchman continued to call me with leads. I never heard again from the medium realtor. I didn't know if it was because my home was not yet emitting the right energy imprint to find me or if she had shifted entirely from real estate to fulltime mediumship and was no longer showing houses. I also knew that it was up to me to read the spirit of the place.

I think we all on some level do this when we are looking for our next abode. And what if, in this case, the spirit of the place had already spoken to me but was not for sale? Or, did I need to think differently about what home really meant? Hadn't I in essence already found it, here, not only in Le Chardon, but also in all of the town and all of the region, in the people, in the land, in the energy? Had not Étienne taken me to the heart and soul of it as a way of telling me about the depth of belonging in a place? And finally, must one own a piece of land or property to actually be able to call it home and thrive in it? Hadn't Neandertals and Cro-Magnons lived here and called it home without owning?

For the rest of my summer in Sarlat, I shifted mental gears entirely from buying to renting and began a new hunt. In so doing, I saw more of the medieval interior of the town and also met new locals who would color my coming days. Nadiya liked my idea of doing comparative shopping as she herself wasn't sure what rent she and I should settle on, if we decided to go that route and Le Chardon indeed were free. She even put me in touch with landlords in town and several other friends did as well.

As deftly as sidestepping pigeon missiles, I sidestepped realtors and pursued the on-the-ground, word-of-mouth network. Only vacation renters went the realtor route. If I wanted to live and pay like a local, getting local prices, I had to do as locals did. Network. And everyone in town seemed to know what I was up to; each market day people came up to me to feed me a new piece of local intelligence that I needed to follow up on *tout de suite* or it might evaporate. Additionally, at each weekly market meeting over drinks, the topic du jour was property prices and old stone homes.

In all this, though, I got an unexpected surprise. Meeting over market coffee with a mutual friend of Aurelie and Cédric, I learned that I was sitting with someone familiar with dowsing, and he could explain how it was used and how it was different from using copper rods to find energy matrixes.

"Both are good for sensing energy, but dowsing has more to do with attraction to water than to energy fields," he explained, going from copper rods to dowsing wands with an ease that a plumber might switch one wrench for another to get the job done properly. "Hazel twigs make the best dowsing rods because they are supple and water rich. *En effet,*" he pointed to his elbow, "one theory is that the lymph gland in our elbow makes us sensitive to feeling the water in the rod that then is reinforced and connects to the water in the earth, that we feel this connection even before the rod bends toward the water."

Dowsing is part and parcel of European lore and has a rich history and respect in France. I looked at the other people gathered, and they listened as if this were perfectly normal conversation.

"You just tune in to the branch and you walk," he continued. "It is usually very subtle, not the Hollywood moment of a great bending branch vibrating toward the ground. The more you do it, the more you will feel what I am talking about, and the more you practice, the more accurate you will get at finding water."

I wanted to practice, find a hazel wand and follow the subterranean stream of Sarlat through town. I was a little self conscious about how it would look, not yet trusting fully that a large part of life here would actually see it as utterly normal, and better, honoring the old ways. I was so happy when I crossed "learn more about dowsing" off my list, but frowned when just above it sat, "find the dancing flower of Temniac," fingering its nose at me, the trail so far cold, but the flower taunting me nonetheless.

I walked that evening across Sarlat imagining the underground water of the town and paying my respects to Mary at her source. Visitors there did what visitors do all across the world at fountains: an ancient Iron Age rite, casting metal, in this case, centime coins, into the water, making wishes.

That night as I lay my head to rest, William Butler Yeat's poem "The Song of the Wandering Angus," played relentlessly in my mind.

> I went out to the hazel wood,
> Because a fire was in my head,
> And cut and peeled a hazel wand,
> And hooked a berry to a thread.

Was it a coincidence that the hazel, an old magical European tree, was connected to the creative sprit, a channel to ground our creative spirit — that fire in our heads — to the earth? Was this happening to me, here? I slept deeply, more deeply than I ever thought possible in that opium addict's psychedelic den. A fire was in my head, and it was touching down deeply into this hazel-wand aided water and rich-soiled earth. I was in Sarlat. This here was a magical realm, a hazel wood.

"Would you like a cup of green tea? I just brewed a fresh pot." This beautiful sprite of a woman with long, silky, black hair was asking me this in her delicate Japanese-accented French that was breathy and fragrant, like the jasmine scent I detected slipping out of the teapot's spout. Her husband, a French man from Bretagne, smiled warmly too, and gestured for me to have a seat in their living room as he took up the little handmade ceramic tea bowls and proceeded to pour tea for all three of us. Two kinds of dark chocolate in similar bowls finished the tray's inviting arrangement.

I looked around and took in a room lined wall to wall and floor to ceiling in books, big coffee table art books, several easels with paintings in progress, and a clothing designer's adjustable dummy, the figure of a woman whose wooden rings had been set to the exact frame of the magical creature before me who had offered me tea, arrayed with an even more magical garment in the making, a sculpted work of whimsical textiles that would make a production of Shakespeare's *A Midsummer Night's Dream* the most mystical of all prior stagings.

Thanks to two other artists, who each August migrated from the Massif Central to Sarlat to sell their art, I'd met Ren and Laurant, both painters, and Ren was also a dress designer. The word on the street among the other artists was that these two were moving to a house in the country and needed to find a renter for their apartment by October. It was right in the heart of the quietest and most magically medieval part of old Sarlat and had an otherworldly stone balcony splashed with a red Japanese umbrella, draping potted vines, and a Mary statue in the corner niche — a composition so fanciful that it seemed only painters and a dress designer could have imagined it and then manifested it.

The apartment was everything a person could wish for to possess a privileged perch in medieval France. Yet, the rent was far outside my range. (I now know that rents in posh parts of rural France compete aggressively with studio rates in Paris, New York, or Tokyo.) And it would come unfurnished, which meant that even the oven, stove, refrigerator, and if I wanted one, washing machine, would have to be supplied by me.

"Never mind all that," said Laurant. "Whether you can rent this place or not, today we are meeting another creative person and that, *voilà*, is the reason for meeting each other. So," he took a sip of his tea, "you're a writer?" In Sarlat, I was beginning to realize more and more, people didn't ask those financial questions. They lived in a town that supported the arts of all forms and respected its creative types, of whom there were many. Here, I'd received more questions than ever in my life about what I was writing about at that moment, not how I wrote and how I managed to make it into a living. The former question gave me energy and excitement. The latter often just made me tired.

I liked these two as soon as they opened their jasmine-scented door. They exuded a calm, peaceful energy, and they took a deep interest in me and the world.

Both Ren and Laurant had come to the Dordogne for *l'energie*. Like Étienne, like me, like Petrus and Jean, like Nadiya, like the realtor-medium, like so many others, they'd felt something here that they'd not felt anywhere else, not even in the mystical spots of Brittany or Japan.

Ren came to France to study pastry making and had been working at her buttery apprenticeship in Bergerac when Laurant walked into her café and felt lightening. Their connection was mutual and strong, to each other and to the Dordogne. When her visa expired and she had to go back home, he followed. A while later he courted her and proposed both marriage and a return to the magical land of the ancient ones. That was how they landed in Sarlat and brought their creative talents to bear, into the broad, supportive creative landscape of a place that sustains artists.

I sipped my green tea, imported directly from Japan, and listened to their tale of kismet. It emboldened me. When I returned in the fall, they insisted, they would take me to some of their favorite and most secret mystical sites in the region.

The autumn was beginning to look like a magical set for *A Midsummer Night's Dream* and I imagined just the right dress to wear.

By the time I said goodbye, I felt like I had known them all my life. Out on the cobblestones, looking up at Mary in her niche with the red umbrella and dripping flowering vines overhead, I marveled at the constant enchantment of this place and the people I met.

Next, I had a meeting with a local, this time a lead through Nadiya. He had an apartment, just vacated, for rent in a building near Le Chardon. Its windows looked out onto a private courtyard whose wall stood on some of the oldest occupied ground of Sarlat. It is actually a courtyard I had retreated to while hunting for property when I needed a quiet place sparse of tourists to catch my breath and cool off. There, I'd recently made a friend in the form of a striped cat, whom I now call Mr. Stripes.

Each time I sat on the stone steps in the courtyard to cool down, Mr. Stripes found me and leapt out from his own cover and sat by my side, and we talked. His grace, in sitting next to me, felt like a blessing.

The landlord and I entered the first heavy wooden door on the courtyard level and went up two flights of stairs. As we ascended, my spirit's hopes went up with me. I had already planned my life here, in this charming stone home with private garden and my favorite feline friend and so close to Le Chardon. And so, I was unprepared for the tumble my spirit would take back down those steps when I saw the dank, water-stained, windowless cave where even the toilet and tub would need replacing, along with the kitchen appliances if I wanted to cook there or keep food fresh.

Adding to all this disappointment, the monthly rent did not include appliances, bathroom repairs, occupancy tax, and utilities. I did the math and discovered that this renting from scratch business was almost as expensive as a robust monthly mortgage. I declined the rent offer. He said goodbye and left, but I lingered, going to the stone steps to sit. Mr. Stripes came soon thereafter and sat next to me. "Don't worry, *ne t'occupes pas*," he purred, using the familiar you because we were now close enough to *tutoyer*. "*Ton endroit te trouvera*. Your place will find you. *Purr-t-être*," he added, licking a whisker, "it already has." Oh how I thanked him for his calming words and rubbed his neck and behind his ears. Cats never lie because they're very comfortable telling the truth, good or bad, in neutral ways.

Thus fortified, I went back to my psychedelic apartment and kept the lights off as I took a cold shower. I then took off swiftly for the Place de la Liberté, sat at my favorite table with my favorite waiter, and ordered a Perrier with lemon. I sat and sat and wrote and wrote in my journal, therapeutically, rantingly, spewingly, sarcastically, and finally, compassionately and gratefully. By the time I was done, I had worked out my final budget and adjusted it to reasonably reflect local prices for studio rentals, minus concierge duties for the care and feeding of sweating stone walls.

Not long after formulating all this, I found Nadiya and made her my offer. I argued how much less work and cost it would be if I paid her a monthly rent and never demanded a change of sheets or towels. I could wash my own sheets and towels. Besides, I would care for the building, look after it, and let her take some time off if she needed.

She thought for about two seconds. "Okay." Then out of the blue, "It's the capacity of floating that makes life better."

I took a deep breath. She smiled her demure and warm Thai smile. Apparently, this was what she wanted too, but she wanted me to know the terrain, to know what I was getting, and what it would take. I agreed to that and to the capacity of floating idea. Now, I knew in my heart that this really was home and that home really was not about owning something, it was about belonging and longing and being wanted somewhere so much that it worked. Floating. A very nomadic notion. Mr. Stripes did nothing but float all day and look at him.

I went back to the square and sat again at that delightful table and ordered *une coupe de champagne*. I toasted the sunset, this time swirling in long, amber fingers that reached their tips into the bubbles of my long, pale yellow glass. To home.

My efforts were so absorbed by home-seeking, home-reshaping, and home-recasting that the hope of finding the flower of Temniac remained a dormant mission, to bloom, I hoped, on my next visit in the late fall when I would inhabit Le Chardon. I squealed with joy.

I returned to the States. There, I remembered another mission, one that now I could fulfill. I wrote to Harold and Dennis and asked how the dig had gone and what the joke was this year on the Delpeyrats. Both wrote back.

Harold said that the summer season went well. "We just opened it up to the point that we found the end of the former excavation and described the levels. Next year we'll start digging for real." He didn't answer the joke question, but Dennis was more forthcoming. "Well," he began, "the joke this year is that there is no joke. We told them there was a really good one so we hope they spend months looking for it."

I carefully queried Aurelie without giving away the joke and found that this was exactly what was happening. They were looking high and low.

In reading those emails from Harold and Dennis, about their dig and about Neandertals, I also recalled something I'd read years ago in *Clan of the Cave Bear*. Whether it was true or not, it struck a deep chord in me and in this business of being human. It was the author Jean Auel's fictitious speculation that Neandertals had a cognition that could access their ancestral memories, a direct line to the people and places of their past. That idea best described the uncanny feeling I got from my first steps in Sarlat and on subsequent returns: echoes of the ancestors, from Neandertals to now.

As I finished the feature story on Harold's work on Neandertals, I couldn't shake the feeling that to learn the true sense of home and belonging was bound up somehow with them. On the one hand, I simply knew that in Sarlat I was home. On the other hand, I also knew that as I wrote about these ancient peoples, they would teach me something about home that would change me.

I held my ear to the stones patiently and waited for even the slightest whisper.

As my train left Sarlat and wended its way to Toulouse, I reflected that in this season I had learned to hold my own with realtors, had gone to the center of the Earth in Sarlat, had learned to make grilled trout in a walk-in fireplace, had learned how to clear and protect my energy, and had gone deeper into a more soulful meaning of home.

I also savored the fact that the coming mid-autumn held the promise of returning to Le Chardon and pursuing, once and for all, that flower of Temniac that had danced in my dream and then on the computer screen.

And my heart danced. I knew I was coming back in three month's time. And soon, Miles would follow. •

FIRST AUTUMN

Le Périgord de l'Esprits n'est pas loin de l'esprit du Périgord. . . . Le Périgord cultive l'imaginaire depuis ses origines. Le sol du Périgord . . . a engendré des légendes que les conteurs ont longtemps agitées lors les veillées.

The Périgord of the Spirit isn't far from the spirit of the Périgord. . . . Since its origins, the Périgord has cultivated the imagination. Its very earth . . has generated legends that storytellers for a long time have animated during long evenings.

— Suzanne Boireau-Tartarat, *Promenades spirituelles en Périgord*, 2007.

Tower in Autumn

Chapter 15

INTERNATIONAL BODY

I felt so good to be home that few things could have added to my pleasure of the moment, but suddenly, through the small gate near the wall came a trotting Mr. Stripes. He had found me from down below in his courtyard and came running up. He jumped onto the wall next to me and nudged me, demanding I rub his neck and behind his ears. He wanted me to admire the new hot pink collar he wore against his gray, black, and white stripes, and then he settled back onto his haunches, leaned into my side, and told me all his stories from the past three months.

Petrus and I turned a quiet bend in the forest and it felt as if at any moment a pterodactyl would fly overhead or a speedy little compsognathus would zip by, brushing our ankles with his long swishy tail. Though, if this were France during the Cretaceous Period when those chaps lived, around 140 million years ago, we'd likely be in an ancient sea and watching a plesiosaur swim by rather than hiking on an overcast autumn day in indigenous oak, beech, and chestnut forest.

Hovering heavy fog reinforced the thick silence of the woods in late fall and partnered with a persistent drizzle, giving my clothes and hair decorations of little watery orbs that clung to every available fiber like morning dew. Every now and then the liquid accretions reached critical mass and became big drops that rolled down my forehead to the tip of my nose and hung there until I flicked them off. In odd contrast, dried-out brown skeletons of prehistoric ferns covered the entire forest floor. They nodded their brittle tips with the slight wind. Overhead towered leafless trees draped in swathes of thick moss and vines. They looked like grand ladies out for an evening of opera in fox stoles and fancy bangles.

Petrus cut sharply to the right, and we entered a narrow path lined on both sides with low stones covered in velvety moss. She stopped and gently brushed back a toupee-like tuft of moss off of one and held it in front of me.

"This isn't a regular rock," she said. "It's a petrified vertebra."

Surely she was pulling my leg, right? The stone was larger than a bowling ball. She understood my disbelief and wasn't offended, oh novice to the ways of the Dordogne.

"Look here," she said, pointing her index finger to what looked like a pattern in the center. "Those are petrified vessels, and here," she turned it slightly to point the vertebra head on toward me, revealing a marble-like core of a different color near the top center, "this is where the spinal cord was." She then ran her hand along one edge and then the other, lifting tufts of moss as necessary to show me the wing-tipped shapes.

Petrus carefully set the petrified vertebra back in its place and swept the moss toupee back over it. A few more steps forward and she did the same with another rock. It became clearer and clearer that this was not an ordinary wall but some giant ancient creature's spine. I soon found myself in that delicious realm between magic and reality.

"When locals around the area cleared this path a few years ago to make a walking trail, they uncovered this stretch, about 50 meters long, of perfectly preserved and petrified dinosaur bones all laying neatly together."

"So, we're talking earlier than 65 million years ago?" I asked.

"Well yes," she said matter-of-factly. "After that, no more dinosaurs, right?"

Right. I grew up in Colorado where dinosaur fossils occasionally cropped up too. As a kid I used to hunt for petrified clamshell fossils from a time some 70 million years ago when an ancient seabed covered today's Colorado. I had forgotten that magic, but in the Périgord, it came back again and again.

Petrus replaced the second petrified bone in the wall and gently placed its moss back over it. The misty air and stones were thick with ancient voices, as if someone had left signs for later visitors, or was still watching from behind the odd-shaped rocks and thick green overgrowth. I just stood and took it in as my brain recalibrated and pushed back the clock to a time some 63 million years before the arrival of the genus *Homo* on any scene. I stood on the ground, or near the ground, where some great beast had died.

A gentle rain began and water drops began to plunk onto my crown, tapping my cranium like a ticking clock. Another drop of water flowed down to my nose tip, this time flicking itself off. Inconceivable time had frozen me.

Petrus waited. She knew the feeling and that this form of enchantment never grew old. This walk had been her idea, a chance to show me the Dordogne in the autumn, my first autumn here. We had already finished off a fine lunch of grilled salmon and leeks in the walk-in fireplace, with a Médoc Jean had saved for the occasion. Thus well feted in the old ways, we were perfectly poised for some deeper time-travel in the ancient forest.

I was struck by how dramatically the color palette and mood had changed, from summer's every-possible-shade-of-green to these riots of warm fire and earth tones against barren trunks and thickets of evergreen oak.

I had marveled at this transition of seasons from the moment I arrived on my train ride south from Paris. It was especially at the point when we passed the tree-covered hills above the vineyards of St-Émilion that the drama began in earnest. Months earlier, my last passage through this territory, the trees wore hunter green and were outshined in the foreground by vibrant new verdant growth on vines of Merlot, Cabernet Franc, and Cabernet Sauvignon. But now the wine harvest had passed and the poplars erupted forward in shimmering translucent yellows as the sun lit them from behind. They danced, thumbing their noses at the naked vines.

And then, as in all prior trips, as the train proceeded east past Bergerac, I began to feel the call of home intensify. At that mystical threshold, the flat land began to swell and pucker and turn into hills and limestone cliffs and dark valleys. We passed autumnal kitchen gardens with kale growing in towering prehistoric-looking stalks and grazing horses who looked like relatives of the painted horses of Lascaux, their coats thickening for winter. Approaching Sarlat, we slipped across the final bridge just before the train station. It arched over the intimate valley that coddled Sarlat, and my breath caught with that first glimpse of Saint Sacerdos holding court in the center of it all. She was stunning, surrounded by trees erupting in the same oranges, reds, and yellows as the limestone of her body.

Richard — son-in-law of the man whose dog Jack killed corks and fancied legs — was waiting for me. As soon as I stepped off the train, he gave me an exuberant hug and jubilant cheek kisses like a relative returned after a long separation. He was Nadiya's keeper of the keys, he explained, because she was in Scotland with Aidan. He grabbed my bag, and quickly we were off driving down the train station road toward the center of town.

Midway down, I saw the leaf lady attacking a solitary leaf that had dared tumble since her last obsessive vigil on the sidewalk moments before. I smiled to myself, happy she was still there, as compulsive as ever, and with the only difference from the spring and summer being that she wore a sweater over her apron. Soon, farther down, I saw the clothesline hung with sexy lingerie, kitchen towels, and apron, and turned in time to see the eighty-five-year-old woman and her husband — still smiling — hanging out on their front stoop, watching the laundry dry on the other side of the street. My smile turned to a full-on grin. It was then that I knew I was really back, really home again. Even though I had gone away, they were all still here, doing their quirky things.

Richard asked about my flight. I did my best to recount in my rusty French that it had been epic. "On one side of me was this Indian woman and her husband," I began, "and on my other side, across the aisle, was this really big guy who turned out to be from North Dakota."

I'd noticed the Indian woman before we had boarded. She was in her late fifties and beautiful and wore her graying hair naturally, letting it accentuate the flow of life on her face, making her wrinkles softer, eyes brighter, and aquiline nose more interesting.

It was my choice too, but because I was the first woman in my family not to dye her hair, I was always looking for role models. When I looked in the mirror, I looked not only at a face that was aging and surrounded by more and more graying hair, but also at one that was making a different choice in the long chain of generations. The Indian woman was elegant. She was vibrant. She made mature women look really sexy. I made a mental note. Stay the course.

When we boarded, as serendipity would have it, her and her husband's assigned seats were just to my left. Seated on the aisle, I looked across it to my right as a very tall man in his sixties arrived and sat down. He smiled at us as we settled in and then pulled out a thick historical novel and began to read. I noticed that in spite of his size, he was mindful not to let his elbows invade his neighbor's armrest.

We all gave each other so much regard and space for this long trans-Atlantic evening flight that we didn't begin to talk to each other until the attendants rallied us with that faux breakfast shtick where the lights come on and, even though it is one o'clock in the morning, you pretend it is breakfast to get in sync with Europe. Along came the attendants with tea and coffee, preparing us to land in France. When it was my turn, I asked for coffee, two creams, no sugar, and a glass of water, please. The Indian woman laughed and asked for the same. "Maybe we're related," she joked, regarding me.

"Maybe," I said, as I regarded her.

"It's funny," she added, "I noticed you before we boarded, and I thought to myself: there is someone like me. I noticed how you also don't dye your hair, and then I studied your hands, the shape of them, and your face, and I felt that you are like women in my family. But then I thought, no, you look French."

Oh, yum.

And, whoa, we'd been studying each other in a quiet mutual admiring way. Sweet.

I told her about my American-born roots with Iranian parents who had immigrated to the USA over five decades ago. She replied triumphantly. "I was right. We are related." She then told me that she and her husband were originally from Mumbai, but that decades ago they had immigrated to the USA and now lived in New Jersey. Their college-aged son was on a semester study abroad program in Paris, and they were going to visit him and to enjoy the city of light.

She then gave me an unexpected gift, a lightening-bolt sentence that entered my skin and careened at high speeds, thousands of feet in the air, into my spine, transforming me on the spot.

"You know," she said, "you are not from one place or another. The way you grew up, you have a different body and a different brain, one that latches on to the international. Wherever you go, you will both belong — because of your own effort and habit — but you will always be just beyond it, international, not of any one place. I feel that, too. But you, the way you grew up, like my son, not me or my husband, you really have this international body." She said body like bodhi as in the Bodhi Tree under which the Buddha sat and attained enlightenment. It was great.

This international bodhi. This delicious phrase rang about in my cranium. I had an international bodhi! It was both nomadic and longing for home at once, and diving into both full tilt. This international body.

This in-between place I had inhabited all my life, mostly alone but at times shared by others with international bodhis, at last had a name. Naming something, identifying it is empowering, both to it and to you.

I wanted to hug her. I had waited half a century to find a name for what this was, all this wandering, not feeling like I fully belonged anywhere, until Sarlat came along. What was this experience that fell inside and outside of ordinary boundaries? This international body.

I felt then and there reborn anew. Finally, after a youth of being chronically betwixt-and-between, I found terra firma in middle age and now knew what to call it. Oddly, too, I'd felt this moment arriving, as if it were ripe to happen, much as the day the armor had fallen off that first winter during my first moments in Sarlat. I'd felt something at work, preparing for this moment's catharsis, when just prior to departure, I'd received independent emails from each of my parents. It felt as if part of the parental genetic code knew that it was time to initiate a crucial rite of passage for their middle-aged daughter that would be fulfilled in midair. In full international bodhi space.

What was weird about those two emails was that neither parent knew that the other had sent me one. Yet, each had written and sent theirs at the same time from their separate offices and separate computers. In both, they reflected on their own journeys of finding themselves in the world.

"Your going away," wrote my mother, "brings the precious but sometimes painful memories of when I said goodbye to my parents. Now I know what they felt and how courageously they kept it inside." But in hindsight, she noted, it had been a very good choice. She'd felt both the sadness of parting but also the excitement of an adventure ahead. One couldn't know the gifts hidden in difficult but promising decisions.

"Just in reading your email about your trip to France," my father wrote, "I feel a tingling in my body as though I am engaged myself in my own trips some sixty years go; my feelings of those years are coming alive and chase yours." He'd been a trailblazer, leaving a certain and successful future life in Tehran for the adventure of America in the 1950s and 60s, building a life entirely from scratch and from his own hard work and earnings. His focus on my trip was all about the adventure ahead, the potential unleashed.

The North Dakotan put down his book and quietly listened to

all this international body talk. He was smiling in a way that spoke of ancestral stories running through his mind as well. We invited him to tell us his story. He explained his own international body, that he had been in the Navy and had been in Vietnam, that his grandparents were homesteaders from Russia and Germany in North Dakota.

"Having land was what made a person rich, and they had left political and economic troubles in Europe for America with the hope of having land. My grandmother traded a horse that was Sitting Bull's. They witnessed the US Army's policy of chasing the Sioux off their lands and into Canada. Their land was in the middle of that. They'd gained their hopes for land but at a price." A non-material price, a price of the spirit, of loss that seemed to always balance gain in this world of ours.

I sat still in my seat with these images moving past me, the pain of poverty, the pain of leaving one's home, the tragic and unjust exodus caused by one people to another. I tried to imagine what his grandparents had gone through and had witnessed. We are all nomads or descended from nomads. I recalled a quote attributed to Leo Tolstoy that says there are really only two kinds of great stories in literature: one is of a stranger coming to town, and the other is of a person leaving. Both stories demanded movement out of the familiar and into the unfamiliar, from the predictable to the unpredictable, and from the mundane toward the promise of adventure.

But what happens when it is you who is leaving town and when it is also you who will be the stranger arriving elsewhere? When you are the protagonist and both great stories unfold together, the impact of the unknown is doubled. At least now I knew that if you are born into that in-between place of leaving and arriving all the time, then, you have an international body.

I realized that in my parents' messages, each had aligned with the part of the story that for each had the most emotional charge. My father tingled with the excitement of going out into the unknown. He at once left town and became a stranger arriving and dove into the excitement. My mother felt the heartache of the people left behind and the sadness of leaving them. She was the other side of the story, the part less told because it will break our strong hearts and expose the high price of adventure: the grief of saying goodbye and not knowing when, if ever, we'll see those we love again.

We arrived at the blue door on Rue Montaigne. Richard ceremoniously opened it and carried my bag in for me. The scent of my grandmother rushed at me in a sweet gust of lavender and linen air. I was arriving again. I was returning. Richard handed me the keys and in Nadiya-coached fashion reminded me how the heating system worked and to close the shutters with the setting sun. He then left me to settle in and rest from my travels.

I pinched myself.

As I stepped into Le Chardon's vestibule, the scent of my other grandmother rushed at me from the kitchen with a subtle gust of saffron and cherry blossom air.

My pannier, my shopping basket woven from stiff grasses with soft leather handles, sat in the entranceway. Nadiya set it there for me to see first. I bought it in the spring, and it sat in storage in the attic since my departure in spring and all through my summer of exile from this studio. I soon saw other gestures of welcome. She had placed a bowl of the season's walnut harvest on the dining table. Handmade lavender soap and a fancy washcloth rested on the bathroom sink's edge. Tears welled up in my eyes by the time I noticed she'd arranged a writer's nook near the big window. A new handwoven Berber carpet lay there, waiting for me to pull up to a small writing desk. There, I was perched perfectly to write and note the world passing through the Place du Peyrou below, regularly, as a permanent resident, a nomad settling in with an international body plan.

I unwrapped the sensuous soap and washed my face of travel. I cracked a walnut to remind my mouth of the taste of the land. I took up my pannier and caressed the firm leather handles and ran my hands over its supple weave. I then skipped down the stairs and stepped out the blue door right as Saint Sacerdos rang her six o'clock-in-the-afternoon bells, six wonderful resonating clangs that vibrated under my skull and made me feel fully planted here and now and fully alive. I might have skipped on my way to do my usual circuit of food shopping along the Rue de la République, *la traverse*, the main drag. Then miracle of miracles, in the little grocery, Madame smiled warmly and welcomed me back. I earned the same from several locals I saw as I passed them while enjoying their early evening refreshment at a sidewalk café. My status of a stranger arriving in town was officially gone. A new and different sort of story was beginning, of diving deeper into the local world. I argued with Tolstoy that this too was a third premise for a great story. He argued back that it was the deeper potential in the story of the stranger coming to town and staying on. My international body conceded. *D'accord, Monsieur Tolstoy. Tu as raison.* (I can tutoyer him for he is dead and in my head.)

My pannier now happily filled with provisions for dinner and breakfast, I fulfilled other rituals of return. I walked to all three of the outdoor, glass-encased, public book exchanges dispersed across town. Called *boîte à lire*, reading boxes, they were an honor system — leave a book, take a book — encouraging a great communal book swap. I loved seeing what books unknown others in town had read, revealing hidden quirks and tastes of the community. You never quite knew what you would find.

Today, there was a stash of just cast-off English mysteries from the 1950s and 60s, all musty smelling as if someone had finally gotten around to cleaning out their sweating stone-walled packed attic. I picked one, slipped the promising book into my pannier and walked back to Saint Sacerdos. I went inside long enough to light a candle in the Bernadette chapel and thank her and the Marys for my return. I then went out and climbed up rue Montaigne. I needed to affect one more ritual of return before going back down and pushing through the great blue door and climbing the uneven stairs to set up house. I went to the low stone wall and sat with the enigmatic conical tower, the lanterne des morts, just behind me like a sentinel guarding my back. Together we looked to the cathedral downhill and the epic pear tree dropping the last of her fruit onto church grounds. I just sat there, savoring that deep sweep and strong sense of rootedness.

I felt so good to be home that few things could have added to my pleasure of the moment, but suddenly, through the small gate near the wall came a trotting Mr. Stripes. He had found me from down below in his courtyard and came running up. He jumped onto the wall next to me and nudged me, demanding I rub his neck and behind his ears. He wanted me to admire the new hot pink collar he wore against his gray, black, and white stripes, and then he settled back onto his haunches, leaned into my side, and told me all his stories from the past three months. Wow, he's a talker. It was impossible to be any happier than I was in that moment. Joy flooded into my heart.

When the sun set, we walked down the hill together, said *au revoir* and *à bientôt* at the blue door, and we each went home. I put my groceries away, happily arranging my provisions on the shelf or in the little refrigerator of the little kitchen as the three huge Gothic windows of my neighbor reflected into my own.

Sunset came sooner than in the spring, and I closed the shutters to keep in the warmth of day and keep out the dropping temperatures of night. But so far, it had been a mild autumn, and the night held on to lingering fingers of warmth that brushed my skin as I snapped the last shutter's latch into place.

In that moment I felt the impact of floating. I was in an odd in-between place where I had no idea what my future held, but I was happy in spite of the risks. It's the capacity of floating that makes life better. On cue, Saint Sacerdos chimed seven o'clock, and the reverb penetrated my body, mind, and soul and nailed me deeply to the very certain present. You are here. You just saw Mr. Stripes! I am so happy. I uncorked a red Bordeaux, made a light dinner of cheese, olives, and arugula dressed in walnut oil, and before Saint Sacerdos could ring nine, was fast asleep.

I heard the swoosh and shovel of ice, the fleshly slap of firm, fresh fish, and the scrape of big plastic tubs and waterproof boots. I threw open my eyes. I glanced at the clock: 6:15 A.M.

She was late.

Next, a crash of ice and an argument erupted below. I jumped out of bed and threw open the windows and shutters. No one looked up or noticed the window's creaking joints because all eyes and ears — the cheese maker's, bread baker's, sausage seller's, walnut oil presser's, fowl farmer's, and wine trader's — were on the man and woman surrounded by fish and a missed shovel of ice scattered all along the cobblestones around their feet. It seemed a jumble of frustrations.

"I thought you brought the extra ice."

"*Mais non!* I thought you did!"

"And where's the trout?"

"What trout?"

"You mean you forgot the trout?!"

I felt as if I were in the middle of an Asterix and Obelix comic book. Then all went silent. I craned my head to get a better look and saw that Madame had clammed up and turned to array glistening fat black mussels from the Gironde in tight-knit rows as Monsieur searched the truck in hopes of finding trout or ice. My eyes went back to the plump shiny mussels. I knew what was for lunch. The usually coveted Aquitaine trout was elsewhere unknown, slowly smelling like day-old fish, unless, of course, it was with the extra ice. I quickly dressed and went out.

A kilo of *moules* later, stored back upstairs in the coolness of my refrigerator, I was out again, now seated at Petrus and Jean's amidst the olives and spices, picking up as if I had never left. Petrus had already plied me with a cup of orange spice tea and a slice of walnut bread that simultaneously filled my hands and heart. I sipped and nibbled and watched as the early morning customers arrived. The longtime loyal shoppers did their shopping early when they could also swap news and trade recipes. As Petrus filled their little bags with olives, they filled Petrus with family and village happenings.

She grew especially attentive as an older woman and her fifty-something daughter stopped to buy dried ginger and spices. I bent my ear to better understand their French, which had a lot of Occitan in it, as they explained to Petrus why they had been away from the market for so long. After they departed, I asked Petrus about them. I was drawn to them both, feeling an intangible pull, as if they were made entirely of kindness and compassion.

"The older woman is an amazing healer and her daughter is stepping into her shoes now because the mother thinks she will depart the world soon." Petrus explained soberly. "The mother hasn't been feeling well, and, as a healer, knows the signs of what can and cannot be done. That's what we were talking about." She paused, saddened by this news. She then gave me an example of this woman's immense skill. She told me about someone she knew in the community who was diagnosed with a terminal illness, someone to whom medical doctors had said there was nothing to be done. She next sought out this very healer who told her, "I can help you but you really will have to want to be cured because it is going to hurt like hell for the two hours that I'll work on you. Once I start, we can't stop."

"What happened?" I asked, unconsciously sliding forward and sitting on the edge of my seat.

"It hurt like hell for sure, but afterward, she really did feel better. She went back to her doctor, he ran tests and was amazed. The illness was gone."

The real deal. Before me was a strong and vital root from the culture growing from the very depths of the soul of this place and this people. I hungered to learn more. There was still a lull between customers, and patiently, Petrus answered more of my questions.

"The mother realizes she has to pass on her knowledge and gifts to her daughter before she dies," Petrus said. "She comes from an age-old tradition of hands-on healers in the Dordogne where it's common that a child will inherit the gifts of the parent. It's usually a mother passing it on to a daughter or granddaughter, or a father to a son or grandson. Both women and men inherit it."

I'd had some inkling that energy healing was a respected practice here but had little idea how it looked. It was already clear that it was far different from our ideas of energy healers in New Age circles in the United States. Something had happened to that person during those two hours of hell, a real battle fought with real energy and matter that resulted in no more pain and a real cure testified by modern medicine.

Petrus saw my interest, and in her inimitable graciousness as one of my primary guides to this magical place, much like with the dinosaur fossils or the orchids, she took me deeper. Jean agreed to cover the stand as we took off briskly through the market. Petrus as quickly came to a sudden stop and pointed out a man who had a bread and produce stand. "People go to him for help. Sometimes over buying bread, they arrange an appointment for a healing." Sometimes, if it is urgent, he'll do a short session right there, such as for a merchant with a bad back. After five minutes with him, it's relieved. But often, he keeps the two industries separate. Healing sessions tax a healer's energy, so he or she has to be careful and take time to rest to regenerate his or her energy. It's a real service, a gift.

As we returned to the olive stand, Petrus told me that there wasn't a payment system for a healer's services, only contributions or doing something for them in exchange. It was a tradition that kept the skill from being corrupted and in the hands of those gifted with it, with no motive for personal economic gain. It was more a responsibility and burden. I thought of Nadiya's mother and the demands the spirits and clients alike made on her at all hours of the night with no great material gain for herself.

Given this ethic, all healers — *guérisseurs* — here had another vocation, such as farming, baking, real estate, or accounting. You could be dealing with someone for years, say, for keeping your books or baking your bread, and not know until you needed it that they were the current inheritor of a long line of family healers.

By the time we returned to the olive stand, it was swelling with the patrons who slept in a little later than the early crowd. Their flow would likely continue until the market folded, so I left my two friends alone and went off to finish the rest of my own food shopping. I looked at the merchants differently, given what Petrus had taught me. How many of these people led multi-dimensional lives with other untold skills that enriched the world around them?

I bought bread from the healer. I figured it was probably pretty vital bread, and honestly, I just liked his vibe. On a sudden health kick, I went next to the organic farmer I liked at the market and purchased vibrant and healthy turnips and turnip greens from him, knowing from Iranian folk cooking that turnips were a cure for everything and often used to prevent and cure colds in autumn and winter. I then fed my soul with vital and fresh cepes ravioli, all in the name of healthy living. Saint Sacerdos' noontime bells resounded through the square. It was time to go home and prepare and devour lunch.

I sweated minced green onions with parsley in olive oil and then added and steamed the mussels in white wine with a hit of pepper and gray sea salt. The salt was pleasurably from the Île de Ré, just north of Bordeaux and just happened to be left in the cupboard by a past renter in Le Chardon. Perhaps it was the renters I'd grumbled so much about in summer? I thanked them in my heart, not only for the salt, but for the sweetness of delayed gratification that I now lapped up from my third-floor perch in the center of it all.

My appetite voracious, I followed the mussels with the ravioli, simply seasoned with good olive oil, sea salt, and cracked black pepper and set on a bed of garlic sautéed mustard greens. My only regret was that Miles wasn't with me, especially when I sipped the dry white from Graves, produced so close to where the mussels had been harvested that I could feel the whisper of salt air and seaweed dance throughout the apartment.

With winter near approaching, with its isolating cold, gray, and wet days, as much as I loved how badminton brought me into the local social fray, I wanted to do something that didn't require schedules, a car, and the commitment of three evenings a week. But I wanted to keep fit, and I wanted to prevent delectable duck fat from sticking to my buttocks and thighs, so I needed to find something that supplemented my long walks into the surrounding countryside. Those walks couldn't be done everyday, not with long stretches of bad weather and the earlier setting sun.

I began by exploring a fitness gym, the only of its kind for kilometers around. I discovered a sweaty world of male expats from England and Holland who seemed to hang out there all day as an English social club.

While this could be edifying, its low ceilings and lack of ventilation made me exit quickly. As quickly, I crossed it off my list.

I reflected next on the few team sports I'd enjoyed in high school — soccer and basketball — that could actually be practiced to a certain degree on one's own. All I needed was a ball and a field or court. Balls were easy. There was a sport's shop on the edge of town, along a path I liked taking for walks. Fields and courts were another matter. I scoured the landscape and discovered that soccer fields were scarce, but that there were two basketball courts within walking distance. One was at the community cultural center and the other a school. Both were available but only when the kids' classes weren't in session (to avoid disturbing them with my ball bouncing through their classroom windows) or when the children weren't themselves at recess using the court for their own unbridled glee.

I ultimately chose the court at the cultural center. It was a bit more private and available throughout the day, but also it was near the corner where a local woman fed stray cats, including one to whom I'd grown attached. His name was Felix. He was a bit bumped around by life and had chewed-up and crooked ears atop his black-and-white panda face. In spite of the blows dealt him, he remained an optimist and came running to greet me before practice. Thus doubly rewarded with muscular thighs free of duck fat and visits from my four-legged friends, I was a regular at that court every other day practicing my hook shot. The best part was that if my skills bit dust, the cats wouldn't tell a soul. That was far better than a classroom full of feisty kids looking out the window at the court at the old American woman.

Once I knew my game, off I went to buy the right ball at that sports shop on the edge of town. As I timidly tried a few basketballs out in the aisle where they were displayed, the shop owner came over to ask if he could help me. As soon as I opened my mouth, he knew my nationality from my accent and gushed like a teenaged girl at a Taylor Swift concert over how much he loved the American game, and soon we were both playing ball in the aisle far less timidly than when I had started. Not only did he give me pointers to improve my dribbling and passing skills but he had me test several balls before recommending a particular orange and black orb, which I made my own and happily carried back into town, cheeks flush with my little adventure.

Excited to try the new ball, I went straight to the court at the cultural center. It proved to be the more ambitious of the two courts. It was on a hill. If I missed the hoop, the ball would continue downhill, no fences to stop it behind the basket, leaving me to run as fast as possible to catch it before it disappeared over a bluff and hit someone on the head. The cats, hanging out by the fence on one side of the court, just looked up and stared, wondering why any creature would worry about duck fat when just eating enough was the only item on their agenda. It's important to note that while they were safe from my errant ball, I was not protected from their ridicule. It was amusing, though, because I would spy from the corner of my eye that their eyes and faces followed the ball, up and down, back and forth. Felix had his usual face on, with chewed-up, uneven ears and crooked grin. Otherwise, it was hard to read what they thought.

Another delight I discovered through basketball in Sarlat was that when I walked to the court with the ball under my arm, I became the center of attention of passing teenage boys. Not in any spicy or mischievous way, but in pure unexpected fascination: they rarely, if ever, saw a middle aged woman with a basketball. They were curious and pulled me momentarily into the world of teenage boys who love to play basketball. We talked game. My being older and female didn't matter. I was falling deeper and deeper in love with the unpretentious, deeply human, and warm side of French culture, a culture rich in exuberant teenagers, giddy grown men in sports shops, and talented baker-farmer-healers.

One Sunday morning, soon after my basketball practice, I went into Saint Sacerdos to light my weekly candle in the Bernadette chapel. It was right before Mass, and I was toying with leaving before Mass rather than staying, but felt a bit of the gravitational pull of all the faithful streaming in. To my surprise, there was the Pantsuit Lady, the one and the same woman in her seventies I'd seen in the spring right before Mass with her sturdy suit, sturdy bowl-cut gray hair, and sturdy manner. She had intrigued me back then, wondering what she was doing at the chapel before Mass and then leaving. But I never saw her again. Yet here she was, doing exactly what I'd seen her doing months earlier.

I dropped my two euros into the offering slot, picked up a blue candle, and lit it with the box of matches nearby. I then went to the lady's left where there was more space, so as not to bother her, set my candle on the metal stand, and stepped back. She turned and looked at it, then at the Mary to her left, and then at me, and said, "Listen. *Ecoutez.* Put your candle closer to mine so your prayers have a better chance." She indicated which one was hers as *quoi* rippled through my mind. She elaborated before I needed to utter why out loud.

"See that Mary, the one in front of us? She shoots your prayers to Bernadette below who shoots them to the Mary to the left who is perfectly placed to shoot them into the nave where they bounce to the apse and up to God."

A three-point shot to heaven? My recent dates with the court had me visualizing her positioned prayers as a big orange ball passed from Mary of Lourdes to Bernadette, who slipped it to Mary of Fatima, who shot it far down the nave. Had I really understood what this sturdy woman told me, or was I making it all up, given my own recent obsession with the hoop? That she was speaking Occitan made me sure I had really gotten it all wrong.

"Really?" I managed, she nodded happily, and so I dived in for clarification. "Do you mean to say that we're playing a game of magical basketball?"

She smiled more broadly and her eyes gleamed. "*Voilà! Vous m'avez compris!* You've understood me!" She exclaimed so loudly that two people who had just entered the church looked toward us in shock. "Glad you get it," she added more quietly. She then turned to go, and I quickly asked her if she was staying for Mass.

"Oh, goodness no. This here is where it's at." And she walked away.

This only reinforced my sense of having found a place where I could really belong, a place open enough to everyone doing their own thing, including rituals in churches where Marys played basketball. Oh, heaven! Maybe everyone here had an international body in one way or another. The experience also deepened my feeling that France may be a secular nation and it may be the birthplace of the rationalists, like Descartes, or a strangely seductive culture that still managed to over-intellectualize corporeal things, like, say, sex, but off the beaten path, it got wonderfully wiggy and pagan and intuitive and deeply spiritual.

Not too many days before this sacred basketball encounter, I had clicked on the television after lunch to find a daytime talk show on the topic of psychic experiences in France. The hostess was Oprah-esque with a big dose of *à la mode Française* — facial expressions that spoke of being scientific and neutral, gelled, spiky, blond-frosted hair with pointy glasses, red lips, and a little skirt — and she had invited before her a panel of respected clairvoyants and a professor of psychology who was an expert on French mediumship.

They spent the hour talking about surveys that had proven that France (and apparently not so much Spain or Italy or those more "mystic" eastern European nations) was the most "psychic" nation of Europe. More specifically, more people in France than other European nations were found to take as a fact that psychic phenomena exist, that ghosts and spirits exist, and that certain people can communicate with them. They also discussed why the Inquisition was born in France, which it was, and not Spain; it was a way for the church to combat witchcraft and sorcery because obviously there was so much talent for it here. Thankfully, they added, the talent remains but the need to persecute it does not.

After the talk show concluded, I felt I had sufficiently made an effort to improve my French, and I switched off the tube. Desiring to stretch my limbs, I struck out on a walk, and it being Toussaint, All Saints' Day, I directed my footfall toward the cemetery. It only then occurred to me why the talk show had aired today: it was the most potent day to commune with the ancestors and the graves promised to be full of life.

I climbed up the rise of the hill at the west end where the tombs stood and looked back at the town of Sarlat below, stunned by the fall colors from the changing forests surrounding the valley on all sides. The cemetery further accentuated the drama, exploding with color from flowers that the living had left to honor their dead.

As before, being here gave me a peaceful feeling of being among happy spirits, today's color only magnifying that emotion. It spoke of a place that has been good to people and people good to it. It was a place that worked one's energy forward and didn't seem to let things get stuck in the past; a place of transformation.

Was this why there were natural healers here who were powerful and respected? Was this why there was a soft but strong spirituality movement with many dimensions? Was this why humans came here so very long ago? Was this also why I felt I belonged so strongly here? I suspected too, as I walked back to town, that Rafaea, Le Chardon's pretty ghost, came and went and that she was not a stuck earthbound soul but one who was a part of the transformative work from the other side of the veil. Perhaps she is a helping spirit whispering prophesies in sleeping incarnate people's ears so that they would wake up fully and take notice of the profundity of life. •

Saint Sacerdos during l'Heure Bleue

Chapter 16

PEOPLE IN BLACK

> The truffle buyers captured my attention on a cold overcast Wednesday afternoon on the main square where several cars sat, trunks open, in front of the mayor's office. Everything about it looked illicit except that it was fully exposed to the best-watched building in town. Hiding nothing, there were still those slinky back-alley, back-trunk glances and exchanges. A man at the nearest open trunk, dressed in olive greens and deep browns, was uncovering various baskets and revealing the best of the season's black clusters as clusters of people in other forms of expensive black — cashmere, mohair, combed wool, buttery leather — moved closer to his car.

O NE SUNNY NOVEMBER DAY, IT WAS TIME. TIME TO TRY again for the elusive church and flower of Temniac. This round, I knew better and left my map at home. Using the autumnal mid-afternoon sun as my guide, I walked north and determined to ask the first local I met for directions. As in fairytales, the first fork in the road at which I arrived, a woman came out her gate to weed her front garden. "Take the road to the right," she smiled and added encouragingly, "it's only two kilometers away, but uphill for most of it."

To the right I went and arrived at another fork in the road just as a youth was returning home from visiting his friend's house. "Take the road to the right," he also said, "and pass the donkeys grazing on your left. Though, they are all over the place so you never know about them."

He laughed and I joined in, wondering about a whole herd of donkeys. I'd never seen more than one or two donkeys together at any one time.

As I committed to the road to the right and saw the hill steepen, I passed a woman taking out her trash and asked if I was on the right track. "Oh, yes, and soon you'll wish there were a café with a cold beer on that road." She laughed and I joined in, thinking she must be exaggerating.

Onward I plodded, angling up. The road steepened. Just as I was beginning to wish for that refreshing café, I noticed something move above me and to my left. I looked up to see a soft nose attached to a long head with long ears peeking over a rise, staring right back at me. And then another head joined it to stare some more. And then another. Soon, more and more heads appeared, and sure enough, a whole splendid herd of donkeys stopped grazing to watch my slow, bipedal ascent. To their credit, not a one brayed a funny laugh. It occurred to me that this herd must be the fabled donkeys from whose milk a local in Sarlat's market makes and sells soaps and facial creams. I even recalled overhearing a shopper explaining that donkey milk was the best youth tonic for a woman's skin. I'd laughed then but did not now. It would have been rude. I made a mental note to try their soap and cream and thanked my new friends for their politesse.

Right as the incline was reaching vertical alignment with my legs, and I was wondering if I were on the right road, for no village and no church appeared as I climbed, I met the most remarkable local of the day. He was an elderly man with a walking cane, going up too. He confirmed and told me to press on, that at the top I would find signs on the roadside leading to the church, but sadly, no café and no cold beer.

"I walk up and then down this hill everyday to keep fit," he offered encouragingly. "I'm ninety, so keep it up and you'll see that it's worth it." He laughed, and then added an elder's wisdom. "But the key is that I take my time, go at my own pace, little by little does it." Thanking him, I pushed upward. Just as I began to think it wasn't so bad, I turned a bend and it got steeper.

No wonder I had missed this village before. It didn't seem to really want to be found. With me, my admiration also climbed for the nonagenarian behind me, and I wished I'd had his foresight to bring a walking stick. Once, I turned to try and see Sarlat behind me, but all had disappeared into my steep narrow path on the road through the forest. After some moments, at last, the forest opened and a black wolf dog offered a welcoming bark from behind his fence. I was on the perimeter of the village. A few more steps and I was at the hilltop and could see the dramatic layers of the expansive Massif Central mountains to my right. And right there, just in front of my nose, I found a sign with an arrow pointing to my left for the twelfth-century Church of Temniac, and there just beyond, it stood in full view. It took this much climbing before it was visible, but now I understood its strategic position, also hinted at by the heavily fortified walls of the church. On the highest spot of the hill, one could see everywhere below but no one below could see it until they were within arrowshot.

When I looked back toward where I had come, I was rewarded at last with a stunning vista of the entire valley in which Sarlat nuzzled, its rippling layers of green, brown, and yellow hills, dips and crevices, and bushy forests meeting in the center of golden stone and the jutting bell tower of Saint Sacerdos. In that virgin glimpse, I fell in love all over again with the place.

I finally pried my eyes away and turned back toward the church, skin pricking in anticipation for what I would find. The flower, the flower, the flower, said I. I stepped up, first coming upon an unnatural mound, just beneath its west entrance, with what looked like a little defunct well on top.

Such perfectly rounded mounds always signaled many layers of human attention worked upon a spot. A well hinted at an underground water source and probably the original reason for building here, in addition to its perfectly hidden position. I thought also of the underground stream running through Sarlat and wondered if it connected with a tributary from here.

Another step closer and I saw a gate with a plaque that stated simply, Centre Spiritualité Temniac. Ah, ah, ah, at last. The spirituality center that originally brought me here, that used the dancing flower as its logo. But I went over to the gate and saw no flower, no logo, peeked in, and saw no one at home. I returned my focus to the church. The key to the mystery had to be there. It was at the highest point and center of this place founded in the twelfth century. Beyond the church, I could just make out another ancient building, a high round tower, and the walled ruins of the fourteenth-century chateau of Temniac. The rest of the village, a cluster of perfect little fairy cottages of golden stone and golden light, gathered around these two, and the whole place was swathed by the very old and very loving arms of grand oak and pine.

Magic pricked the air. Had I entered a fairyland, fallen through a veil where the illusion of time was suspended? Would I return to Sarlat twenty years later this very afternoon?

I found the large western entrance of the church firmly bolted shut, but a smaller southern door sat ajar. I pushed open its heavy wooden and iron-studded gate and stepped through a low stone archway into a single chamber whose acoustics took my footfall and echoed them perfectly along walls and ceiling.

Simple, beautifully proportioned, filled with celestial sounds just from quietly breathing, I felt good standing there. I felt all my cares slip away and seep into the earth below, alchemically transformed into something more fertile. I sensed that this place had power and secrets to share, but in its own time. I hoped one would be the flower I'd seen dancing in my dream.

I walked down the nave to the apse. A *mésange bleue*, a titmouse, who had been gripping the lead edge of one of the stained glass windows with his acrobatic feet, suddenly took flight and flew arches over my head. He was the same species of bird who had flown into my window the past spring, and his yellow and blue flashed across the air, a stunning match to the blues, reds, and oranges around him. He landed again on a window as I found myself standing before a thick prayer book laying on the floor beneath the altar.

Someone had set it there and laid it open to a page for that day's inspiration. A small stone rest on the page to hold it open. Next to the book sat a little basket with slips of paper where people had folded notes of hope, prayer, and blessings. For such a small place, there were a lot of written-on slips in the basket already. I joined the crowd and took up a blank slip and poured my most intimate hopes onto it, folded it, and slipped it into the basket with its community of hope and faith. In my solitude, I felt connected. All the little details — the bird, the book, the stone, the slips of paper — wove me in. I wanted to light a candle and looked about, seeing to my left a wooden stand with two-foot taper candles for the taking with a two euro offering.

I dropped the correct coinage into the offering box and was just drawing out one of the long candles when a sudden burst of light flashed onto my right side. A motion sensitive light had come awake and revealed, also to my right, a subterranean passageway. I carried the candle unlit and as in a dream followed the lights. I would surely be returning to Sarlat that afternoon twenty years later. Time-travel has its risks. At least I had a candle.

Down I went, deeper along narrow and deep cut stone until I arrived at a round crypt set exactly beneath the altar. Mary was there to greet me, in that light taking on the mature and weighty form of a subterranean goddess of the earth, a counterbalance to the sunny and airy image of the sky Mary that stood directly above her in the altar. Notre Dame de Temniac. This church in name and practice was devoted to Her, above and below ground, the sky goddess and the earth goddess, heaven and earth at once.

I found myself mesmerized by the life-size statue and a golden stained-glass window just beyond her shoulder. I sang a small sacred chant, and my voice returned to me amplified with harmonics as it washed across the walls and released an ethereal energy emanating from the vibrating stone. The space above defined acoustic perfection; this space below surpassed it. The only thing that released my feet from the spot was seeing the dimming light of the setting sun through the low round window. I knew I needed what was left of it to make my way safely back down that steep hill to Sarlat. I thanked Mary for Her grace and moved to a passageway I saw parallel to the one I'd arrived on, on the other side. As I approached, it erupted with light and guided my feet back up and out, a full circle of arrival and departure from the underground world of the goddess. Something more was there, pulling me to return, but for now, it had to wait.

Back above ground, there was just enough time and light to search for the flower. I looked at every corner, every wall, every paving stone, every ceiling curve and joint. I did not find it, but in looking, I came across two plaques at the back of the chapel explaining the church's history and why it was wholeheartedly in love with Mary.

Since the founding of Our Lady of Temniac in the twelfth century, the church and Mary have protected its people many times, but the apex miracle occurred in 1627 when a deadly plague hit Sarlat and the surrounding region. The desperate Sarladais made a pilgrimage to Temniac to petition Mary for a cure. The sick and the still hale gathered and walked up the hill, much along the path I had taken this day, paying homage to Mary. She quickly answered, and people were cured. Unlike Saint Bernard of Clairevaux, she didn't need a loaf of magic bread as intermediary, her access to heaven so much more direct. Ever since then, more than ever before, this site became a deeply venerated and magical place hidden here in its curious reveal-and-conceal on this highest hilltop.

I carefully made my way back to Sarlat, down the steep hill in the low light. Going down was harder than up, given the sheer angle, but I was full of the luster of wonder, pondering the experience of that place on the hill and its healing miracle. Miracles. When I stood in the crypt, the walls were covered in plaques of thanks and gratitude inlaid in marble. The dates on the plates indicated decades and centuries of healing miracles from Our Lady of Temniac. I wondered, as I reflected on these signs of gratitude while descending in waning light, if I had missed the whole point of my dream. Perhaps I was to look for something symbolic, not physical? Wasn't this Mary above and Mary below like the intersecting triangles of Solomon's Seal, heaven and earth meeting into a six-pointed star, or, in this case, a flower? Had I not just visited the Mother underground and above, a sky and earth goddess as once, intersecting in my heart? What could possibly be a more stunning dancing flower of Temniac?

But still, I had seen the flower dance in my dream just as I later saw it dance on the computer screen of the spirituality center next door to the church. It had a physical manifestation in this world and I still had to find it. When Miles arrives, I said to myself, by now approaching the level ground of Sarlat proper, we'll come back; two pairs of eyes are better than one. I smiled. I knew he'd enjoy the nutty adventure of hiking to look for an elusive flower in a whimsical-if-wifty dream from months ago. If it really existed.

I stepped into Sarlat's golden market square just as the last drops of light dissipated into the darkening blue night sky. It was *l'heure bleue*, my favorite time of day, especially right here when the setting sun left a lingering and deep cobalt blue in the sky that complimented the glowing amber stone and the gently flickering lights of evening. I loved how everyone was finished with work and buying their evening bread, some doing some window shopping, and some meeting friends for a glass in a café. I loved it especially now, this week, the third week in November, when the year's new wines were being released all across France.

It usually came in the form of Beaujolais Nouveau. The new bottles appeared overnight, arrayed at the entranceways to wine shops and grocery stores, whispering an excitement only found in autumn — the sun is setting earlier, the air has a slight chill, but early evening spent out with friends is still electric.

It is the perfect time to gather in a local café and try the year's new red.

"The new wine is how we learn what this particular year tastes like," I recalled a Parisian friend telling me. "It's a review of the year," he'd said, "wrapping things up in a flavor that succinctly defines it." He then confessed that he wasn't a fan of years that tasted too much of banana, a risk of the young Beaujolais.

I wanted to taste this year, the year of my first spring, summer, and autumn in Sarlat. I wanted to note it well, reflect, and remember forever its taste in one sip of wine: the flavor of the year that changed everything. I too hoped it was less ripe banana and more forever.

I rushed to Le Chardon, splashed some water on my face, and changed my clothes and shoes. I then asked my neighbor from Liverpool, Simpson, who was renting the apartment across the hall, and Nadiya and Cédric, after their evening badminton practice, to join me at Le Bataclan, a locals' bar in the heart of the town, to taste the magical year together. The first round would be on me. They agreed.

Deep into the blue hour we arrived. As I pulled the door open, I could see that the bar pulsed with the energy of a group gathered to watch a heated rugby match. But tonight, the monitors overhead were off, yet the crowd was really pumped up. Excited to find out what was all the buzz, I excitedly stepped in. Simultaneously, my face rammed into a high-velocity backhanded fist of a burley man at the bar.

Crack!

My head flew back. Simpson caught me. I saw birds and six-pointed stars everywhere (but not flowers). This wasn't my idea of a first round, but it was definitely on me.

I don't recall much of those initial seconds except that I didn't think my nose was broken and I felt Simpson step forward and angrily demand an explanation. I think I heard him say, "What sort of man hits a woman?" As noted, he was from Liverpool, and I could feel his fists warming up for a fight. As the stars and birds cleared from my vision, the man hurriedly apologized, and his two buddies quickly stepped between their friend and Simpson and explained that it had been an accident, that their friend was too deep into his cups, intoxicated over the new wine, the Gaillac Primeur, and was animatedly expressing his love for it with arms swinging hard and wide and backwards when I walked into the line of jubilant fire.

As my head cleared, it made sense. That seemed to be what had happened. I also was relieved to confirm that my nose wasn't broken and the punch hadn't drawn blood, but I was going to have a swollen snout and maybe black circles under my eyes for the next couple of days. "So, this Gaillac," I managed through throbbing sinuses, "is that much better than the Beaujolais?"

The whole bar went silent and looked at me in astonishment. The bartender broke the stillness by explaining that while he'd be happy to find a bottle of Beaujolais Nouveau for me, if that was really what I wanted, that yes, truly, the young Gaillac, "primeur, it's called," was superior, worth flailing arms and gesticulating fists.

"How?" I asked, finding that talking about wine diminished my pain.

"For such a young wine," the bartender began, "it has less of that thick fruit taste, the banana that often dominates a Beaujolais Nouveau."

"And more minerality," added the heavy hitter, "also remarkable for such a young wine." He was quite eloquent for being so tipsy.

"And from the south, near Toulouse," added one of his buddies, "making it our wine, not theirs." Ooh. Ahh. A cool reference to the *oui*-saying northerners. Those were fighting words. And so I had to try it.

"Well, then, I really could use a glass of Gaillac Primeur right now. A round for me and my friends, *s'il vous plaît*." We four then went and took a seat toward the back, safely away from the door.

When the bartender arrived with our glasses, I could see the color of the wine was different too. Gaillac was deep garnet where Beaujolais Nouveau was medium ruby. He set them on our table, and as I pulled out a bill to pay, he said, "This first round is on the gentleman who hit you."

In any other context, those would be strange, dark words, but here they were bright and appropriate. We turned to the big fisted man across the bar, who by now had stepped away from the door and worked his way around the bar counter to a safer place for inebriated burley men passionate for new wine, raised our glasses, and smiled. His eyes met ours, he raised his glass, and we drank.

I savored the strong hit of young mineral. Where Beaujolais Nouveau flirted with tastes of fleshy tropical fruit, Gaillac instead punched with quartz-and-iron earth followed by cherry and currents. The throbbing in my nose subsided. This year tasted earthy and grounding, real and substantial. "This is so much better than, *plus que*, all the Beaujolais Nouveau I've ever tried," I declared to my three friends.

Cédric lingered over his sip, savoring it, then looked at me. "I've been meaning to tell you, you have to watch out how you use the word *plus*. Sometimes it means 'more' and sometimes it means 'none' or 'no more.'"

"It can mean the opposite of itself?" I asked, and added, "Why is French so hard?"

"French is a very subtle language," he offered nonchalantly, as if that were helpful. "That is its beauty and its danger."

He then went on to show how many frightening ways the meaning can change in using the word *plus* in different placements and with different preceding words. In that horrifying moment, I realized that half the time I used *plus* I was actually saying the opposite of what I'd meant. Subtle was not the right word. Subversive, yes. Just as I was catching my breath at that, he smiled, swept back his long, fashionably styled French hair, adjusted his French designer glasses, and said, "It gives us French men an advantage, *n'est-ce pas?*"

Nayida rolled her eyes. Simpson glared. I did my best to ignore him, even if he had been the messenger in that weird prophetic dream I'd had before ever coming to Sarlat nearly two years earlier. And soon, the second round of Gaillac was on me. Simpson switched to beer like a good Liverpool lad. He'd have *plus*.

I noticed with November an increase in people in town dressed in black. They seemed to belong to three separate tribes: truffle buyers — but not sellers, who dressed in the colors of the forest — filmmakers, and funeral goers. Telling them apart wasn't always easy and context was everything.

The truffle buyers captured my attention on a cold overcast Wednesday afternoon on the main square where several cars sat, trunks open, in front of the mayor's office. Everything about it looked illicit except that it was fully exposed to the best-watched building in town. Hiding nothing, there were still those slinky back-alley, back-trunk glances and exchanges. A man at the nearest open trunk, dressed in olive greens and deep browns, was uncovering various baskets and revealing the best of the season's black clusters as clusters of people in other forms of expensive black — cashmere, mohair, combed wool, buttery leather — moved closer to his car. Collectively they looked like a very big high-grade truffle themselves. A dog joined the fray and forcefully pushed his nose through the thick forest of human thighs. The image was complete.

Next, several armed police arrived. Rather than busting up what in any other context would be an illegal drug sale going down, they instead surrounded the cars and offered extra protection. Their presence confirmed that the cars held the legendary funguses that brought in around twelve hundred euros per kilo. As I inched closer, I learned that many of the users, I mean, customers, the ones who had physically come to buy for themselves, were celebrated chefs and restaurateurs from the culinary capitals of France.

Another sea of people stood off to the edge just beyond the police. They too shimmered in the blacks of cashmere, soft leather, wool, and silk. They all were fused to slim black cell phones with bidders at the other end, high-end buyers so wealthy they had others do the buying for them. I imagined the clients at the other end dressed not in black but nautical blue and white stripes with deep bronze tans, seated on their yacht in azure seas off the coast of Corsica and Cannes. Black attire suddenly took its traditional place in Western history as the uniform of the working class, even the high-end working ones, and not of the self-sufficient truffle hunter nor the outrageously independently wealthy. I see Cro-Magnons, and especially Neandertals, scratching their heads at the social reality of this modern hominid.

I learned from a policeman coming off duty that this scene would unfold every Wednesday afternoon for the next two months, or for as long as the black truffle continued to offer such quality that winter. He looked at my lack of black and added that sellers of the more ordinary grade truffles, averaging at the more modest rate of around eight hundred euros per kilo, would continue to sell them at the Saturday market, where ordinary people purchased them for their own home-cooked savory dishes.

But people in black were appearing throughout town on other days of the week. There was an especially high concentration around the movie theater. That was when I learned that Sarlat had an annual international film festival that opened for a week of short and long film debuts in mid-November. These black attired were filmmakers (leather), actors (cashmere, silk, and wool), and film students (cotton). One night we were well rewarded when Audrey Tatou walked by us in a slim short black dress as we stood in the long line waiting for the doors to open at the theater. She was there for the screening of a movie in which she starred. We held our breath in that moment of sheer magic, for she was exactly like her ebullient self we have seen on screen — quirky, warm, funny, smart, and beautiful. And yes, her eyes and smile are that stunning in person. In French fashion, we simply stood still and enjoyed her passage; no one inundated her with requests for autographs or smothered her with proximity.

Funerals, too, seemed to be picking up or were no longer punctuated with the many weddings and first communions celebrated at Saint Sacerdos in spring and summer. Those latter rites of passage had cheerful bells that rang to announce them, but the church had also doleful bells, ones that now rang quite a lot on any given afternoon and announced only one thing, a funeral. Each time I heard them I would head to the big window in Le Chardon and witness rites of departure — a loved one leaving town for good, not a story Tolstoy noted perhaps because it would happen to us all no matter what — in a somber sea of black. The funeral processions always concentrated first at the church entrance, surrounding the coffin. Sometimes they were a small intimate cluster, like a bouquet of black anemones; at other times, the whole square became the night sky. Loud mournful bells stopped all other life on the Place du Peyrou.

But color, robust and riotous color, also exploded onto the scene through the weekly markets and my treks and explorations out into Occitan country on foot. I savored heartily being here and practiced more and more the art of being fully present. This helped push away occasional black thoughts, unbidden anxieties that at times erupted to the surface over the insanity I'd just accomplished: packing and leaving and risking all that went before me to inhabit here. When these worries haunted me, I'd remind myself to breathe, to savor, to walk, and to connect, and the fright would be held in check and balanced with why the risk was oh so worth it. I was here, wasn't I? Yes, I had gambled everything to be here, but how splendid that I actually could, what a great thing, what a gift, a stunning stroke of chance. Life-affirming-being-present-color flowed back. It also arrived in daily doses through the deepening of established friendships and the arrival of new ones.

Most certainly, the most hue-rich connection of my autumn came in the form of Bernadette. I met her at the Wednesday market, a petite seventy-eight-year-old woman with sparkling blue eyes and brown-gray hair that she always pulled into an elegant chignon. She wore only long skirts with elegant lacy and silky blouses, stylish sweaters, and colorful scarves, almost always accentuated with a broach of a lion.

"I wear only long skirts," she explained, "simply because anything else is uncomfortable. I'm old enough to skip being uncomfortable anymore." I was drawn to the way she owned herself and knew what she liked and didn't like. "Why the lion you ask?" she went on, "I'm a Leo and I like being a Leo. I've worked hard to know my mind and honor it. I no longer care what others think about me. My life is my life. I also don't talk to dead people anymore."

"Dead people?" I had to ask. She took the cube of sugar from the edge of the saucer holding her espresso. "Watch," she said, and dropped the sugar in, took up her spoon and stirred. I watched and waited. "Does the sugar still exist even though it has been dissolved and is no longer solid?" She asked.

"Yes?" I nodded and questioned, knowing there was more.

"Well, the soul is like that." She stated matter-of-factly. "We may give up the body, but the soul is still there, like the sugar, dissolved into the hot rich liquid of the universe. Anyone who does not get that, who lives as if they are only flesh and bone, tires me out. I just don't talk to them anymore. They follow forms and are not yet alive. Nothing but themselves can wake them up from their living death."

"I'm so glad you're talking to me," I said sincerely. "I don't want to be dead."

She laughed, took a sip of her coffee, and added, "Now the sugar is a part of me and soon it will pass on to the waterways, and from there back to the earth to reincarnate. Isn't it beautiful?"

I was falling in love with this clear-talking, no-bowing-down-to-other-people's-opinions, soul-talking, luminous, and beautiful French woman. Bernadette was to become a pivotal person in my life. In many ways she was the role model for the kind of older woman I wanted to become: strong, unafraid of life, unafraid to be beautiful at any age, certain in what was right for her, and owning it without pushing it on others. She had similar interests to mine and had made similar choices in her life, even though she was originally from Paris via descent from Burgundy and I from Colorado via descent from Iran.

She told me early on in our friendship that she had married twice. The first marriage was to a very wealthy man who gave her great material wealth but conventional, rule-filled love. Her second husband was a poor artist who made just enough for them to live on but gave her rich, soul-filling, life-feeding love.

"My marriages reflected Siddhartha's path toward enlightenment," she once said, "going from wealth and giving it up to find freedom, real freedom. That gift I received from my second husband. He may have been materially poor, but he gave me a rich life."

It was thanks to Petrus that I met Bernadette. On one cold Wednesday morning in November, she invited me to join her for a hot chocolate at one of the cafés in the main market square. When we got there, three women Petrus knew were seated at the one booth tucked near the big picture window. They invited us to join them and we sat down, feasting our eyes on the colors of the market on the other side of the window while warming our fingers and toes.

All the women were in their seventies, self-assured, and elegant. I liked all three but was especially drawn to Bernadette. She would state things straight on — no wobbling around, they would just tumble onto the table with a solid thunk — and stir things into the conscious mind that most people habitually kept locked in the subconscious.

Our gathering warmed up with hot chocolates, espressos, and camaraderie as one of the women told me that her family name came from Basque and a town in Navarra, Spain, a town on the pilgrimage road to Santiago de Compostela. She elaborated that her family was originally Jewish and had been so for a long time after they came to the Périgord, and while today they were Christian, she still felt an affinity for being Jewish. She fast forwarded from the Middle Ages to World War II and proudly stated that her family had been part of the Resistance, as was their local parish priest. "He wore a rifle under his robe at Mass," she said, "to be prepared to defend his flock in more ways than one."

Another, Vivienne, originally from Brittany, was a vegetarian and was studying English because she had a daughter who lived in Texas. She had a perennial cheer about her, as if one ought to see only the bright side of things even if life dealt heavy challenges. She explained that when she retired and was already divorced, she realized she could live anywhere she wanted, so she decided to move to a magical land.

"But Brittany," I felt compelled to state the obvious for many people, even in France, "is considered the magical land of France. It's where some say King Arthur lived and died and where you can visit Merlin's forest . . . "

"Bretagne certainly is magical," offered Vivienne. "In fact, one day I'll have you over to try my buckwheat savory crepes." She chuckled. "But. *Mais*. It's not as magical as the Dordogne. The magic here is really old magic. Cro-Magnon magic." Everyone nodded their heads in agreement. "There's something extra here, some *je ne sais quoi* here . . . " She continued to search for the right word.

"A powerful pull," offered Bernadette.

"*Voilà.*" Answered Vivienne.

"Like a special energy," Bernadette elaborated. "The one that nurtures artists here. My husband was an artist, you know, and picked this place for that. I also think he knew he would die before me and he wanted me to be somewhere that supported me." She gave me a knowing look, to read the word "support" at its deeper, more spiritual level. "You're in the right place. Keep writing," she added with emphasis. And then with the sweetest grin said, "I don't think it's an accident that we're meeting. You know, I love Iranian culture and can't believe I am meeting an Iranian-American here at the market in Sarlat. Petrus was sure we'd want to meet."

I looked at Petrus, looking very pleased with herself, and smiled in confirmation. "I am so glad we did." I said to Bernadette. I felt a powerful pull.

I soon discovered that Bernadette read only mystical literature and each year she applied herself to the spiritual and esoteric traditions of one culture in the world. One year she'd read the *I Ching*. Another year she'd read the *Mahabharata*. She'd then read the Torah and studied Kabala. She'd read the Bible. She'd read the Qoran. She was presently reading everything she could find written by Henri Corbin, the celebrated French scholar of Iranian mysticism, Iranian Sufism. She added that she loved Iranian mysticism more than anything else, that it made sense to her. Petrus volunteered that Bernadette was also an artist, not only her aforementioned husband, and that she painted Persian-style miniatures, which she'd been wanting very much to see. She asked Bernadette if we could stop by her place to see them.

"When can we come see your paintings?" I asked, echoing Petrus.

"How about after the market folds?" She offered. To this we agreed.

To accelerate the meeting time, I joined Petrus at the end of the market and helped her and Jean pack up their van with olive containers, spices, tables, and umbrellas. We then crossed to the other side of the medieval town and walked up three stories to Bernadette's apartment with a view of the entire town below. Her home was small but a perfectly ordered universe of a life lived fully and still in ripe progress. One wall was covered in heavy books and another with sacred statues of world deities from all faiths. But it was the remaining wall space that stunned us. Her detailed miniature paintings interwove with paintings she'd done of sacred geometry, creating a large mandala in its own way displayed across the apartment. It was as if we'd walked into a secret gallery in Paris. She began the tour, telling us the story of each.

Her miniatures were based on Iranian or Indian miniatures, but she then added her own mythology to them. The Lady and the Unicorn was mixed in with the Buddha and Simorgh, the mythic and mystical bird of Iranian mythology. It was exquisitely executed and very fine work, a reincarnation of the original painters' workshops that first produced this style. I looked more closely around her apartment and found that her bookshelves were overflowing with books on Islam, Buddhism, Kabala, the mystics of Christianity, Tarot, Carlos Castaneda, shamanism, even the Swedenborgians, and on and on. She had books set behind books because she had run out of shelf space.

I asked her how she started painting miniatures. "I really began by painting mandalas." She said, pointing to the other paintings. "That led from one style of meditation to another. I would begin each painting by meditating on an Iranian miniature I liked, and then, when my own images and stories began to appear, I painted my variation of that work."

I walked around the space, looking more closely at the paintings with this new knowledge. In them I saw worlds of Iranian landscapes, with some people dressed like medieval Iranian princes and peasants, but most were in European attire and enacting a European fairytale within the folds of an Iranian mystical framework. My favorite was of the beautiful European princess surround by the thirty birds of a classic Persian story about a mystical journey to find a leader, their king, Simorgh. These thirty birds went through seven stages of hardship. At last, in their most alone and darkest hour, they realized that they collectively became the great Simorgh, and their odd characteristics and quirks that had often caused problems within the group were parts of what completed them on their individual and collective journey. It's a story with a mystical word play built in. In Persian, *si morgh* means "thirty birds." The king Simorgh is the thirty birds. Bernadette loved the spiritual cleverness coupled with the depth of the story.

We finished our tour by sharing a freshly brewed pot of Moroccan tea using fresh mint Bernadette habitually bought at market for this very ritual. I asked her why she loved Moroccan tea so much. As she pushed the fresh mint leaves into the pot with a good handful of gunpowder green tea and sugar she said, "I'll tell you about my life in

Morocco on another visit." I understood for certain then and there that small talk was not an option with this woman. Come here and speak of mystical truths or don't bother. I was in love.

After tea, Petrus had to run home, and it was time for me to repair to Le Chardon, get some work done, and continue my preparations for Miles' arrival. Bernadette walked me to the door and told me to stop by any time I felt like it. "We have a lot to talk about and we can take our time." She smiled. Her blue eyes sparkled. She then gave me a warm hug that felt as if I had known her forever. I did not want to let go.

As I made my way back to the other side of the old town, I realized that everything I had ever experienced in my life, from life in the Rocky Mountains to Tehran to Spain, to the east coast of the United States, to Germany, Morocco, and Portugal, had prepared me for this time in France, here in Sarlat, and for meeting people like Bernadette. Sarlat was feeling more and more like the epicenter of it all. As betwixt-and-between as I was, every day when I stepped outside my blue front door, I had the uncanny feeling that I was born here and that anything was possible. It was a delightful mystery. I marveled at the magic of how our lives can unfold, especially if we trust that strange inner knowing and take that leap of faith and risk.

I made one small detour while heading back home, carrying on that little ritual I'd developed, to see what books had appeared in the three *boîte à lire*. The first two came up with nothing, but at the third I was drawn to a beat up and abused book at the bottom of the stack. It's spine was so worn that its title had peeled off a long time ago. But there was something about it, perhaps its binding that spoke of an old, well-made book, that made me reach for it and dislodge from the other books. Its cover lettering and image had long rubbed off, and its binding was of quality cotton string but was coming undone. I cradled it and carefully opened it. I had stepped into *The Thousand and One Nights*, confirmed by the inside title page. Beyond it were familiar stories and numerous illustrated plates, almost identical to Bernadette's miniatures. It was a French translation from an English translation and had been published in 1957 with elaborate plates on thick vellum. Inspecting the book's hardcover again revealed a now heavily worn but illustrated design, almost as if it had been hand painted with an enamel-like paint. I carefully slipped it into my pannier and determined to keep it there until I saw Bernadette at the next market day to give to her.

I walked toward Le Chardon and wondered, had I found this book on any other day, would I have seen the consequence it bore now, a direct coincidence with my meeting with Bernadette, the one person in town who would delight like no other in this book, a direct link to my own lineage? Did it matter? For today was the day it appeared. Perhaps this was no accident, no coincidence. "This," Bernadette would surely explain, seeing her bookshelf with the volume by Carl Jung in my mind's eye, "was synchronicity, pure and simple."

I turned and walked across the big market square and could just see the ledge of my beloved studio's big window when Saint Sacerdos rang out two low-timbered rings for the afternoon hour. They penetrated my soul and resonated with the profound well-being and belonging that rooted me to this place and to these people. Color, glorious color, swirled about me on the square. •

Dancing Flower of Temniac

Chapter 17

THE DANCING FLOWER OF TEMNIAC

It was quiet and subtle and utterly beautiful, and I would not have wanted to first see it any other way than this. We were inside the circle defining the outer limits of the flower, and it felt as if the original meanings of that six-petal symbol, of balance, heaven and earth, male and female, light and dark were coming together in that moment of perfect harmony.

A FEW DAYS BEFORE MILES WAS TO TOUCH DOWN ON French soil, I woke up to the faint tinge of pine in the air and an unusual early morning scuffle going down on the cathedral square. I hopped out of bed to see what was causing the stir and saw the town crew with a tractor hauling and setting up a towering tree. The four men dressed in orange jump suits were working together like interior decorators to get it positioned just right. Then two went up in the bucket arm to layer on white lights. The tree was so close to my window and so big that the need to find a Christmas decoration for Le Chardon was trumped by the square's grand Advent tree. Christmas was coming and I could feel the charge in the air like the days I was five and six and viscerally knew that Saint Nicholas would visit.

A stroll about town later that morning confirmed that the Advent season was officially here. After righting the tree, the crew began building small wooden cottage-like kiosks for the Christmas market on the south end of the old town. It would open in a few days and go on until Epiphany, assuring that the Three Wise Men had gifts for all. As if to add to the festive air, the temperatures dropped more and it grew very cold, not an easy thing for the building crew, but the town was abuzz with excitement over the coming of the season's first snow.

Market day that week delivered another delight on my doorstep. When I opened the blue door and stepped out, I was greeted with four huge crates of oysters of different sizes sitting right in front of my door and at one end of the fishmonger's market offering. Huge orange crabs, plump plum-colored sea urchins, cockles and whelks, clams, giant prawns, and glistening fresh trout, salmon, and snapper also peered at me from their beds of ice. The oysters were so fresh and so inexpensive that I decided to buy a dozen and make it my Advent tradition to have oysters for lunch every market day in December.

I then went off for a rendezvous with Bernadette and Petrus and asked how everyone was so sure that we would get snow. Where I grew up in Colorado, it could change its mind at the last minute in either direction, to snow or not.

"Oh, it's simple," began Petrus. "I look out at the Massif Central to the east of our house, and if it has a thick, ominous layer of cold clouds, they will soon work their way toward us."

"The Pyrenees to the south," added Bernadette, "also play a role and snow can come from there, which is seen for a day or two the same way. Sometimes, both ranges have a storm coming and that's when you do extra market shopping and stay home." The two women laughed.

"But the coming front," finished Petrus, "is a freezing air wending its way to our valleys from the Massif Central. It has the smell of snow on its fingertips."

The smell of snow, the tree on the cathedral square, and the building of Christmas kiosks stimulated a flurry of festive things about town. Town merchants decorated their shops in the agreed-upon colors of green boughs wrapped in blue ribbons and silver-white lights. One shopkeeper had wrapped several bundles of cinnamon sticks with velvet blue ribbons and tied them on to a little tree next to realistic renderings of snowy owls and electric blue lights. Everywhere I looked, green, blue, silver, and white were dusting the town with its wintery cheer.

I enjoyed how people really liked talking about the weather as if it was a sporting event, dynamic and engaging, not just a source of chitchat. And Bernadette was not a chitchatter. After our snow study, she launched into her current reading, all of Henri Corbin's studies on Iranian mysticism. That's when I realized I'd left the book I had for her on my dining table in Le Chardon. It would have to wait until the next market, then, for me to give it to her.

"Why Corbin?" I asked.

"Because he was a true mystic himself. He understood Iranian culture and Iranian Sufism and he also saw its universal expression, that it was something for all humanity."

"For example?" I was intrigued. I'd rarely talked to a non-Iranian about Iranian mysticism for it seemed as if there were too many layers of explaining before arriving at the meat, the oyster in the middle of the hard shell. But Bernadette had shucked her own oyster and was now slurping in its plump glistening meat.

"For instance," she began, "that a person must find God directly. That God is everywhere. That this is everyone's birthright, not just a handful of people following a label or a ritual or a group leader. That's why the Sufis were often both esteemed but also radical elements in their societies. They listened to God's heartbeat, not the king's! They spoke of love, universal love, which unites, never divides, and so the dividers of the world are out of luck." She sat back with a big satisfied grin.

In all my years growing up in rural Colorado, this was the instruction in my household. When some classmates in school asked me what my religion was, I was stumped. My parents never forced a label on me. As true mystics — my mother with her poetry and my father with his classical music — they wanted me to find my own relationship with God and insisted that the most important thing was to be a good person, that this was religion's main purpose. The rest was personal and spiritual, not religious. But in school, a non-answer to these questioners, who were usually from homes anchored in organized religious certainty, my inability to answer with a clear protective name was often taken as a sign to try and save me.

If I didn't have a child's brain that was simply confused by the illogic of these encounters, I would have spoken my truth, paraphrased right out of the mouth of Rumi. "My religion is Love and love for all of God's creation." I think this is also something Jesus would say. So would Abraham and Moses. So would Mohammad. So would the Druids and the followers of Artemis. As a matter of fact, I think that is pretty much what all the prophets, avatars, and wise people would agree upon, even if some of their followers were still piecing it together. And I suspected that this universality came out of experience, an open heart and mind, and compassion, not books and ordained rules.

Love.

I'll tell you about love.

I was in love with Bernadette.

Hot-mulled wine also appeared on chalkboards throughout Sarlat's cafés. Add the smell of wine, cinnamon, and citrus to the pine and snow-tipped air, and the festive season had officially begun.

An oyster stand serving champagne along with the little mollusks from Aquitaine and Poitou-Charente held the center of the Christmas market, right next to the chestnut roaster and carefully attended cauldron of spice-mulled wine, *vin chaud*. It became a ritual among friends to meet there after work and sit down to oysters and champagne or buy a paper cone filled with hot chestnuts and a glass of hot wine and meander through the little Christmas town. Kiosks were filled with beautiful local handcrafts, from felt ornaments to hand-knit hemp yarn sweaters and scarves, to silks painted like watery landscapes, to silver and gold jewelry, to preserved foods such as black truffles, truffled fois gras, blackberry or fig jams, chestnut chutney *(confiture de chataigne)*, and locally crafted beer.

The latter came from a boisterous, impish, French-speaking Irishman from Dublin, Stephen, living in the Dordogne for many years who decided wine country needed a good local beer. His presumption paid off. His stand was always pumping with business and nearly all the buyers were French. One day as I mulled about the market with my vin chaud, I had to step quickly aside as a man from Alsace-Lorraine rushed across my path and bear-hugged Stephen in his kiosk. I went closer and learned that the northerner was visiting relatives in the Dordogne and had sampled the Dubliner's beers and that there was hope for the holidays down south. He was back to buy in bulk to stock up for the holiday season.

"At last, a good beer in the south!" he exclaimed. He bought two cases filled with a mix of the five beers, from blond to stout. He swaggered away under the weight of his acquisition shouting a cheerful *a bientôt* intending to be back to resupply through the long Advent season.

As a break from a session of writing, as a warm up to a walk, or as a cooling down after a game of hoops, I was at the Christmas market practically every day, gluttonous and bibulous, and I wasn't alone. I would run into friends there and we would join forces. I also met new people in the community, and we soon began to greet each other with the daily repetition of seeing a face that was becoming familiar with each pass through the *marché de Noël*. Indulgent food and drink taste so much better when the whole community is involved.

The truffle season also carried on, each week sending the waft of pheromones through the market square. And the twice-weekly markets also carried their mandatory meetings over coffee and glasses of wine with friends. I settled deeply into my life in Le Chardon and the festival rhythms.

It was a time of deep and rich experiences, but it was also a time of supreme in-between-ness. Everything was now in storage back in the States, Miles was about to join me, and our physical anchor on the earth was now this temporary foothold here. Both exciting and incredibly disorienting, I felt at once the nomad's sense of freedom as well as the desire for stability and home, something I hoped more fully to experience as my age drew closer and closer to the half century mark.

I reflected again on what really defined home. Was it owning a piece of property? Was it having a family and community to which you contributed? Was it feeling a strong sense of belonging in that effort, in that place? I suspected it could be all three things but that the last two were more important than the first, even though that was the first one that made most of us feel somehow secure. So I also thought about what it was to be secure. I liked security, that sense of protection and safety, of having enough and, with luck, a warm glow in one's mind, heart, and belly. But to seek it as the primary focus of one's ambitions also seemed, ironically, the riskiest thing to do. It was fickle company if treated as an external force. Home, by contrast, felt good any which way I turned the idea in my head. It seemed poetic that Miles' arrival would occur just before the winter solstice and when my experience of each season here would come full circle and enter my second winter with his first. Home, here, would become something for him to try on.

And so, I was also nervous in the midst of my excitement for his arrival.

After I'd said goodbye to Bernadette and Petrus that morning after they'd filled me with mysticism and snow-casting, I took up another market ritual I'd come to count on every Saturday. I went to Vincent's bookstand to peruse his used books, looking for gems while hoping to overhear more energy, chakras, and New Age conversations with his customers. There I found Laurant, the artist from Brittany I'd met while apartment hunting in the summer. He was holding a large crystal tumbler with whiskey in it and flipping through Vincent's formidable collection of coffee table art books.

Vincent came over to greet me in the midst of a conversation with a woman about the healing properties of crystals. The whiskey was his and that he doled it out on cold days to favorite clients. I was thinking what a lucky dog Laurant was when suddenly Vincent pulled another tumbler from under his table and poured me a dram of Black Label. Laurant and I clinked glasses and soon Vincent, finished with his talk, retrieved a third tumbler resting on a stack of New Age books and joined us. We perused books, sipped, and talked. Laurant was curious what I was writing about and Vincent went to dig up a couple books he thought I might like to see when he learned I was researching the deeper mysteries and histories of the Dordogne.

I'd noticed all day that I was going through a low cycle with my French, on a spectrum where some days were good and other days I retreated backwards in skill. Yesterday I had been feeling super fluent. Today, like an infant. I apologized to my two erudite companions but they said they understood. Learning another language is like that, with rises and falls.

Vincent, I learned, also spoke Italian and Spanish because his grandmother was born in Argentina before she came to France. Laurant spoke some English and Japanese and a bit of Bretagne. Both reinforced what I'd learned on the ground long ago in my efforts with Spanish, that monolingual people are the first to criticize a foreigner's efforts in their language, but those who had worked to learn other languages are the first to defend and support such efforts, knowing how hard it is.

"Language is for communicating, right?" Vincent kindly mused. "So who cares if you make mistakes? If I understand you, you're successful, and if you sip the whiskey," he added with a smile, "I am sure your skill will improve."

We clinked glasses again and I sipped. I can attest to the fact that the healing power of crystals is real, especially when it holds whiskey within. Before long, to my surprise, I noticed my whiskey was gone. I noticed two other things: I was not as cold, and my French most surely had improved.

I wasn't the only one to notice the disappearing whiskey. In the coming days, I learned what a small town Sarlat is. Rumor spread that the American writer downed her whiskey like Marian Ravenwood in the Indiana Jones film *Raiders of the Lost Ark*. While stunned at the reputation over an innocent glass of golden drink on a frosty market day, inside, I beamed. Marion Ravenwood! Yes. I liked that association, and I would do my best to hold this unintentionally earned status. My heart warmed even more toward Vincent and Laurant and their kind welcoming rituals of the faulty French-speaking foreigner and their spinning of tales.

Among the late autumn produce pouring into the market was a beautiful little dark-orange pumpkin-like squash called *potimarron* (red kuri squash). At first I bought one because it was so pretty, and I just wanted to set it on my kitchen counter and look at it, but soon I bought one each week because my young market friend, Céline, shared her favorite soup recipe. With it, I'd fallen in love with the rich, more delicate and complex flavor of the potimarron compared to pumpkin or other squashes. Céline told me to begin by caramelizing two well-minced shallots in butter and then adding in the peeled and cubed squash and letting it sauté until slightly softened and browned. Next, I added grated ginger, a peeled and cubed potato, a splash of white wine, salt and pepper to taste, and water or broth to cover the vegetables. Once it reached boiling, I lowered the heat and let it simmer until the potimarron and potatoes were soft. Then, advised Céline, I was to puree it. When serving it, once in individual bowls, she said a splash of heavy cream and a showering of minced chives on top finished it nicely. And, if one wanted to perform le chabrol after the soup was gone, this was a perfect soup for it where the red wine would mingle with the creamy remnants stuck to the side of the bowl.

It seemed the perfect welcoming gesture, so just before Miles' arrival I made a pot of Céline's soup with a pretty little gourd I purchased at the Wednesday market. Two days later I received a final email from him before he departed for the airport in Philadelphia and turned in our keys to our now former landlady. All the boxes were in storage, he said, our whole life of reduced material goods in one place, a four-by-ten-foot storage unit, now dormant, waiting for the next move, the next home to come alive in. After that ordeal, a person needed a hot, rich, and nourishing, soul-feeding meal, and the creamy ginger-laced potimarron would kick it off.

Also in anticipation of his arrival, I wanted Le Chardon to be perfectly fitted to everything that would make him love it here, want to stay, and to feel it as home. Nadiya brought me a new set of pressed, thick cotton sheets to place on our bed. At the prior Saturday market, I'd purchased a small round Provençal tablecloth with a pattern of green leaves and olives and yellow lemons and sunflowers that fit perfectly on the table in the large room. I bought yellow mimosas from a gardener who had set them up that market day just beneath my window on the square below. Their feathery, sun yellow stalks lit up the lemons upon the cloth when I set them in a clear vase on the table. I found a locally milled soap of lemon verbena and set it out on the side of the sink, its grassy lemon smell filling the porcelain space. I fluffed the pillows. I picked up a bottle of locally roasted and pressed walnut oil and another of truffle. I found fresh local pasta made from chestnut flour and set it in the refrigerator, next to the fresh duck breast to grill with mushrooms and red wine. I located the farmer with the early harvest of winter spinach and cleaned it to be ready to make a hot salad with lardón, walnuts, and local blue cheese. I bought a bottle of the Bergerac region's most coveted red, a Pecharmant. X. I would pop the cork just before running off to meet his train.

After this whirlwind of ecstatic activity, I stepped back to take in the apartment. It felt like what my grandparents' homes smelled and felt like upon arriving for one of our long anticipated summer visits. Come, feel so welcomed, you'll stay awhile and, with luck, never leave. For a nomad, it was shameless pandering to settled peoples' comforts. Or was it? Maybe it was perfecting the idea of home because home was so elusive that it had become idealized.

Early the next morning, I got the call from Paris. Miles had landed and had located a rare pay phone. He had his train ticket and would arrive in Sarlat at nine in the evening that day. My heart pumped hard. Sophie called, saying we were to have another freezing night and not to walk to the station; she would pick me up, and we could drive there together to greet The Man.

There was one more thing I could do to perfect Miles's welcome: get good beer. That should seal the deal, thought I, and the only one that would assure the magic of my snare was La Croix du Rat, the name of Stephen's beer, inspired by magical religious stone crosses he'd seen erected on the outskirts of surrounding medieval towns and villages to protect the residents from the plague and the rats that bore it. A Rat's Cross ought to do the trick, and off I dived into the Christmas market. I found Stephen at his kiosk holding court over his five brews and doing hand-over-fist business as usual. He looked up at me and implied I ought to throw my order into the mix, that he could multitask.

"Okay. One of each of your brews plus two of your special Christmas Ale."

"Ahh," he smiled and made eye-contact. "Your husband is on his way, isn't he?"

"Yes," I said, "and I think your beer will help him get over jetlag and feel welcomed here."

Stephen handed me my selections to place in my pannier. "I'm sure you will help your husband recover from jet lag, too." He said pointedly and accompanied his statement with a sultry swishing of up and down eyebrows.

"I'll do my best," I offered shyly, trying to ignore the eyebrows. I then rushed back toward Le Chardon to chill the blonde and amber and set the stout, chestnut, and Christmas ale on a cold spot on the kitchen floor. I was smiling ridiculously without caring who saw it. I loved our quirky little town with its diverse mix of colorful characters.

The Man arrived well and all the elixirs, including that of love, worked well on Miles. Well-nourished and well-rested, we made the initial tour of the town late in the morning the next day. It was Saturday and he met my friends at a central café surrounded by produce tables and cheese and sausage stands where we shared a glass and toasted his first day. All around us swirled the riotous colors of the market in winter, an even more potent enticement to all I had done in Le Chardon. He met the golden lab who slumbered on a high wall of his people's thick garden wall, granting an ear scratch when in the mood — he immediately allowed Miles the honor, a good omen. He met Nadiya, Aidan, Petrus, and Jean, and soon they hatched many plans for winter fireside dinners, all cooked in the fifteenth-century fireplace. He met Bernadette and saw immediately why I loved her. He then met Mr. Stripes, who was waiting for us on our return to the big blue door and who tried to come inside and up the stairs with Miles. I took that as the ultimate blessing for this new chapter together, here.

In those first days, to make things feel normal, that is, that we were aspiring and productive residents, not tourists or holiday visitors, and also to temper all the dinners and lunches to which we were invited thanks to the appearance of The Man, we established early the discipline of working. In a studio with one table, we arranged this to share the dining table, now drawn out and its lengthening leaf inserted, he at one end and I at the other. We practiced leaving each other alone so that we could concentrate, I on my articles and book writing and he on his film and music projects. We rewarded ourselves with excursions out into the colorful and quirky world around us, from the delights of local food shopping to going for good long walks into the surrounding countryside. We often wound the day down with an early evening stroll through the Christmas market, grabbing a glass of Advent cheer with friends as *l'heure bleue* wrapped us in a darkening cobalt cape speckled with stars.

Over the days I realized that having Miles here also gave me someone like me with whom to talk about Sarlat, someone who was experiencing it as I was, an American outsider who was warmly welcomed in. One thing our conversations made me more aware of was how Miles also noticed those little things that the Sarladais had not forfeited to modern life that made day-to-day life so rich:

Such as being able to buy our food everyday nearby, on foot, and it being so fresh and mostly locally grown, caught, or raised in the free, open air.

Such as being able to strike out in any direction for a walk and land in a beautiful country landscape and meet engaging people speaking Occitan and being perfectly understood through their smiles, gestures, and warm eyes.

Such as the pull from Saint Sacerdos to visit everyday and sit and meditate in the candle glow.

Such as the joy in climbing to the tower, the lanterne des morts, and greeting Mr. Stripes or hearing the *rouge-gorge* break out in territorial song at dusk.

Such as those unconsciously delivered but reliable little acts of everyday life that seemed small but were so significant, like the expected *bonjour* upon entering a café, restaurant, or shop and *au revoir* upon leaving. To not deliver these rendered a person rude, to deliver them opened the doors to a universe where all were helpful, patient, and kind. These little simple things wove and rewove the social fabric of the community powerfully everyday, and that cloth was a strong cloth.

What was also remarkable was that while people took time to greet each other, they also respected each other's boundaries, and so a greeting was pleasant, but everyone still got their errands done. If one of us simply longed for company but not a gathering, a stroll down Sarlat's main traverse was all it took to feel connected to others while at ease to move at one's own pace.

Miles also fell immediately in love with the region's grilled duck. Over the years he had made duck a special comparative study of his and liked to order it when he found it on a restaurant menu. After a sublime duck grilled then simmered in an Empordà red wine and plum sauce in a village in northern Catalonia, Spain, years before, no other duck passed muster. But in Sarlat, the first place I took him to was a little restaurant near the Mary fountain that specialized in grilled duck. They prepared it the classic way for the region. It was grilled *à point* so its center was rosy but its edges crispy and browned. It was then sliced thinly and served with *pommes Sarladaises*, potatoes sautéed in duck fat with garlic and parsley, and a green leaf salad. He ordered it, inhaled it, and declared it the best duck yet. He inhaled it both because it was so delicious and also because it was not so very big a serving. Miles enviously had retained the metabolism of a teenage boy in his middle years, along with a teenager's figure and appetite, so this entrée's four delicate thin little slices of duck breast was, in fact, more of a very nice appetizer, and I knew he left hungry when we stepped out into the tiny cobbled street.

So hungry, in fact, that he suggested we head off *tout de suite* to the local household goods store on the main drag and purchase a good duck-grilling pan. We did and, after some deliberation, we picked out a hefty cast iron piece that had some fancy labeling about mineral content and heat conduction. It was a serious piece of equipment with a serious price tag, but as he paid for it he said, "I like it here. I see this as an investment in our new home. We may not have the house yet, but we have the pan."

Home. The magical word. I said nothing. There was no need. Happy. Moreover, I couldn't recall such interest in skillets before. Even better, when we got home, he researched the internet for the best way to grill duck *à point*. The next market day, he was up early and set out to buy a thick, fresh duck breast with its mandatory layer of subcutaneous fat. As I finished shopping, he went home and began the quest.

I am pleased to report that his first effort was as sublime as that duck in the restaurant, only it was better because he had made it and it came in larger portions. "After I grilled the duck breast to its perfect rosy-crispy balance, *à point*," he explained, "I got online and learned what it means to deglaze a pan and did so with the Pecharmant." At the last minute and in a rush of inspiration, he also threw in currents, a crushed clove of garlic, and a pinch of thyme. He then reduced the liquid to make *une sauce remarquable*.

This was only the beginning. After the duck adventure, Miles grew more intrepid in the kitchen and began to look forward to shopping daily at the market or the local grocery on the main traverse and coming home with just enough food for that day, and then masterminding dishes in the small kitchen for big lunches and leftovers for lighter dinners. That special red wine current sauce spawned his own idea for a rice dish to compliment the duck. He used short-grain brown rice, red rice, and black rice, and made something of a red wine current and fresh herb risotto a la Périgordine with walnut oil and a touch of duck fat, which locals again and again stated was as healthy for the heart as was olive oil, and not like other animal fats. They would back this up with national statistics that proved that the people from the southwest, the biggest duck fat eaters in France, lived longer and rarely died from heart attacks and strokes.

"What do they die from then?" I'd ask, curious and also taking notes for my own older life, if I was lucky enough to make it here.

"Old age," they'd offer point blank with no further details and so left it to my imagination to come up with what death from old age looked like here. In my mind I saw a person walking along a lane in the distance, entering an evergreen oak and pine forest, and slowly disappearing, dissolving, as their particles became a part of the earth again. That's what death from old age looked like to me in the magical Dordogne of duck fat eaters.

About a week after Miles' arrival we visited the Irishman at the Christmas market to replenish our beer supply — and receive saucy comments, this time eyebrows directed at The Man. As soon as we stepped into his stand, Stephen handed us cups of hot apple cider that he made from his own apples. He and Miles then launched into talking about his beer, which he referred to as living liquid. "The beer inside these bottles is alive," he said, holding a bottle of golden ale to the light. "And the character of the beer grows as it sits in the bottle. If opened and allowed to oxidize, it gets finer and finer, mingling with the air but it never stops becoming something." He spoke with such passion that you could feel the yeast responding to him through the glass. It was liquid love.

We walked toward the Place du Peyrou laden with good beer and good cheer and stopped at Saint Sacerdos to enjoy a quiet pause for meditation and prayer. It was that *l'heure bleue* time of day when the cathedral took on a special stilling blue glow inside. Stepping the short distance to our blue door and up to Le Chardon, Miles said he agreed that Le Chardon was as much home as was Sarlat. He too wanted to live here, and if one day we could afford to buy the studio from Nadiya and Aidan, and they would sell, *tant mieux*. That made me happy. By then I had also relaxed. Before Miles' arrival I was nervous about sharing this space, which up until now had been my solitary retreat and sanctuary, my room with a view, my room of my own. I both wanted him to enjoy it and also wanted it to not lose its special writer's retreat magic.

In the early days with Miles in Sarlat, in Le Chardon, I discovered that he had fallen into a similar deep, creative, peaceful retreat mode and was fully enjoying doing his own creative work from his corner of the big table as was I from my opposite corner. It was gratifying to see that he felt nurtured by being here too and that my experience of the place was the same as before, only better because I had him to share it with. We let each other work, we did not interrupt the other's flow. That powerful pull of place was working on us both and grounding us each deeply in our creative lives. While we could hit that flow anywhere and were practiced at it as an imperative means to get work done, here it took very little effort.

This all felt good, however dreamy. But actually buying Le Chardon? That was beginning to feel more and more farfetched. In the months since spring, there were very quiet, soft rumblings beneath the surface of Nadiya and Aidan's lives that silently implied that their marriage was being tested and likely coming to an end. Neither spoke of it, but it was palpable when I was around one or the other or both. In those unspoken rumbles I began to hear subtle murmurs that possibly they would be selling Le Chardon, but not as a separate apartment. If they sold, they would sell the whole building just as they had originally bought it.

Before they owned the building, a doctor and his family had lived here, and it was a large single family home. The medical office was on the first floor, and the doctor and his family lived on the two upper floors. The property was still seen as a whole house, not three independent apartments. That made it far out of our reach if it ever did sell. More saddening was the idea that they actually would sell it, give it up, render it not our home as much as rendering it not theirs anymore either.

After some sadness over these possible future changes, I decided to simply let it go and enjoy being here, now, and not worry about the future, and work harder at learning about this place and its secrets and work harder in my writing about it. In those moments, the Buddha on the mantle reminded me to just be present. I would work my way into a Bernadette state of mind, and I was happier for it.

I was also tickled in knowing that on the other side of the medieval town was a woman who meditated like the Buddha while reading about Iranian mysticism and painting miniatures — as well as Tarot cards, I recently learned — while simmering a perfect pot of Moroccan tea to sip through creative works. In all my travels and in all my lives in far-flung places, I'd not met a soul so close to an older version of the person I imagined myself becoming. I had so much to learn from her. Home, again, I reminded myself, was here, not Le Chardon per se but simply here as well as that moveable and more permanent home we all possess that truly makes us all nomads and well-settled at once. I just wanted to be sure it was always somehow connected to and inhabiting Sarlat.

It's the capacity of floating that makes life better.

I couldn't wait any longer. Miles was now well rested and well fed, thanks largely to his own efforts and those of friends who feted us. One day, despite the clouds and drizzle, I said to him, "Let's walk to Temniac. I want you to experience the little church for yourself, and I need help finding that flower, if it really exists."

We took off after breakfast and climbed the hill. The drizzle held to its stick-to-your-face method, but we stayed reasonably dry and were sweating and peeling off layers by the time we ascended the steep hill and arrived at Temniac church's side door, again, ajar. We went in. No one else was there. After Miles took in the upper level, we each dropped a two euro coin in the votive box, took up a tapered candle, lit them, and went down the same passageway whose motion sensor lights flicked on as before.

I could tell from Miles' face that he loved the church already, that its intimacy, harmony, and beauty had struck a chord in his heart. He simply grew very quiet and his face glowed with joy.

We went down into the crypt and set our candles on the stand next to Mary and stepped back. "Listen to this," I whispered and sang a piece of an a cappella sacred song I learned a while back when I walked on the pilgrimage road to Santiago de Compostela in Spain. I learned the piece when, enchanted by all the acoustically beautiful little chapels along the way, I discovered that they were best experienced in song and sound.

After the last note echoed off the stone walls, I noticed that Miles had closed his eyes and hung his head toward his chest to listen. He then opened his eyes, still looking down, and quietly said, "Uh, Bee? Look down."

I looked down. Shazam! Right where we both stood was the dancing flower of Temniac. It was inlaid in a mosaic pattern with smooth river rock, a cobbled floor I had taken as just cobbled before, so caught up by what was above it, thinking that it was nothing but rows and rows of stones, so much so that I ignored it while being right on top of it. Twice. More astonishing, it marked the perfect center of the crypt, making me more concerned at my skills of observation and how I had missed it. But then it seemed more perfect that Miles should find it and it be he who reinforced my wacky dream. And there we were, our feet standing together within the flower's outer circle.

It was quiet and subtle and utterly beautiful, and I would not have wanted to first see it any other way than this. We were inside the circle defining the outer limits of the flower, and it felt as if the original meanings of that six-petal symbol, of balance, heaven and earth, male and female, light and dark were coming together in that moment of perfect harmony. It danced and we danced, its pulse a three-four beat.

Neither of us was able to say another word until we finally uprooted ourselves and climbed up the other passageway to ground level and exited the church. As soon as we stepped outside, the drizzle turned into thick, heavy rain. We hadn't thought to bring umbrellas, so we sped down the steep hill and made our way back to Sarlat, elated, laughing, and completely soaking wet. After a quick stop in Le Chardon to change into warm, dry clothes, we went back out, to the Christmas market, where hot mulled wine never tasted so good. •

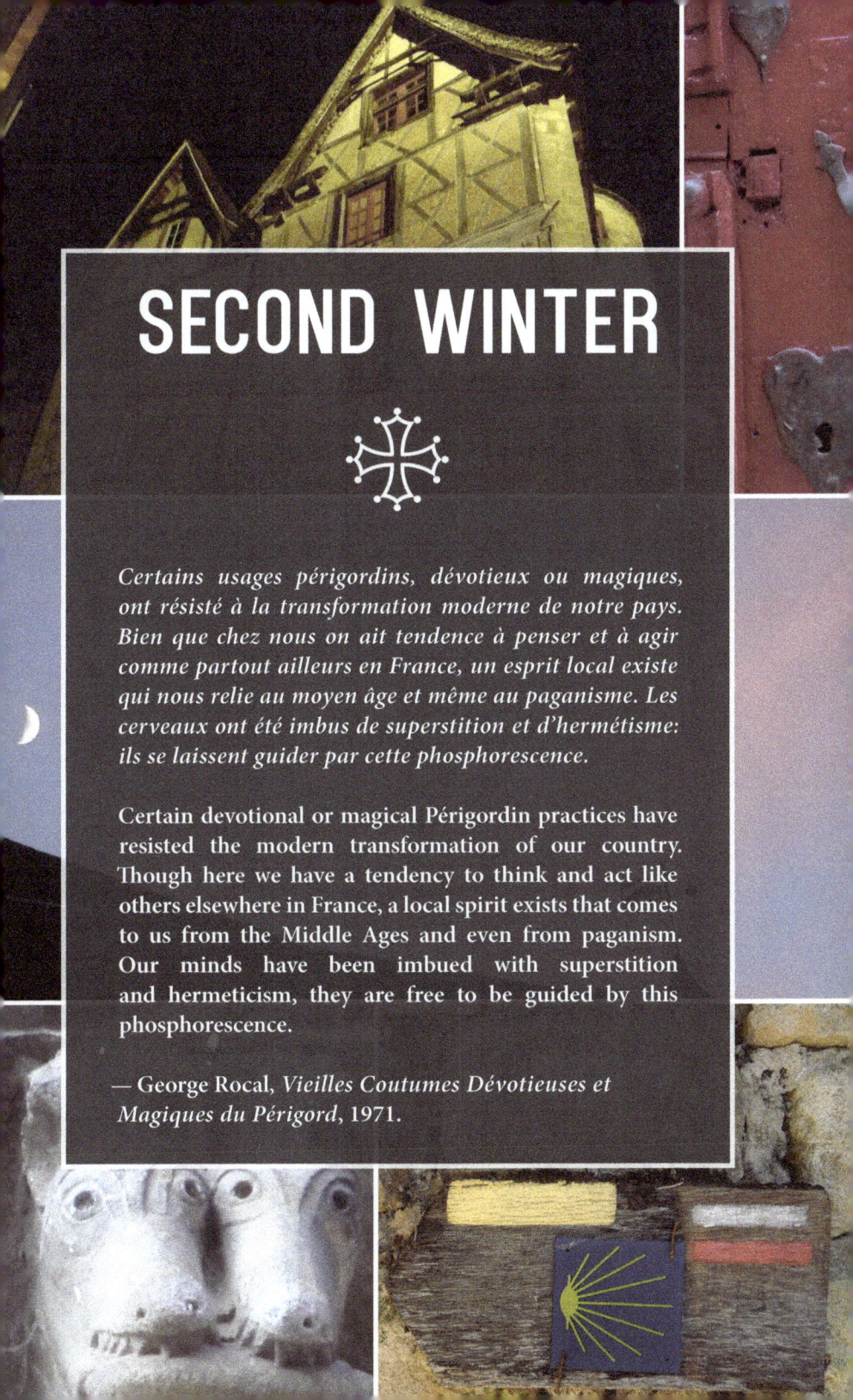

SECOND WINTER

Certains usages périgordins, dévotieux ou magiques, ont résisté à la transformation moderne de notre pays. Bien que chez nous on ait tendance à penser et à agir comme partout ailleurs en France, un esprit local existe qui nous relie au moyen âge et même au paganisme. Les cerveaux ont été imbus de superstition et d'hermétisme: ils se laissent guider par cette phosphorescence.

Certain devotional or magical Périgordin practices have resisted the modern transformation of our country. Though here we have a tendency to think and act like others elsewhere in France, a local spirit exists that comes to us from the Middle Ages and even from paganism. Our minds have been imbued with superstition and hermeticism, they are free to be guided by this phosphorescence.

— George Rocal, *Vieilles Coutumes Dévotieuses et Magiques du Périgord*, 1971.

La Roque Gageac on the Dordogne

Chapter 18

HIKES, HEALERS, ANCESTORS, AND SPIRITS

Our new friends organized two separate days with Monsieur Pémendrant because his ancestral land held two caves and we visited one on each meeting. After each rendezvous with him, we then spent the rest of the day trekking deeper into the area's forests and learning about the native plants and animals. These two adventures led to others, and we kept trekking through the winter into early spring, visiting medieval chapels and castles and learning about their folklore, including some in prehistoric caves or with prehistoric caves at their base, or an ancient Celtic well in its heart.

M ONSIEUR PÉMENDRANT WALKED AHEAD OF US, THE twig he used as a pointing tool stuck behind his trouser back's waistband and moving like a tail swaggering right to left with each footfall. I'd noticed that while our group — seven trekkers, three of whom were professional outdoor guides and new friends — wore state of the art hiking boots, he wore well-worn men's dress shoes for all his tasks, from feeding his cows and chickens to playing ball with his dog, to this, showing us his caves.

In his mid-eighties, he was a force. I observed early in my introduction to him that this farmer-turned-amateur prehistorian knew a lot more than most scholars but was modest about his knowledge. He also had a wicked sense of humor and kept us on our toes. Case in point, as soon as I thought this, he took a turn and went straight up the hill to our right. It was steep and our path appeared to be a goat's ad hoc route of rocks and narrow footholds. But up he went in his leather lace-up dress shoes like an ibex easily flitting up a steep mountainside. We seven followed as if waddling ducklings coming to the water's edge and hitting hard earth with awkward flat feet.

Monsieur Pémendrant inherited a great Périgordin legacy, family farmland that upon exploration of its caves in 1902 revealed that early humans had also called his land home some 16,000 years ago. Two caves in particular held engravings that excited prehistorians and expanded our ideas of early modern human art.

He stopped at the cave opening to set down the canvas bag he'd hauled up on one shoulder, again, with more ease than had we with our tailor-fitted trekkers' backpacks evenly placed on both shoulders and synched ergonomically at the chest and waist. His bag held a small motor battery that was attached to a car headlight with a thick coated electric cord. He hit an on-switch he'd also rigged to the contraption and the light came to life. He saw my curiosity.

"I played around with how best to light the cave tours," he said softly. "After some trial and error I hit upon a car headlight, a perfect size, strength, and shape, and the battery rarely runs out like those new-fangled headlamps." He chuckled, pleased with one more triumph over posh modernity. His light lasted a good long while. I touched the crestfallen headlamp on my head, even though he had politely not cast an eye at it during this exchange, and nodded in admiration. My lamp ran out inordinately quickly, almost after a single day of use. This farmer was an inventor and explorer too, and he wasn't done with me on the wicks and lamps theme.

We formed a single-file line behind him and went into the narrow cave opening. Behind Monsieur Pémendrant went Thierry, then me, then Miles, then Béa, then Petrus, then a friend of hers, then the tallest of us all, Bruno.

It was thanks to Petrus that Miles and I were included on this private visit. She knew Béa, an avid outdoors sportswoman, naturalist, and professional photographer who founded a popular tour company, Dordogne Fellow Traveller, and collaborated with Bruno and Thierry to offer adventures in hiking, biking, and canoeing as well as guided visits to caves, medieval churches, and castles, often combined with some form of physical adventure to get there.

All three grew up in the region, bounding up trees, into caves, through ruined castles, and up and around crumbling old stone walls. Béa loved to run and cycle and often discovered new places through her daily jaunts, places she would then research and include in her tours. Thierry, an avid waterman in kayak and canoe, would discover new places from the bow of his boat, and Bruno, through weekly hikes into the woods, often as much in search of mushrooms and firewood as of old caves, chapels, and Celtic fortresses. They were always researching and exploring the region as much as sharing their mastery with others. They were also boisterous and funny as hell.

But today, they were oddly silent. I think they sensed from the start, when Monsieur Pémendrant drove up and tucked that twig like a dog's tail into his backside waistband, that they were in the presence of a master. It wasn't that they were intimidated but rather waited with anticipation for what the elderly man would say next. Monsieur Pémendrant was also a trickster. His humor often came out as a practical joke chortled over in Occitan.

Well inside the cave now, we stopped and he pulled the twig from his backside with one hand and with the other swept his headlight up and along the wall to our left and stopped at eye level.

"Do you see what it is?" He pointed with the twig, letting our eyes work out what we were looking at. Intentionally engraved lines were everywhere in various directions. I tried to calm my excitement and willed my eyes to slow down and look for a pattern or a shape. I followed a big curving line at the top and soon realized I was tracing the head of a human, a very big headed human, for the lines then continued into a body with wing-like arms and hands and fingers, then legs and floating feet. There was something flighty about the composition, as if the human was half fairy.

"Is it a woman?" I asked, almost breathy and dreamy, surprised at the sound of my own voice in the subterranean space.

Monsieur Pémendrant chuckled and moved his headlight a little lower to highlight the torso of the human and simply said, "*Non.*"

Thierry whistled, Bruno chuckled, Bea laughed aloud, as Miles, Petrus, and I inched more closely to study the very long and very thick protrusion coming out of the very male loins. It was so big it was obviously the central point of the *oeuvre*, if proportions were any indication of priorities and importance.

Looking at our three faces nosing in closer and closer to phallus *extraordinaire*, Monsieur Pémendrant was now bent over laughing nonstop, the twig anchored under his hand on his knee, wagging up and down. He then stood straight again and clicked his light off. "It's best not stare too long at it." He then as quickly switched the headlight on again and laughed even more. By now Bruno had tears in his eyes, and Thierry would have been rolling on the cave floor if the boulders around us allowed it. Béa looked at me, clearly enjoying my novice's initiation to true prehistory in the Périgord and said with a straight face, "Do you still think it is a woman?"

As my new friends collected themselves, Monsieur Pémendrant retucked his twig in his pants and pulled out a modern pointer from his pocket, a red laser, and set to gleefully retrace the entire human form with it, saving the biggest limb for last. He then went on to show us other creatures engraved nearby, creatures who had been overshadowed by the sexual antics of our own species. The cave was packed with depictions of life, a remarkable ancient art gallery.

One market day not long before, while sacking olives, Petrus had said that there was someone else I had to meet, Béa. She sensed a kindred spirit between the two of us. By now I was known for wandering off and walking on my own into the wild in the name of close-to-the-ground research. That I also had walked several routes of the Camino, the Way of Saint James to Santiago de Compostela across southern France and northwestern Spain, including along remote forests and mountain passes of the Atlantic coast, Petrus was determined that I meet my female French counterpart in the Dordogne.

Petrus was once again correct. I was smitten when I met Béa, also over olives. She wore trekker's pants and hiking boots with a fleece top and her long blond hair was un-fussed-over but elegantly pulled up in a pile on her head the way only French women seem to be able to do. She wore no makeup, but the natural elements had colored and enhanced her face to a beautiful earthy glow that makeup artists covet but never achieve because it comes from fresh air, movement, and sunshine.

Our friendship was sealed with her first sentence after hello, "Would you like to go on some hikes with us, let us experiment with new material on you for our tours, and explore caves and Romanesque chapels?" Oh, God, yes. She said she would organize it and be in touch. As she walked away, Petrus looked especially satisfied. I was halfway through asking her how she'd met Béa when she replied, "The olive stand. It's always the olive stand. We meet so many fascinating people just by being here every week. To think that something so small as an olive facilitates so many adventures!"

It certainly was one of the important doors that opened to me here: Le Chardon, the olive stand, and the Lébérou Café. All were magical thresholds, portals like Alice's rabbit hole that opened so willingly to me and led me to deeper and deeper connections with the people, creatures, and the earth of this ancient and enchanted place.

Our new friends organized two separate days with Monsieur Pémendrant because his ancestral land held two caves and we visited one on each meeting. After each rendezvous with him, we then spent the rest of the day trekking deeper into the area's forests and learning about the native plants and animals. These two adventures led to others, and we kept trekking through the winter into early spring, visiting medieval chapels and castles and learning about their folklore, including some in prehistoric caves or with prehistoric caves at their base, or an ancient Celtic well in its heart. We saw forest frogs, bats, moles, hawks, the occasional wild boar, deer, and fox. Sometimes a village dog would join us and spend the day with us until we found its owner or took it back to the village. We'd uncover vast old vineyards and shepherd's huts hidden by forest growth that took over after the vines were destroyed due to the aphid-like phylloxera epidemic that struck down many of France's vineyards in the late nineteenth century. We'd kayak and put in wherever the whim struck us, Thierry at the helm. Our treks always involved a serious picnic, including homemade soups Petrus hauled in her pack in three thermoses, or a hearty meal at night.

The land never ceased to offer up yet more layers of secrets and intrigue, and Béa, Bruno, and Thierry were its keepers, masters of the land's knowledge and wisdom, along with old-timers like Monsieur Pémendrant, the old wine-whisperer of La Canéda, and the *oc* folks of Café Oc.

On one hike in the midst of a Middle Earth forest, beech and oak trees dripping with green moss and dressed at their legs with thick fern undergrowth, Thierry saw a small cave that intrigued him, and he slipped off the path to investigate. The rest of us continued on. Thierry was impishly prone to poking into crevices here and there and we got used to simply slowing our step a little to give him time to catch up.

I hadn't noticed that Miles, also an intrepid explorer, had trailed off behind him to see too.

I turned around in time to see that Thierry had caught up with the tail of our group, but there was no sign of Miles. As soon as I'd noticed he was missing, like someone stepping on a full tube of toothpaste, I saw Miles squirt out the cave opening that Thierry had left behind and then run like the dickens to catch up to the rest of us.

"Badger!" he exclaimed excitedly. "Badger." He repeated, more flatly, as he neared Thierry, looking at him accusingly.

Thierry had no idea what he was guilty of but the stunned look on Miles' face sent Thierry into fits of laughter. Béa, more concerned for Miles, quickly asked, "Badger?"

"Well," started Miles, looking askance at the now out-of-control-and-howling Thierry, "when we went into the cave, I behind Thierry, we found nothing. Thierry made a loud shout to see how deep it was and how the sound echoed. It was deep. It was dark. It was narrow. And then he left. But I stayed to feel the quiet of the cave and see more once my eyes adjusted to the dark. That's when I saw two eyes flash open in the back, followed by the low warm-up of a growling dog that then crescendoed and peaked into the frightening screech of a very angry alley cat. That's when I ran for my life."

By now all of us, including the more dignified Béa, were gripped with uncontrollable laughter, wiping tears from our eyes. When the last bursts of glee subsided, Thierry realized he had awakened a badger from a deep winter's nap.

Later, I recounted the badger incident to my brother, an avid mountain biker in the Rocky Mountains. He calmly said, "That's why it's usually the second mountain biker who gets bit by the rattlesnake."

"Really, how so?" I asked, not connecting the dots.

"Well, the first biker gets the warning, but the second gets the strike."

That evening, after the badger incident, Bruno's mother invited us all to her home to have a home-cooked meal, Périgordine comfort food. Bruno grew up a local in the heart center of all things prehistoric and Périgord, a mere stone's throw from the major prehistory sites along both the Vézère and Dordogne rivers. His whole family was passionate about this remarkable ancient geography. When we arrived at the front door, his mother warmly greeted us. As we stepped inside, I noticed on her entryway table a piece of mail, opened so that the flyer in it was on top. Sex in the Time of Cro-Magnon, it said. Oh yes. That was eye-catching.

"Sex in the time of Cro-Magnon?" I asked and heard my hiking companions *ooh la la* behind me, hoping to coax the proper older woman to reveal her secrets. But she calmly shrugged and said, "Sorry, but it will more likely be about the exchange of DNA, not anything to take notes on for application in the boudoir." She said this as she walked back into the kitchen and invited us to join her. She explained over her shoulder that the flyer was for a special conference coming soon to the nearby prehistory museum in Les Eyzies. It was far less about prehistoric sex, which we can only speculate over, and more about its consequences. And here we are.

"*Et voilà*, here we are," said Bruno's mother gesturing toward a wonderful long table, the kind that we Americans fantasize about when someone says, "French country cooking." It was set and arrayed with soup bowls and a big loaf of bread in the center. She picked up a ladle and suggested we sit, and then she began to pour homemade beef consommé into our bowls, saying modestly all the while that she'd really only made a very simple traditional meal.

We were famished from a long day of hiking out in the sunny but cold winter. The steam from the thick, earthy broth hit my nostrils, and I made a mental note to redefine the word "simple."

We were silent, savoring the fatigue-curing, frost-eradicating broth. That masterpiece was followed by a wild mushroom tart, with mushrooms she and Bruno gathered from the surrounding forest in a flaky, layered buttery crust she had been making for decades. She discounted the compliments we gushed at her with the flick of a hand.

She wasn't done. A just-picked-from-the-garden curly endive salad showed up at our table with a perfect vinaigrette — white wine vinegar, minced shallots, mustard, olive oil — and a wooden board with three kinds of local cheeses. Then, "a simple dessert," she said as she stood to make, one by one, crepes from a homemade batter for dessert. These we filled with a selection of her own homemade jams: melon, orange, and fig.

We went home satiated and content. What is more satisfying than concluding a day of exploring the wild world in winter than with a wonderful meal? That evening, as Miles and I returned and walked into the medieval center of Sarlat, we found that in our absence the town had been transformed. The approaching weekend was the annual truffle festival, Fête de la Truffe. The same crew that built the Christmas fair and set up the Christmas tree took everything down and set up white cooking tents in the Place de la Liberté.

Other venues throughout town set up chalkboards and posters announcing when famous chefs would hold cooking demonstrations and truffle tastings. The most dramatic change was on the northwestern side of the cathedral. There, the crew had hauled in tons of dark brown dirt and piled it onto the old cobblestones, raked it smooth, and placed a little fence around the pile. They then planted live little oak trees, striving to mimic a little forest. I learned, upon asking one of the shopkeepers whose store was right across from the new forest, that this was for staging tomorrow's truffle-hunting contest. Hunters in the region would bring in their talented truffle dogs for demonstrations so that visitors could see how a dog sought out the elusive truffle hiding under the earth. There would even be prizes.

Her raised eyebrows were equally matched by mine. We wondered who had come up with this idea, because even the locals, who knew better, were dubious about the faux forest's effects on the dogs. Dogs were smart. Their noses sensitive. Something about all this manhandled dirt would strike them as off. It was something ancient and ancestral, deep in the real forests of the Périgord Noir that triggered olfactory intelligence. But we were excited nonetheless just to see dogs.

The next morning, from our perch in Le Chardon, we watched the contest along the side of the cathedral. We were initially amused as the serious professional dogs took umbrage at the strange truffle forest. They, more than not, refused to be a part of such artifice. The thicker the crowd drawn to the event, the more they staged a strike and resisted. One sat firmly on his haunches outside the spectacle and refused to budge no matter how enticed, even with treats.

One man at last encouraged his hunting dog with extra treats to bend dignity and offer the gathering crowd a demonstration. He did, very grudgingly.

We left our window seat and slipped down and into the crowd, moving away from the faux forest and toward the white tents. The smells of truffles and cooking thickened the air. To our delight, hunting demonstration now fulfilled, culinary events featuring the coveted famous truffle were erupting everywhere, just in time for that all-important French tradition of taking a little *apero* with friends before lunch. We went toward the market square and all the tents were operating at full steam.

A helpful festival reveler initiated us to how it worked. We were to purchase booklets at ten euros a piece that contained ten tickets.

Each ticket could then be exchanged for a truffle-inspired appetizer or a perfectly partnered glass of wine. Each with booklets in hand, we entered into the thick of the tents and began to graze, sample, drink, and declare the truffle festival a piece of brilliance, bringing the truffle more democratically to all palates and budgets.

What was better, Miles and I compared notes, the simple fluffy creamy scrambled eggs with shaved truffle or the Chinese-inspired truffle wonton stuffed with duck and cabbage and the black dust? What about the ham and pea soup topped with truffle freckled fresh cream? I held off a verdict until I applied my last two tickets for the *pièce de résistance* for which I'd guarded them. Thinking of my friends at Café Oc, I knew the litmus test of truffle perfection was the canapé.

I spied a chef from across the square who had decided that this was his single dedicated contribution to the hedonistic festival. As libation, all he had was champagne to match the canapés. *Oc. Oc.* I made my way to his table covered in a sea of black on butter white: thinly sliced black truffles generously fanned on buttered rustic bread with a hit of sea salt, right next door to an expanding grid pattern of little glasses shimmering with bubbly brut. It was a perfect day at the seashore, the sun sparkling off the sea, a salty breeze. I handed over my booklet and received my treat, which took on, from the first bite, the same effect as oysters and champagne. There is something about the mix of salty sea with buttery earthiness that makes our taste buds sing and our being feel so good that it is small wonder that both food items are considered aphrodisiacs.

I smiled at Miles. Miles smiled at me. We declared the fellows of Café Oc to be spot on in their assessment of the perfect truffe. We clinked our champagne flutes in their honor and walked home.

People here call this life, *la vie normale*, and it feels as if the rest of us are not normal because we have forgotten how to live, that the basics of fresh air and healthy earth and engaged community are what make life rich and very worth living. A life dedicated to thriving, not achieving. A man who speaks to his vines. Another who gives his bird friend some water as he weeds in the garden. Dogs who have citizen's rights. Food that is grown by you and your neighbor and not trucked in from across the continent. Saying *bonjour* and *au revoir* habitually, as par for the course upon entering a public place and leaving it. Truffles handled simply, without a lot of chefs' fingerprints to make them more chic and coveted by the elite. A glass of bubbly that costs only a euro. It's really not an argument, la vie normale, but a statement of a basic truth.

Three weeks earlier, before great adventures with Monsieur Pémendrant and gorging on truffles, we enjoyed Christmas Eve's midnight mass in Saint Sacerdos. It was a singular moment in the year that revealed all the cogs that make this community whir, that make this place thick with *la quirky vie normale*. Everyone was there, everyone had come out of the woodwork. I was sure that even the basketball lady of Lourdes would appear.

When we arrived, a few minutes before *minuit*, the cathedral was overflowing into standing room around the back and sides and the pews were packed in like sardine cans. We managed to find a small space to squeeze into and joined the masses two thirds of the way back from the altar. As we settled in, I noticed a man to our left who I learned was Welsh, wearing a shoulder-to-almost-floor-length royal blue and white poncho that appeared as if it came from the American Southwest. He had shaved his hair on each side, leaving a thick strip of long gray hair running down the middle of his head, from his forehead to his neck, where it ended in a long ponytail that he had fastened with a leather cord decorated in beads and seven large hawk feathers. On his left ear hung a long black feather earring. Next to him was an Ethiopian man and French woman and their two children. From the Welsh shaman hippie to the Christian Orthodox Ethiopian, I felt the love in the church, our diverse little universe in the ancient land of Cro-Magnon. I shivered with joy from the tip of my head to my toes for I realized that I was in a place where it was no longer weird but normal to be an American-born, Iranian-Coloradan progressive who read Castaneda as much as Corbin.

Sweetening the thought as it unfurled in my giddy brain, the priest walked past us and made eye contact with me, then looked at Miles, and barked a jovial *Joyeux Noël* at us. He had often seen me coming in during *l'heure bleue* to light a candle at Bernadette and the Marys' feet and then sit and meditate, usually right before he planned to lock the church for the night, but this was the first time he'd spoken to me. It warmed me more than he could ever know. He then proceeded to his hidden room on the side of the nave to prepare for that magical realism of shifting seemingly ordinary stones into sacred space and transcendence. Light this night was born into the dark world. The crowd pulsed with the expectation of this miracle and the collective energy in church that night shouted, *Let us rejoice!* The Welsh shaman hippy turned to us and smiled.

I turned quickly to the left to see if the holy basketball lady had come to do her usual pre-mass illumination, but I did not see her. I had already lit my candle and set it where she had taught me was the optimal hoop-shot prayer spot. It stood flickering alone.

The service began and everyone was full of good voice and sang robustly. The energy was pulsating and it was as if we were at a sacred disco. I had never been to such an exuberant midnight mass in all my life. When it was over, after the children and teenagers enlisted into the service had taken the roles of angels and we sang more lung-filled cacophony, everyone warmly wished each other *Joyeux Noël*, and we began to stream out into the crisp, starry night.

As we filed out, I looked to my right, and sure enough, there was her candle at the Bernadette chapel, positioned snugly next to mine, the edges touching. She had snuck in and disappeared. I wished the bowl-cut-hairdo lady a Merry Christmas in my heart, knowing she'd get the greeting in her sturdy mystical way.

New Year's Eve soon followed and Petrus told us we would stay overnight at the farmhouse and she would organize the feast and festivities. She was preparing the Dordogne's most traditional dish for the event, *la mique*. Petrus labored all day and by nightfall our little group of friends arrived in festive finery, anticipating a long night of fine food, song, stories, and wine. We were also instructed in the Dutch tradition of lighting firecrackers at midnight, herded unexpectedly by the neighbor's sheepherding dog, Tango. Thereafter, until five in the morning, back around the fifteenth-century fireplace, a friend's daughter serenaded us in a warm mezzo-soprano voice and accordion in traditional French and Occitan song.

But throughout the long merry-making night, *la mique* was held as the climax of the evening. Perhaps you've heard of pot-au-feu or cassoulet and it makes your mouth water? Then, think of the two together in a big, black, cast iron kettle hanging from a hook over an open fire and sealed over with a big disk of freshly kneaded sourdough bread, which will bake into a fine loaf of bread, golden and crunchy on top while chewy and warm inside, sealing in the bubbling pot's ingredients and absorbing the fragrant steam and sauce below. This process goes on all day, the pot brimming over with winter vegetables, sausages, meats, garlic, herbs, spices, and wine, with the bread being laid on the top for the last two hours of cooking. All night we'd been inhaling the fumes that penetrated every crevice of the grand stone sitting room, and so it was a moment of great ceremony and watering mouths when it came time to eat. Petrus carefully lifted the bread seal and set it on its own plate for us to break off savory chunks as we spooned the robust stew into our generous bowls. Preceding this, we had not suffered. We'd enjoyed Petrus' secret recipe for perfectly prepared foie gras and thin slices of smoked cured duck with a peppery arugula salad.

But *la mique,* even more than foie gras and duck confit, is the Dordogne's mythic dish, imbued with alchemy and ritual with that big black iron kettle and bread lid. It is also incredible satisfaction in all things good — vegetable, animal, and mineral — that go into it.

And so we lay about the fire, satiated and serenaded, with firecrackers detonated and well herded by Tango who had long since, as reasonable creatures are wont, gone home. Throughout the entire evening, Ferdinand did not leave Miles' lap. It felt like another good omen.

Then we slept. Late. And awoke on a sunny, cold New Year's Day to eat more around Petrus and Jean's generous table. Ferdinand continued to sit in Miles' lap. *Oc.*

One day, shortly after New Year's, Miles came back from the Christmas market, which was in fuller swing because Epiphany was almost here, the day gifts are exchanged in France, saying that I needed to go back with him. He had just met the bookseller with a kiosk there, and they had talked about the esoteric Dordogne. I must meet him.

"He's originally from Paris," recounted Miles, "but lived for years in Japan as a businessman. Now he and his Japanese wife and their three sons have resettled here. I liked him." I trusted his instincts and pulled on my jacket, scarf, and gloves and followed Miles back to market.

We approached the bookstall of a plump, pink-cheeked, and very jolly man with Harry Potter-like glasses. Miles introduced me to Gerard who greeted me enthusiastically. "Ah! I hear from your husband that you are a writer and that you are writing about the Dordogne, especially the more spiritual aspects?"

"Yes," I nodded. "And I hear you know a good bit about the less known esoteric stories of the land and culture?"

He beamed. "Yes! We decided to come here when we moved back to France after years in Japan. I'm from Paris but I didn't want to go back there. We came here because the land has a special energy.

I think some places have spirits as much as people." He elaborated that the Dordogne, the land itself, is, as a person, a whole being with a personality. He then added that this spirited and personality-rich aspect of the land can include houses. With this he said, "Wait until you meet my house!"

I was intrigued, and a little nervous. Before I could wonder what meeting a house might entail, he began talking about the possibility of reincarnation, and that many people who come to the Périgord had earlier, past life connections to this land. He looked at me knowingly, implying anyone who had the strong feelings that I had for this place was a part of that returning tribe.

By this time his kiosk was beginning to fill up with customers again, and we needed to let him return to his work, but not first without a jubilant promise from him to show us "some of the magical places nearby." We agreed to fix a date in a few days, after the Christmas market closed and he had more time. "I want to invite you two to stay overnight at my home," he added. "You must experience it! We can share a good meal and set out early the next morning for our magical adventures. I have two friends I want you to meet, local experts on the region's mysteries. I'll arrange it."

My intrigue deepened, and I was grateful. But I was still wondering what he meant by experiencing and meeting his house. We said goodbye, but as we walked a few steps, he excitedly called to us, "We have ghosts, you know, and they'll let themselves be known." Gulp. What had we just committed to doing with a perfect stranger? But Miles squeezed my hand; he had a good feeling about this. One thing was sure, I knew that my future sleepover would involve little sleep.

There are some experiences everyone seems to talk about here that almost never will make their way into a guidebook on the Dordogne. The frequency of living in places with spirit inhabitants is one of them. People here talk a lot about energies, spirits, presences, and ghosts. It is part of the local culture as much as foraging for mushrooms, self-sufficiency, and good food and wine. It's not all sunflowers and lavender here in the south of France. It's also lots of layers of history, a good dose of it dark, and here in the Dordogne, add the lesser understood and mysterious aspects of prehistory, and it leads most residents, native and expat alike, to have a pretty healthy respect for the disembodied weight of the past. In the Dordogne, belief in ghosts is for novices, and experience replaces mental constructs. There can be a thick intensity to living here that stems from the long occupation of this land, since the time of Neandertals. It's not always an easy bike ride through rolling hills, sipping wine and eating duck — though, that helps. It's also a geological cycle through layers of time where people liked it here so much that their ancient imprint is still here, peeking from behind trees and rocks, haunting buildings, and asking the living to live with them.

I mentioned this realization to Petrus one day as she was bagging some olives for a customer. After the transaction was finished, she said, "It's a place that's been inhabited for so long that ghosts are a normal expectation. The flip side is that because of the many layers of human occupation, with their persisting influences felt in the present, it's not always an easy place to live. But," she brightened, "the effort is worth it because it is a rich place to live. Everyday is a mystery and you feel so alive. Everyday I discover something new that I didn't know." This was the essence of that special energy, this never-ending mystery unfolding even after decades of living here. One always felt alive; routine and ordinariness were inherently banished from the land.

Not long after Epiphany, Gerard the bookseller organized an evening at his home with his family and the two friends from Bordeaux who were well-versed in the esoteric Dordogne. We were all to come for dinner, stay overnight, and embark on trekking adventures the next morning.

Miles and I took the train to St-Cyprien, where Gerard picked us up and took us to his village home nearby. As we arrived we saw an all stone and slate roofed house that looked as if it had been built in three different times. It was complete with a small tower and a beautiful stained glass window depicting a medieval knight in full armor. As beautiful as it was, I felt an inexplicable denseness around the house immediately upon stepping out of the car. It was a bone dry and sunny day, but it felt cloying, cold, and dank. His warm and very welcoming wife, Kazumi, came out to greet us along with their three sons, all trilingual in Japanese, French, and English. They then gave us a tour of the place before we sat down to lunch.

That general feeling hovered but got no stronger as we went from room to room, until the room Gerard saved for last, which was right next to the kitchen where we would eat. It was the one with the tower where Gerard stored all his books. At its threshold I was hit by an unearthly cold. I noticed that Kazumi and the three boys had opted out of following us there and that the dog, who had been glued to our heels, retreated very quickly and went to his bed and curled up. That clammy cold penetrated deeply and made me feel very uncomfortable. It wasn't the normal straight-forward physical damp cold of a stone house near a river in a valley in winter. It was different. It had the non-rational feeling of someone standing right behind me, even though no one was there, and just sucking all the warmth around it. I noticed too that the bookseller had been watching my reaction. There was nothing about the room physically that could explain its dramatically different temperature from the neighboring rooms. All were built of the same stone, the same thickness, with the same heating system in place. I quickly retreated back into the now unusually warm kitchen. Instinctively, I surrounded myself with light and warm thoughts. Miles seemed equally disturbed and joined me.

We next gathered for lunch around a hefty wooden table in the center of the especially inviting kitchen. I noticed that the dog still looked a bit skittish and still lay curled tightly on his mattress. The bookseller saw me studying the dog and finally spoke, "That room is the house's most haunted part. Our dog refuses to go near it, and it makes him nervous. It's occupied by a spirit that refuses to leave." He said this as casually as his next sentence "Would you like some roasted chicken and vegetables. Kazumi is a wonderful chef." *Oui*, I said softly, my brain still processing the phrase, "most haunted part." It meant, there were still other, albeit lesser haunted, areas in the house. Great. This was one time I wished we had a car, wished we could explain that sleeping over was out of the question. But we were committed. I looked at his three sons, eagerly tucking into their mother's roasted chicken, carrots, potatoes, and green beans and decided to relax. If they lived here all the time and were happy and well-adjusted, I could surely spend one night.

"The spirit just won't leave," Gerard continued. "It sucks all the warmth out of that room no matter how much I insulate and heat it." He had invested quite a bit to weatherproof the room. In fact, it was better heated and insulated than the rest of the house, but to no avail. "It's as bone-chillingly cold today as it was the day we bought this place," he concluded.

Over lunch, over delicious food that made me forget temporarily about transparent onlookers, we learned that the house was quite old and had been expanded several times. A stone inlay inside the house had 1557 engraved on it and established one of its foundations as sixteenth century. Gerard thought that maybe a judge had lived here and built the house. He added that it had blue paint underneath later paint, a color that was used only in the homes of those loyal to and in the ranks of the king of France. He then went on to speak of the many other occupants of the house and its earlier incarnations, dating all the way back to the Merovingian period of the seventh century.

"The 600s," he explained, "is when this plot of earth began to take on its human color." That was as far back as historical documents took it. Before that it was also in the heart of ancient Iron Age Celtic occupations, and before that a crossroads for Neolithic and Paleolithic occupations as far back as the Neandertals and perhaps earlier. From solid historical sleuthing, though, Gerard found the house had first been a hermitage, from the seventh to the eleventh centuries. Someone installed the cellars in the eleventh century, not an uncommon thing to do in the Middle Ages if you had money and something to hide.

He and Kazumi bought the house while in Japan, sight unseen, but had a good feeling about it. On their first night sleeping in it, after they finally relocated to France, Gerard said that his dreams were full of visions of walking into the cellar and seeing instruments of torture on the walls. When he woke up, he knew it had been a place where people were held for crimes before they were heard by a judge, who came and heard the cases on the floor just above the cellar. He looked into it, and historical documents corroborated his dream.

Miles, a wholeheartedly rational, well-grounded, sane, and reasonable person, said that he had felt a strange sort of upstairs-downstairs energy when he first walked in, as if there were some great division of power in the house.

By dessert, Gerard summarized his detective work in one bite: The house had been a hermitage, then the residence of a wealthy fiefdom, then a judge's home, and later, through poetic justice perhaps, an abode of prostitutes during the Napoleonic era. How had he arrived at that last likelihood? "There are simply too many sinks here," he explained. "That's not normal. No one needs five sinks for one farmhouse, and not in all the rooms upstairs." After the brothel, the home lay abandoned until WWII when Nazis took over the farmhouse for their nefarious occupation. After the war it lay abandoned again for decades until our hosts bought it. They admitted they were looking for a place thick with layers of history. They certainly got their money's worth.

With the setting sun, the two friends from Bordeaux arrived. Pascal was a stonemason skilled and certified in restoring historic homes and was sensitive to the earth energies of the places he worked. Fréderique, his wife, was a healer who used horses in helping to diagnose what was wrong with people. As Pascal restored a home's body and soul, Fréderique restored people's.

We again sat down to eat; feeling energies and spirits requires energy. Having dinner with a stonemason schooled in sacred geometry led me to ask about the six-petaled flower of Temniac and why this ancient symbol appeared in so much Old World art and architecture. Pascal lit up. Well-versed in freemasonry, he said it was a very important symbol, the symbol originally of Isis and her manifestation as the original Mother Earth, Gaia. It was the flower of "the mistress of the universe, the master builder" as he called Her . . . and Her, not Him. He smiled, loving being the rebel. "Most people think the master builders were men, but the original one was a woman."

The flower, he said, preceded and inspired Solomon's Seal, these days more popularly called the Star of David, but that one ought never forget its more ancient and primary origins, the Mother Goddess. "Some masons took the flower as their symbol to honor Her, the original Builder." A fire was in my head. This ancient symbol was reminding us all along of our origins from the womb of the original Builder. How stunning and beautiful. The red horses of Lascaux galloped forth, birthing us from the womb itself in that narrow subterranean space. I also understood why Fréderique enjoyed Pascal's company so much: he honored women. They also shared a passion for the region's mysteries and explored them together.

As my mind reeled, celebrating *La* Builder, Pascal was just warming up. "You know the lanterne des morts in Sarlat? Beyond the historical explanations given, it was built in fact for the purpose of concentrating and transmitting earthly and heavenly energies, a lot like a Buddhist stuppa works to concentrate and transmit prayers. It is the physical manifestation of the flower, Solomon's Seal, heaven and earth meeting at that point and channeling energy above and below." Right there, at the wall near where Mr. Stripes and I often met, and where Miles also enjoyed concluding his days, just sitting on the wall as *l'heure bleue* descended.

After good food and satisfying conversation, through which I'd entirely forgotten about ghosts and being cold, it was time for us to turn in. Kazumi and Gerard showed us each our rooms and we said goodnight. Pascal and Fréderique slept in a room off the kitchen on the same level, and Miles and I were above, where the rooms each had a stone sink. As we climbed the stairs, Gerard called up after us in a loud whisper. "I look forward to hearing about your sleep . . . and whom you meet tonight."

Crap. Great.

After squeamish tossing and turning, I finally fell asleep. Miles was out cold from the moment his head hit the pillow. How did he do that? I did not have a good night's sleep. It was probably my mind playing tricks on me. I recalled many times that the human brain can be quite the con artist. Still, after odd, restless dreams, as if I were sleeping in a central train station, I woke up to the sensation of a heavy and cold weight on my left leg. In heft and size, it felt like a cat that had climbed onto our bed. But instead of the warmth or solidity of a living cat, it was invisible and stone cold. Even after I woke up and moved my leg, I could still feel the weight on the bed. Once I even think I felt nimble little feet. About this time, Miles woke up too and was having a tough time having a peaceful sleep. He pulled me closer to him and offered the one source of heat in that bed that night.

Almost as soon as I fell asleep again, I woke to the sensation of a sentinel, some young man who kept coming and going, pacing back and forth near the window on my side of the bed, as if it had once been a door. I tried to sleep again and succeeded long enough for a lucid dream filled with a lot of people coming and going from the room. I then had a very strange dream, one in which I felt a man dressed in a seventeenth-century military uniform with studded collar standing next to my bed and asking politely, "Can I step into your dream and join you, *partager votre rêve, s'il vous plait.*" What?! I said *non*, firmly and loudly enough that I woke myself up. Miles seemed to keep sleeping, and I could see that he was finally getting a deeper level of sleep.

I almost laughed at the absurdity of the situation, but stopped laughing when I felt a chill near my bed begin to retreat as if stepping away. Thankfully, if it were a ghost, he was rather polite, asking for permission and even using the *vous* form, even if he did want to slip into my dream.

I sit on the fence as to whether I completely believe in ghosts, or if, as noted, the mind is a bullshit artist working with subtly planted suggestion, but I can say this: I don't think I could sleep over in that house again. I like my dreams, and some of them are weird, but I don't care to share them with peripheral characters wanting to step in, imagined or not.

When the sun finally shone through the window, sleep deprived, I jumped out of bed and sought out my first bowl of coffee; I was going to require a lot of coffee today. Miles also looked worn from his night. We went downstairs and toward the judge's quarters, above the cellar. There, over a warming and delicious strong bowl of coffee, sat Gerard at the kitchen table, offering us our own steaming bowls full of brew. We accepted and sat down.

"*Alors*," he said, expectantly. "How was your night?" I took a deep sip of the life-giving liquid, and before I could answer, Pascal and Frédérique came out from their room. "I'll tell you," the stonemason said, who had heard Gerard's question, "It was a busy night." He rubbed his eyes. Frédérique nodded agreement and added, "People were coming and going. There were footsteps in our room, but also overhead, right by the upstairs window in Miles' and Beebe's room."

"Yes," added Pascal, "it felt like being in a station."

My throat closed. I set my coffee bowl down.

"That's interesting," smiled Gerard, "because there used to be an exterior entrance to the upper floor, right over where you slept. The window in that room was probably once a door."

I got a chill. I picked my bowl up again, warming my hands. I then told them about my night visitors and my sense that someone paced near my bed as if it had been near a door, which it seemed, now in the stark light of morning, it once had been.

They kept looking at me, so I unloaded the rest and told them about the dream interloper and the cat. Gerard said he knew the cat, that he'd encountered its presence a few times. Crap. Great.

"It might have belonged to one of the madams," he offered casually, "or to one of the noblemen who lived here. It's not clear which." Or both, I thought in an off color way. It would have been sweet, the way it nimbly padded its little soft feet about the bed and curled up on one's legs, if it hadn't been so darned cold and eerie.

Thankfully, before us lay a warm, sunny, and cheery morning. I knew I would need a nap once we got back to Le Chardon, but I was energized by what the friends from Bordeaux had planned for us: several visits to hidden shrines, all built over mineral springs and to which locals for a long time had quietly made pilgrimages. So quiet were they that they were not found in the usual guidebooks on the Dordogne.

Not all shrines are the same, Fréderique taught us, but all are potent, each in their own way. Some are for ridding a person of addictions, others of negativity, and still others, are for the usual garden variety of sought-out health cures and boosts to one's well being. At one, difficult to locate as it was tucked in a lush, narrow valley surrounded by evergreen oak, she warned me not to touch the water of the spring flowing beneath the shrine. It was known for removing negativity and was doing it not only for individuals but also for the entire earth, constantly, a cleansing portal sucking away all our psychic trash with which we pollute the earth and ourselves. The water is so concentrated with our refuse that, "you should never touch it, or, heaven forbid, drink from it."

A small opening, like a window, was erected right over the water's flow beneath the shrine, and people had left items symbolic of what they wanted cleared, plus offerings of gratitude, such as candles, now spent, and flowers, now in different states of decay. At the center of this window was a statue of Mary, one that had taken on a dull gray hue. The chapel near which the little watery shrine stood had a white stone Mary standing at its gateway, free of blemish or wear and tear. It seemed the two were in a dance, one taking on the burden, the other, free and outside its reach.

As we walked away, an elderly man appeared who seemed deeply troubled by something. We greeted him formally and left him be. I turned to watch how he approached the shrine. He didn't touch anything, but he stood as close as he dared to the flow of water and closed his eyes, letting it pull from him that which he had come here to release.

At the shrines, there was one strikingly similar feature: all had statues of the Mother Mary, usually more than one, and not one of them had Jesus anywhere to be seen, except by suggestion with an occasional cross here or there. They were exactly like many shrines I witnessed across northern Spain, also without the Son and all dedicated to not only Mary but to a more ancient name of the feminine divine, one that preceded the arrival of Christianity.

Fréderique confirmed this and pointed to small details hidden to the casual observer, features that survived from pagan practices or Christian ones that took on local expression, such as stone statues with particular hand gestures not commonly found among more popular or universal depictions of Mary and the different saints. Then, some sites needed to be walked around a certain number of times in a certain direction in order to activate their energy.

At one site, when I entered, I felt my throat tighten and grow congested, and I kept swallowing, hoping to clear it, but it seemed to stick until I walked to the altar. As if someone had massaged my throat, it cleared and I sang a soft song to hear remarkable acoustics softly whisper throughout the entire chapel. I asked Fréderique about the sound effects but said nothing about my throat sensation. "Some places are associated with a certain chakra," she stated matter-of-factly. "All a person has to do is find the site's center and stand there to activate the area of the body associated with chakra energy of the chapel. If there are any blockages, standing there can clear them."

"So this chapel is associated with a chakra?" I asked and fished at once.

"Why yes. The fifth chakra, that of the voice, and more profoundly, of finding one's voice." Interesting.

Growing up in Colorado in a town labeled "New Age," it fully occurred to me now that those New Age ideas were really Old Age ideas for people residing in ancient traditional places and were based on generations of folkloric practices and knowledge. There was nothing wifty or navel-gazing about these places, and no one felt any need whatsoever to defend the logic of their practices to outsiders. These shrines today still have annual pilgrimages and festivals and draw a lot of people, local people and few, if any, tourists. My mind reeled pleasantly, my throat hummed, I'd found my voice, and I also had a lot to contemplate and weave into my ideas of reality.

So stunned by the morning into early afternoon of explorations with Fréderique and friends, we did not need a nap when we returned to Le Chardon, though, I was grateful to live in a house with only one spirit who came and went and who had a good sense of boundaries and cheer. •

Market Onions and Beans

Chapter 19

WEDNESDAY MARKET CAFÉ

"Being human, let's face it, is murky business. It's beauty. It's pain. Even trying to be good, doing the right thing, can be so subjective. It's not really about the obvious extremes of good and bad is it? It's about navigating the ambiguous stuff, the gray area of everyday life." She shrugged and added, *"That's simply what being here on Earth is about."*

I CARRIED THAT BOOK AROUND, *The Thousand and One Nights*, in my pannier for several weeks, waiting for my next chance meeting with Bernadette and Vivienne. But I didn't see them around town or at market throughout the winter holidays, later learning that many older residents of the town found it difficult to navigate the uneven cobblestone in winter, especially given the thick tourist presence on market and festival days and the frigid weather. The Three Kings had come and gone, the truffle festival had folded, and the goose festival was about to kick off when a slight warming trend arrived. With it came the songbirds of late winter and early spring and soon my two friends were again passing through the market square during the Wednesday market.

I caught up with them one day and the three of us settled into our booth at our favorite café and reestablished our market meetings after finishing food shopping. Petrus flitted back and forth between us and the stand, depending on the number of customers clamoring for olives. I pulled at last the book from my pannier and handed it to Bernadette. "I found this right after Petrus and I left your apartment in December. It was in the *boîte à lire* near the Mary church. I thought of your collection of books and wondered if you could use it."

Her face flushed with wonder. She took it and held it like a newborn. She then carefully opened it and turned the pages. Her eyes grew larger as she opened one page to the next. After a few moments she looked up. "It's perfect. It's really remarkable. This volume fills a hole in my collection. I've been searching a long time for a book such as this. And did you know, I learned long ago to restore old books? This is going to be fun."

"This was no coincidence," declared Vivienne. "It's too perfect. That the very day you two met and you had just come from Bernadette's home to see her miniatures, you found this near the Mary church?" I shook my head in confirmation as she looked at Bernadette and they shared a knowing look. "*Non,*" she decided, "this is no coincidence."

I had to know what that knowing look was about. "The Mary church?" I asked. They smiled. The magic spot. Of course this book would appear there, at that *boîte*. They explained together that while the church was now converted into the daily covered market, it had been a beautiful church dedicated to Mary. But not Mother Mary, as everyone believed, but the other important Mary, the Magdalene. It gave the church a special extra aura for them because it included all women, not just the ones who were blemish-less or had become mothers. It also stood over that underground stream in Sarlat, coming off from the fountain dedicated to the Mother, flowing under the church and on to Saint Sacerdos and the Tower, making magic happen. I smelled the strong waft of feminism. I loved these two.

"Isn't it curious," said Bernadette, returning to the book, "that here in the heart of the Périgord Noir, you should find this? That there are three people here, at least, who are interested in Iranian mysticism and miniatures."

"You mean Petrus?" I asked, but simultaneously Vivienne, who understood Bernadette's meaning, said, "I wonder who that third person is?" I then realized the third person referred to here was the unknown former owner of the book.

Who indeed? Were they someone we had yet to meet or had they left this earth and was a family member cleaning out their attic full of old books? We would probably never know, unless the Mary church performed some more manifestation magic.

We finished our coffee, and Bernadette went straight home, jazzed to commence work on the book, to coax it back to life. She stayed up late several nights. She made a lot of pots of Moroccan tea. She repaired the binding, cleaned the pages, patched the missing pieces of the cover, and repainted the lost or worn parts of both the cover and the inside color plates. A week later, at our usual perch in the market, she pulled it out of her pannier, covered in a supple protective plastic sheath. What I had given her was so worn that hardly anything was left to its cover and binding except the worn threads of the canvas. But here Bernadette presented a perfectly bound, polished book with repaired velum, restored and ornate paintings, and perfectly repainted gold lettering.

"It's ready for my shelf, where it fills a hole in my books much as our friendship fills an important hole in my life. It feels complete." We clinked coffee cups. I told her it was the same for me. We sipped, very pleased with ourselves.

As Wednesday markets were reserved for gathering with this small circle of remarkable women, Saturday markets continued as times to gather with the growing array of friends from all ages, genders, and senses of humor. Many were friends I'd made during my first winter forays onto the badminton court with Nadiya. While my game was still abysmal, the birdie of my new friendships sailed beautifully over the net in a delightful returned exchange.

With my second winter in Sarlat nearing its end, both Miles and I had been there long enough to establish other habits, rituals, and patterns. I stepped back one day to reflect and noticed that my week was defined by delightful daily rituals, more than I could recall from anywhere else I had ever lived:

We bought fresh food everyday from local vendors, many who had grown the food themselves, and we bought only enough to cover a few meals, knowing we could go out and purchase fresh food on foot within minutes any day, market day or not. Neither Miles nor I missed having a car, and we loved the freedom and simplicity.

We met up with friends in cafés throughout the week and felt plugged in to the life of the town, while also having wonderful vast stretches of solitude in Le Chardon to work. The café visits served as incentives for getting a lot of work done during the day. We would wake up very early in the morning so that we could finish a half day of work by the time life stirred below our window and we could join it, then return to finish the second half of the day's work. Upon doing that, we often went for long, exploratory walks, sometimes alone and sometimes together. On each of these I still learned something new that deepened my understanding of the land and the people, including a few new Occitan words from farmers and vintners met along the path.

I made sure to visit the frogs in the stream north of town, the donkeys on the way to Temniac, and the black wolf dog at the village entrance, and I went and sat next to the six-petaled flower often, waiting for Her to reveal Her secrets. I walked to Carsac, still rushing past that one eerie cold spot, and revisited the warm Romanesque church there and sang in its transept.

Miles and I often set off on new footpaths, which began to appear more and more as we furthered our understanding of how locals traversed the land on foot. We found three different ways to reach and revisit the Templar church in La Canéda. On many walks, where it was fair game, we gathered chestnuts to take back and roast over an open skillet with a rewarding glass of Vin de Domme red, a very local wine.

On Sundays I also became attached to a new habit, one of walking at noon to the nearby newsstand, the tabac, and buying the Sunday edition of *Sudouest*, the regional newspaper with its two weekly magazines. I'd next settle at a table in the sun in the market café, order a dry Bergerac white, and slowly sip and read and watch the world saunter past in their Sunday finery. Sometimes Miles would join me and sometimes he would go off on his own explorations, such as seeking out more footpaths throughout town. They were an invisible web of networks most people missed, and they opened up paths throughout Sarlat that took a person to places they had no idea could also exist in town, such as orchards and hidden kitchen gardens, rows of blackberry bushes, narrow and high stone walls, shepherd's bories, and sheep and horses grazing on a hill that was someone's expansive backyard hidden from the paved roads.

Miles and I also had been in Sarlat long enough for other ritual magic to take hold. The fishmonger who woke us up with her ice at 5:30 A.M. no longer rang our bell at 5 A.M. to see if it was we who had illegally parked a car that blocked her spot by the cathedral wall. She at last knew that we had no car and that we knew the rules, and so we got to sleep an extra half hour. When I bought my weekly dozen oysters from her, she began to throw in a few extra plus a whole lemon. *La vie normale.*

The initially reticent Occitan lettuce seller and his wife now greeted me warmly, even if not as enthusiastically as the cheese vendor and the honey man. I had now been there long enough that the baker, too, had decided I was not too much of a moron, and he allowed that maybe my French and even my Occitan was gaining some small centimeters of skill. No, some millimeters of skill, but still, it was an acknowledgement.

The waiters and owners at my favorite cafés had begun to impart sweet little gestures that touched my heart in ways they may never know. They smiled and treated me like an old-time local and greeted me warmly even when I walked by and could not stop and sit. When I did take a table, they sometimes topped off my wine or gifted me a glass just because. On Sundays at noon, Carlos would see me sit and arrive and perfunctorily ask, "*un blanc sec*"? And as soon as I indicated, *oui*, he had the golden glass in hand and ceremoniously set it on the table before me.

Into late winter, Mr. Stripes and the golden lab were greeting me sooner than they used to. Mr. Stripes would see me and come running and gently run into my legs and purr. The golden lab would offer a friendly woof when he saw me climbing the street toward his wall and then lower his head so I could scratch behind his ears. At the fruit stand on market days, the mischievous half-border terrier, half-Jack Russell would make a point to come out from behind his crates of cantaloupes to greet me warmly.

And the *rouge-gorge* and the *mésange bleue*, the red-breasted thrush and the blue titmouse, sang often. They were either perched nearby on the cathedral right over the windows of Bernadette, Bernard, and Philomena, or in forests and gardens through which I walked.

Saint Sacerdos and the Tower pulsed their warm, earth energies more definitively underfoot and spoke of how they really held us all up, along with the good vibes of the town's underground water streams and the ancient ancestry of the land. The cathedral's bell retained and deepened its Tibetan prayer bowl resonance as it penetrated one's brain and loosened one up for a life more fully felt.

Every moment now was rife with rituals, ones that were alive and vibrant and real and that filled my being as never before. And it never grew old or tired or routine. I prayed to the gods and goddesses of this land to let this be so, forever, amen.

Another ritual I held to was attending the monthly meetings of Café Oc. The mid-February meeting brought eleven of us out into the cold night. I was warmly greeted by all and kissed on the cheeks by the flirty eighty-five year old. The same nice lady who translated Occitan to French for me on prior gatherings sat next to me again. Tonight, the group had asked a local art historian to come and speak about Maurice Albe, an artist who moved to the Dordogne at the age of three, in 1903, and who lived the rest of his life here, creating some of the most expressive woodblock prints of the land, people, and local folklore. He lived to the age of ninety-five and by then was quite the regional expert as well as celebrated artist.

He also lived and breathed Occitan and so did the art historian who passed around copies of his block prints. Though stylized and black and white, we were astounded by how evocative they were of this land. I was immediately attracted to his work—it spoke about both what you can see and what is there but invisible, that energy people kept talking about as real and present.

My favorite woodblock was of the village and church of Temniac. I knew that on the day that he engraved it, it had shown itself to him in its full magical splendor, revealed its Shambala, so that he could capture its truth. My other favorite woodblock was of the mythic Lébérou. I am sure Albe had seen one in the forest during a full moon. It looked as one would sketch a familiar.

The Fete de l'Oie, the goose festival, was also soon upon us. In mid-February, overnight, where once stood the faux pas faux forest for faux truffle hunting, the dirt had long been hauled away and in its stead stood a reed and twine fence containing a cozy space spread with fresh hay and occupied by a flock of geese. Soon appeared below our window a tall and long-haired goose master in poet shirt, leather vest, pants and boots, and a flowing wool cape. He opened the twine fence and marched his geese out and along the square and cobblestone streets in intricate, controlled patterns with voice commands, a herding dog, and the slight movement of a wooden stick that looked like a pilgrim's staff. One gesture and, as an ocean wave, the geese flowed as one to his will. It appeared that geese are far more herdable than sheep or cows: one slight coaxing in the man's voice, and as a well-trained army, geese moved as goose.

Nearby, the same white culinary tents for truffle tasting were up again but this time to feast on fowl. I wondered if the geese sensed the cause and effect, if they smelled their kind on the spit next door or if they were blissfully oblivious to the smell of bird flesh all around them in different states of seasoning and dress.

And as the world arrived to gorge on foie gras, confit, cassoulet, and magret de canard, I realized that this would be Miles' last festival before heading back to New Jersey. He was leaving a little earlier and taking on the task of setting up another foothold in New Jersey for us as we worked out our peripatetic ways, while contending with the relentless perennial demand of making a living. We still had not uncovered the magic bullet that would allow this dream to come fully true. Internet access made a big difference, but a full geographical shift was still a work in progress.

Doubts flooded in. Maybe, as Market Man whispered to me when other friends were engaged in other conversations, over steamy market coffee and fresh chocolate croissants, "the fantasy is more interesting than the reality." What a whammy of a double entendre, *n'est-ce pas*? Or, as another friend, a transplant from years ago from up north, said, "Once you achieve this great dream, you'll find this place is troubled by the same troubles as any other place." True, maybe, but. This place has called to me like no other and this place is like no other. And, being a semi-nomad means that one can make adjustments as they go, or go away and come back while still being rooted here and rooted there. *Oc.*

Still, Miles would be gone by the time Carnival rolled around, and then, soon, so would I. I tried not to think about that. I comforted myself in the permanence of things of the Périgord, its annual festivals, its warmth, our friends, this magnificent ancient earth.

Before his departure, we decided on one last epic journey into the forest and prehistory of the Périgord. One sunny but frosty winter's day we took the train to Les Eyzies, prehistory central, with the main ambition being to visit the cave of Combarelles and its remarkable engravings of animals and humans dating to around 13,000 years ago. It was not far from the Font de Gaume and equally unique and important. Whereas Font de Gaume could undo one upon witnessing the two elk, one licking the other's nose, in Combarelles, one's undoing arrived in the far back of the long, sinuous, seemingly-single-tube cave where another engraved elk was bowing his head and just touching the tip of his nose to the opening of an underground water stream. It was old magic. It was still present and still strong.

We secured tickets for the guided visit to the cave slated for the afternoon and then spent the morning paying homage to Mr. Magnon's old hole, his cro of fame, visiting the comprehensive National Museum of Prehistory, and enjoying a sturdy lunch in the café situated right below the museum. On earlier visits I'd fallen in love with this café, seemingly no different than other cafés in the region, but its situation and the town together made it feel like favorite mountain cafés in the Colorado Rockies. It was run by warm and welcoming people, the food was excellent, and there was that same solid cowboy and hearty mountain frontier-freedom-feel here. Fortified with duck cassoulet, lamb chops, and garden greens, all from a farm nearby, we walked to Combarelles.

Ours was a small group of five people. Soon we all discovered, including our polite but exhausted guide, that one of the visitors was an incessant talker and know-it-all. At first he made us feel claustrophobic in the narrow tube of the cave, but eventually, we tuned him out and instead drank in the magic of the ancient engravings. Dating to between 13,680 and 11,380 years ago, we had to go seventy meters into the cave before encountering the first drawings. Thereafter, it became a Bayeux Tapestry in stone, a long, unbroken narrative that seemed meant to be taken as a single story. Our guide pointed this out, too, as he showed us the section where all predators appeared, together, concentrated in the same stretch.

We passed several human forms that were almost abstract while the animals were very realistic. These made us really wish we could know what the original engravers were thinking. There were numerous horses, mammoths, deer, bison, then some oxen, wild goats, ibex, rhinos, and a wild donkey. Deeper in we arrived at the section of the stone tapestry with the predators — a lion, a bear, and a wolf. Then deeper still, at the tapestry's end, there stood elk taking his eternal drink.

I secretly thanked the know-it-all in our group, for as we arrived at the end and stood before that stunning elk and the opening to an ancient water source, his incessant yammering with the guide gave us a longer pause there to take it in. I tuned out the world of noise and became deeply entranced by the delicate nose marking a source of life. This water had to have been important, and so far back here in the cave, as both a safe place and a portal to another world. I snapped back to the present when our guide announced that our tour was over, extricated himself from the talker, and quickly led us back through the long passageway and out into the shockingly bright open air.

There is a part of the cave that branches off from the main passage midway, but that part was off limits to visitors. The guide explained that it accommodated only a few people. It led to a small chamber with more engravings, leading experts to wonder if this was the destination of a teacher and a few initiates. Perhaps, the whole of the cave was a didactic instrument, and that tunnel served as a deeper journey, a gradual education that culminated in initiation from youth to adulthood?

Over coffee one day, Nadiya looked at me and the lighting crew was back. I uncrossed my legs and sat straight, grounding myself as much as possible.

"When you first came to Sarlat," she began, "I thought to myself, 'I see Beebe here, this is where she will live,' and then I thought, 'and Sarlat wants Beebe. She ought to come and live here.' I just saw it and felt it." She then sat back and smiled, pleased with herself.

My heart sang. I reached across the coffee cups and touched the back of her hand and simply said, "Thank you."

Maybe the lighting crew had taken a vacation for the winter holidays, but now that the truffle festival and the goose festival were done, they were back on the job. A week later, Nadiya hit me with a one-liner. We were running errands together in town and stopped to do some window shopping to see what the clothing shops on the main traverse had in mind for spring. As we gazed at dreamy, warm weather attire, my mind wandered. I wasn't thinking about what the window display was telling me, that spring colors this year involved a lot of hot pink and lemon yellow, both colors I don't look good in anyway. Instead, I was staring at the riotous colors and thinking to myself how much I loved even the little things here, the daily stuff, as well as the big stuff, the deep friendships, the deep earth pull, the sense of destiny, and, oh yeah, how on earth was I going to be able to really live here long term?

I was so lost in these thoughts that I'd missed the cue from the lighting designer. I did, however, begin to feel Nadiya's eyes drilling into me. I turned to look at her.

"Yes?"

"Just this. If something is going to happen, it is going to happen, just take your time."

How could you not love her?

Then, two weeks later, we met up during the Wednesday market and went together to the fishmonger's for the last of our shopping. I was just finishing paying for spanking fresh salmon when I felt the slight shift in lighting, and out of the blue Nadiya said, "Now is your time to write. Write your best work yet, and that will direct all the rest. This is your time."

Then the lights dimmed to normal, and she resumed her search for the freshest shrimp as if she'd not spoken. I smiled and only then noticed that the fishmonger was trying to get my attention. She had been holding out my change for who knows how long. After I apologized and took it, I wanted to hug Nadiya right there, but because she was Thai, which made her more reserved in showing emotions than both the French and the Americans, and because my hands were full with a pannier of greens in one and a bag of slippery fresh fish in the other, I said, "Your mother would be proud." To which she rolled her eyes and reiterated that she had no interest in following in the family talent.

Nadiya wasn't the only one who had begun to tell me my destiny. One market day I joined Petrus and Bernadette at our favorite café. It was warm enough to move from the booth inside to a café table outside on the square's cobbled stones, right in the midst of market exchanges. Vivienne was away visiting her daughter in Texas. Petrus was frequently leaving her drink on the table and dashing back to the olive stand when customers began to gather, and then flitting back. At one point, as Petrus rushed off to take an order, Bernadette leaned toward me. "I have some things to tell you."

"I'd love to hear them," I replied and leaned toward her in a conspiratorial hover. I tried to wipe the giddy smile off my face but I savored these precious moments with her.

"I see something in you," she said. "Do you know what you are?"

I shook my head *oui* then *non*. I still didn't breath. I didn't want to pop the bubble of this magical moment, one that felt like initiation, like crawling into that tunnel in Combarelles with a wise teacher who was about to give me my real name.

"You are a nomad. That's the word. *Une nomade*. Your willingness to explore, go beyond what may be ordinary, has led you here."

I breathed deep and fulfilling pure air. She retold a story from her life that she'd shared before, but this time she went deeper.

She leaned back in her seat and her eyes went to a place that was inside her memories, not out on the market square.

"I've told you that my second husband picked this place for me?"

"Yes."

"He knew that it would be a good place for me to grow old, especially if I were to be alone, without him. And it is a good place to grow old. I am happy here. There is so much more here than meets the eye, and I think it draws people like you and me, nomads." Yes, I said again, but then left the space for her to continue. We were members of the same nomadic tribe. I realized I was holding my breath again.

"Let me tell you about our time in Morocco," she continued. "We traveled around a lot, in a caravan. One day we decided to drive down to Morocco. We went south and then drove deeper into traditional Berber territories." She looked at me knowingly. "You lived in Morocco, so you'll know what I mean when I say that it is a deeply magical place, a place that has more enchantment than most. Isn't this why we're nomads? Looking for those magical places that wake us up and take us deeper?"

"Yes. Like here."

"Yes." She paused. "Like here. But Morocco is something else too. For a long time I was drawn to Morocco, and then my husband said, 'Let's go.' One day we drove our caravan to a place that looked empty but had an uncanny pull. We both felt it and knew it had led us there. Next, we came to a village. It felt like home to me. We lived there for a while. It was such a beautiful place. The village's origins, its name, you'll find curious, were actually Persian." She paused, then added, "Nomads, always nomads." They, her, me.

Saint Sacerdos' bells began to ring at midday, the hour we usually bid each other adieu until the next Wednesday market. We stood and hugged each other and then Bernadette paused and looked at me. I felt a lighting shift not too different from those uncanny moments with Nadiya. I held my breath and waited.

"We are connected to a great source," she said, "to the Spirit of this world and beyond. As the Sufis say, we are connected to the sacred earth and to the sacred sky in a flow that is all the Divine's creation. A lot of it is not visible to the physical eye, only the inner one." The last ring of the noontime bell struck and reverberated through the air and I felt a pleasant buzz right between my brows. I hugged her again and held on a little longer. The mysteries of this existence were many and many were invisible but real, including this beautiful friendship with this beautiful woman. And it felt as if Bernadette was telling me through her own experience as a person of many pastures seeking home that *you're home, you've been called here, been greeted by the spirit of this place, and you'll always be a part of this place, even when you can't be here.* It was the best going-away gift anyone could bestow.

After a rainy but warm start to the last week in February, the Wednesday market arrived with cheerful bundles of early-blooming miniature daffodils. Nearly all the merchants had splashes of yellow on their tables, some for sheer beauty and others for sale. I bought two bundles, one for Miles and me, and one for Petrus. She always liked having fresh flowers on her stand, usually from her own garden, but it was still too cold for that.

As spring approached, the moderately small winter market began to expand again, slowly growing into its warm weather proportions. As more merchants came out of their winter hibernation, soon it would be as in summer, with all the streets inside and around the medieval town lined with tables and kiosks selling anything you could possibly need within walking distance. My heart pulled at this thought because I knew I would not be here. Still, I knew it was no accident that this place had pulled me to it so strongly, and somehow I would find a way to come back. How still eluded me.

A few days after the mini daffodils arrived in market and colored our table in Le Chardon, Miles departed and flew back to the United States. I was happy for the joyous life of those little flowers for they cheered my melancholy over his parting and soon mine. Adding to the longing, mornings were dawning more and more beautifully as the world came out of winter's slumber. The lanterne des morts looked sublime in the golden glow at sunrise. It felt more alive than it had all winter, and I wanted to look at it every day, all year long.

Birdsong was everywhere and the *mésanges bleues* were back at their acrobatics around the cathedral's bell tower. The next Wednesday market, Nadiya joined Petrus, Bernadette and me again over hot drinks as we waited for Vivienne to arrive. It felt as if all three knew I was feeling tender about leaving but didn't want to draw attention to it. Bernadette soon delivered the perfect medicine, as if reading the misty thought bubble over my head.

"Being human, let's face it, is murky business. It's beauty. It's pain. Even trying to be good, doing the right thing, can be so subjective. It's not really about the obvious extremes of good and bad is it? It's about navigating the ambiguous stuff, the gray area of everyday life." She shrugged and added, "That's simply what being here on Earth is about." She then touched my hand and looked at me the way only she can.

"For me, I find my guidance and solace in reading good spiritual books. They remind me of the magic that truly is a part of life, right here, right now. Wherever you go, remember, you are always connected to all that matters."

Wherever you go, remember, you are always connected to all that matters. This line rang through my soul, over and over, taking root to draw on at will for comfort. Better guidance I could not have received. I also noticed Nadiya looking at Bernadette and smiling a smile known only to the lighting crew. It might have been the same one-liner she was about to deliver, but Bernadette had nailed it so well that Nadiya sat back and took another sip of coffee and gave the crew the day off.

That evening, when the sun was setting and no one was looking, I went to that place along the wall between Saint Sacerdos and the Tower that had special magic for me. I pressed my palms against the old twelfth-century stone structure and closed my eyes, uttering a statement and a prayer. Wherever I go, I shall also be here, connected to this magical place. I will come back.

In that moment, I heard the *rouge-gorge* sing overhead in the one pear tree growing on the cathedral's hill. Simultaneously, I felt a gentle thump around my legs and opened my eyes and kneeled down to greet Mr. Stripes. •

The View from Temniac

Chapter 20

INTO SECOND SPRING

Yes, it is a cliché but true, home, like happiness, is an inside job, but the community in which one weaves it can make a big difference in how one engages the interior. Feeling this interior confidence, I determined to be present wherever I was, while finding a way to return to Sarlat, the nomad, as always, moving between pastures. Home, I now knew, for a nomad, was liquid, not solid.

A MAN WAS PLAYING SEVERAL MEDIEVAL INSTRUMENTS during an afternoon of courtly twelfth-century troubadour music. We were all in a room in the old mansion next to Sarlat's cathedral, which once had been the residence of Sarlat's bishop. Contemporary with La Boétie's sixteenth-century house across the square, the bishop's house shared a wall with Saint Sacerdos on its southern side. A lot of the music from the modern troubadour was familiar to me from Spain, Portugal, and now, France. All were in one variation or another of old Romance languages from across the world that I loved so much, from the Atlantic to the Mediterranean shores, from Galicia to Italy's Piedmont, peaking at its extraordinary center in the valleys and mountaintops of the Pyrenees. This great geo-cultural swath was Café Oc.

He sang in Occitan or her first-cousin languages of Galégo-Portugais, Asturiano-Léonais, Aragonese, and Catalan. As he did, we learned that nearly all the songs boiled down to a couple of universal themes about romance that were fairly radical and new, at least in the twelfth century. One was that there was always a noble lady at the center who was desired by someone who could not have her due to his social station. Making it a truly engaging story, the noble lady also usually desired him. Second, oftentimes, our scholar-musician informed us, it wasn't just the troubadour, as we so often think, but a Moor, someone entirely from outside the noble lady's society. And she longed for him to come and whisk her away.

Cédric had come to the event with his two children. I loved watching them together. He was a loving father and his seven-year-old son was leaning comfortably against his father's left side, engrossed in the music with eyes rapt on the instruments. Next to him, his five-year-old sister sat straight up on the edge of her seat, listening intently to the story of risky love while securely holding her beloved and very worn-out stuffed, floppy-eared rabbit close to her chest. Occasionally, she would assure her big-eared friend that they would never part. Seeing these two like that sent happy waves through me, speaking of a vibrant past still alive and connecting powerfully to its young inheritors in the present.

Living next door to the cathedral offered these weekly chances to slip across the square for little lectures and concerts, either in Saint Sacerdos, with its ethereal angel-like acoustics at the transept, or the bishops' house, with its more earthy and wood-timbered walls.

A local historian told me one day that the building in which I lived was built over the likely earlier residence of the monks who originally founded historic Sarlat and had possibly been their own sleeping quarters or simple rooms for sleep and prayer. A few steps and they could be in Saint Sacerdos within seconds to carry out the sacred rhythms of daily chanted devotion in between chores. My mind reconstructed the area around the square into a bucolic country scene of monastic gardens, one a bee keeper, several hoeing, planting, weeding, pruning, and plucking insects off of leaves and working quiet magic from heaven and earth to coax all to thrive and feed body and soul.

Now with Miles' absence, I too had a somewhat monastic daily life that was punctuated by the bells that tolled every hour, reminding me of the passage of time and the moment in the day to pause and be present. I still loved that the bells made their biggest broo-ha-ha at seven in the morning, at noon, and at seven in the evening. Old agrarian rhythms that said cyclically, get up and go to the fields, break for lunch (and *bon appetite*), and stop your labors and enjoy the evening gathered with loved ones around the fire. Those gatherings probably involved music, too. These three times of day, received fifty-plus chimes from the bell tower, when all the other hours of the day received bell clangs for the exact number of the hour. It folded me into an old cadence of life lived through the old cycles of the land and people.

Other deep cycles flowed through this monastic perch. From my big window I witnessed nearly all the funerals, weddings, and baptisms arriving and departing from the cathedral. While chopping vegetables in my kitchen I would fall into easy meditation with the sound of the knife and board and the contemplative mood of the three stained glass windows across the way and their stories of deep passion, love, and will. And I never grew tired of, could not resist, the sublime pleasure of pushing open the wonderful blue door and walking the few paces to the cathedral's great wooden door and stepping in for daily prayer and meditation.

My spiritual practices actually got better by living in Le Chardon and Sarlat because the setting inspired a desire, not a discipline, to meditate regularly. I wonder if this had been so for the monks and nuns who chose such a life and lived so close to their temple of choice. Moreover, if I did not go to Saint Sacerdos even one day, I missed my friends there, the personalities written in glass and stone who were now eternal and very much alive.

Best of all, like clockwork, there would be Mr. Stripes waiting at the wall between church and tower for an evening rendezvous just after the seven o'clock bells finished their exuberant jostling.

But my monasticism was soon to take a filmic turn. One morning, Nadiya knocked on my door, a huge smile stuck on her face. "You have new neighbors. I've just rented the other two apartments in the building to the director, producer, and scriptwriter." I looked out the window and saw their trucks rolling in and parking next to the cathedral. They were going to use sections of Sarlat for several sets and also other nearby towns and the countryside, ideal because never having been industrialized, the landscape still looked medieval. They were also using Sarlat for their home base so this was where the film crew would wind down every day. Below my apartment was where they would gather after finishing a glass on the square.

As the days unfolded, my first interest was what they were shooting.

I pieced it together from snippets heard and flyers announcing the project posted on select historic walls, announcing to the public the film schedule and when that section would be blocked off and transformed to look fully eighteenth century.

It was a dramatic and semi-tragic saga of a stunningly beautiful and savvy young woman of noble birth who was falsely accused of a crime and shipped off to a French colony in India for execution. The spine of the plot was her finding a way to return home and exact justice upon the person who had framed her and taken her inheritance. She does return, quite the skilled and cunning fighter and revenges her betrayal and wins the day. The Dordogne and its historic sites served as the pre- and post-India sets for the story, from fall to return and redemption. The crew would then head elsewhere to film the middle portions of the story.

It was exciting to get glimpses of the beginning and the end, like cheating with a novel and peeking to read the last page. Because Miles was in the film and music business, both incredibly tough and mystifying areas, I found it a fascinating world, even if it moved slowly, was executed in nonlinear sequences, and required incredible attention to detail and loads of patience and resources. I never saw the crew face to face in the building; their hours were very early and very late. I did smell brewed coffee in pre-dawn hours and late-night cigarette smoke drifting up through the balcony.

As my days diminished before my return to the States, I found myself taking walks that would offer closure for me, to make this sublime journey through the full seasons complete. I visited places and creatures that now felt like old friends to say not goodbye but see you soon.

I took the northern road to Temniac, passed the frogs in their creek and the old man staking climbing green bean vines in his kitchen garden. The frogs were more riotous in their chorus, and the old man was enjoying the warming thaw of spring on his bones. By now I knew they each had their way in each season. In summer, I now knew that his green beans would be heavy and tall, having climbed on the stakes and engulfing them. There would also be tall mustard greens languidly swaying in the late summer wind as the frogs added their sultry summer song from their warm, wet mounds in the middle of the creek, lots of little froglettes clambering about. In fall I knew that the frogs would retreat, and the man would begin cultivating winter greens. In winter, there would be barely a peep from the slumbering frogs, though they may come out into the sun on a crisp sunny day. The old man would also be out only when the sun was high and the skies clear, to prepare his field for spring and to pluck a few green leaves from the now nearly naked mustard green stalks to add to his winter soup.

I also took the southern road to the train station to say my see-you-soons there. As with the northern road, here, too, I now knew the full seasons and could imagine their complete cycle. I knew now that in winter, people closed their windows and doors but still watched carefully what and who passed by, waiting to open a door quickly and welcome a newcomer with panache as he or she slopped down the hill from the train. In spring, the octogenarian lady would hand wash her very sexy and expensive lacey lingerie and hang it across the street on a clothesline strung between two plane trees as her satisfied husband looked on. I now knew that through spring, summer, and fall, another lady would make it her top priority to eradicate every dry leaf that tumbled down onto her sidewalk within the hour of its transgression. Her two brooms were at the ready when I walked past, leaning against the tree that produced the most leaves. I noticed that the winter pansies were about to give over to the spring pansies, poppies, daisies, lilies, and narcissuses, and they to the summer Russian sage and lavender when it would sweep in the wind, its tips pointing the way toward the train station, waving to those departing and welcoming those arriving.

If the road north and the road south were so rich, the center was equally engaged with rituals of parting. I spent as much time as I could with friends, including Mr. Stripes, who seemed to know something was up and tried to come inside the blue door with me. As a rule, on those last days, I would end the day with a good walk and then would go and sit and write at dusk on the Wall between the Tower and Saint-Sacerdos. Often, that was where Mr. Stripes and I found each other. He would hop up on the wall with me and peek over my arm to see what I wrote, sometimes placing an encouraging or editorial striped paw on the page to influence the outcome.

Market days began to swell again, strawberries were back at market stands and elsewhere, and the markets began to take on the crowded proportions that would build to full impact in summer. But instead of feeling melancholy that I would not be here for their fullness, I instead felt deep gratitude for how utterly lucky I had been to get to know the market in winter when the locals came out more and the merchants had more time to talk.

For me now, even with so many visitors diluting the mix, the market was full of stories about the people who bought and sold there year-round. There was Bernadette, Vivienne, and Petrus. There was the cheese seller, the baker, the Occitan lettuce sellers, the fishmonger, the sausage maker, the walnut oil presser, the beekeeper and honey seller. There were Vincent and Em-man-u-elle. There were Cédric and Aurelie and all our market friends on Saturdays. There was indisputably Nadiya and all her Xs that had held the test of time and seasons. There was Gerard the bookseller and friends and the ghosts. There was the energy healer and his bread. There was the root lady who sold diverse, not-ever-seen-in-the-supermarket winter vegetables from her organic backyard. There were so many, many more, and all these people and their stories were now the market to me.

So I counted my blessings as strangers poured in who did not know the tales behind the lettuce or the bread or the cheese. Full circle had indeed arrived, but it was not a circle, it was a spiral, and I was twirling my way slowly into the next ring and going toward the center. Deeper in, deeper down.

My dreams were also indicating that there had been a breech between my prior worlds and this one and that they were now blending, working out a way to come together into a whole instead of separate parts.

In one dream, Miles and I were in Sarlat, and his elderly uncle from New Jersey was there in Le Chardon preparing a Japanese dinner for us. Next in the dream, or a dream that followed this one, I was food shopping at an American grocery store I often shop at, but I was not in America, but in Sarlat, and Cédric had come to join me and help me shop. Outside, Carnival was unfolding for Mardi Gras and there was a parade down the main street with people in all manner of costumes, just like the actual carnival that had just passed. In this geographical fusion dream I looked out the shop window to see that it was both Sarlat and the town I lived in at the southern New Jersey shore, a hybrid place bringing all that I loved about both places into one place. This dream was one of many like it in those last days; sometimes my hometown in Colorado, instead of New Jersey, appeared in a fusion dish with Sarlat. But always Sarlat. But this last dream added a new piece. As I was about to wake up from it, a word popped into my head. I opened my eyes and wrote it down quickly in my journal that I kept by my bedside.

Grignoter.

I had no idea what it meant. I didn't think I'd ever heard it used, or if I had, it had registered subconsciously. What I did know was that my worlds had woven together so completely into my being that now it was time for me to consolidate that fusion more fully into the physical world. Somehow.

Being a big undertaking, I did what I could do. One step, one word, at a time. So, I climbed out of bed and went to my dictionary on the dining table. Grignoter, it said, means "to nibble." Was that the answer? Nibble my way, little bites at a time toward fulfillment? Ground myself in these rich places of being, this place of my spirit, a mouthful at a time? It was exactly like something my mother used to tell me when I had a huge, at times overwhelming, undertaking ahead of me. It was a Persian phrase. "Drop by drop, it becomes an ocean." Drop by drop. Nibble by nibble. *Grignoter par grignoter.*

I slipped off one last time to La Canéda and its Templar church and visited the elderly man weeding his garden with the *rouge-gorge* sitting on the water bowl rim next to him. They greeted me warmly as I passed. I said hello to the curious white horse and donkey who inhabited the same field and were amorous and playful, and I left them alone out of courtesy. I walked by the wine-whisperer's vineyard and found it pruned and ready for this year's growth. He was nowhere in sight but his sheep and geese were feeding just beyond the vines among the plum and cherry trees that were in bloom. It was a perfect snapshot of bucolic country life, and I tucked that image into my mind as a reminder of life in beauty and balance.

I then walked briskly back to make my date with Sophie, one last meeting "until next time." As we settled in to our table on the market square and Carlos brought us our order of beers, she asked, "When are you coming back home?" I was so happy at her casual use of the word "home," that I landed her a big bear hug but couldn't give her an exact answer other than, "As soon as possible."

My last night, Nadiya and Aidan had me for dinner with Petrus and Jean. I had already said goodbye to Bernadette and Vivienne, who had made a special Bretagne lunch at her village home just outside of Sarlat in honor of our friendship. We sat to savory and sweet homemade buckwheat crêpes, mystical talk, and probably too much hard cider, if that is possible. Similarly, at Nadiya and Aidan's, we laughed and ate and drank — too much, and Aidan would cheerfully say that it was all the American's fault.

Late that night as I returned home, Mr. Stripes ran to me and tried to squeeze in through the blue door when I opened it to go inside. He knew. I stayed with him for a while, and we walked up to the tower together. I asked him to please not forget me, even when other charming visitors came to stay in my studio. He handed me a striped paw. We shook. I hoped to return soon to greet him in a new season.

The next morning, early, I was on the train north, bound for Paris. Mr. Stripes came to say goodbye as soon as I opened the blue door, and Nadiya took me to the train station, reminding me of her classic encouraging one-liner, "You see, you do." Stepping off the metro in Paris and into the neighborhood where I would pass my last day in France, I went into shock. People moved too fast. They had no interest in what season it was, even if the songs hailed Paris in the springtime, and what does that mean if you don't see the cherry trees in bloom or hear the *rouge-gorge* boast about his mate? Worse, they made fun of my southern accent, not to mention that they scoffed when I ordered a *chocolatine*, not a *pain au chocolate*. Worst, they didn't seem to know about *la vie normale*. Even with the beautiful neighborhood markets abounding in the city, all the food had been shipped in and a good deal of it from very, very far away.

The human scale of time and patience that I had experienced in Sarlat altered me, made me slow down, and removed the need to prove anything to anyone because I had been so wholeheartedly accepted as who I was by the locals of an enchanted place untouched by the industrial world. A place where Neandertals and Cro-Magnons still lurked behind the trees and waved hello. I missed it miserably, but then recalled market-day words of wisdom from Bernadette. "Earth is messy," she said, "and perfection and clarity can happen in heaven, but not here. We're here to be imperfect and inquisitive and to dive into unknown territory, and then to do our best with it."

Another balm for my spirit arrived when I arrived at my little hotel run by a nice family. I set my bag down and suddenly out from behind the front desk ran a little gray and black striped cat who sniffed my bag and then came to me in a warm and robust greeting. Mr. Stripes had left a note when he'd rubbed my bag it seemed, one that extended to the city cousins, asking them to make me feel at home. It worked. I almost broke down in tears.

Two days later, I landed in Philadelphia and returned to our little island in southern New Jersey. Miles had rented us a lovely little beach cottage and set up a warm temporary new home. I was warmly welcomed home by him and an intimate circle of friends who had cheered all along my quest to find myself in the world, and when I determined it was Sarlat, could see themselves being a part of that trans-Atlantic adventure. As I stepped into our cottage, I was overwhelmed by gratitude for the wealth of places to live and the blessings of community and self-sufficiency in them all. I realized then and there that the common factor between all three geographies — the place of my birth in Colorado, this oceanside perch in New Jersey, and my home of homes, Sarlat — was in fact my quest for self-sufficiency and community, for seasonal pastures that allowed movement but also depth, commitment, and personal authenticity.

Curiously, the confidence of having Sarlat — I would always have Sarlat, the place I felt most fully myself — gave me the ability to fully come home to myself, to occupy more fully the geographies in which I found myself. I at last saw that my life journey had been about striving for self-sufficiency all along, a very nomadic thing to do. I was persistently seeking to rely on myself and on resources of my own making, no matter the fickleness of the exterior world.

Yes, it is a cliché but true, home, like happiness, is an inside job, but the community in which one weaves it can make a big difference in how one engages the interior. Feeling this interior confidence, I determined to be present wherever I was, while finding a way to return to Sarlat, the nomad, as always, moving between pastures. Home, I now knew, for a nomad, was liquid, not solid. It was very real and touchable but fluid.

Months later, as I worked more deeply this epiphany and wondered how and when I would return to Sarlat, I received an email from Harold. He wrote that he liked the feature story I'd written on him and his work on Neandertals. He added that he was often asked if he would ever write a popular book on Neandertals, based on his wealth and depth of experience over several decades. His reply to this repeated query was that he felt it was important but that he himself just didn't have the time to write it. "Then it occurred to me," he continued, "would you be interested in writing the book?" If so, it would be important that I visit him again in the field and get to know the whole team, possibly become a part of the crew.

Would I be interested? *I would be ecstatic, riveted, thrilled.* It was a dream come true. I thought to myself, giddily, it meant I would have to spend summers in the Dordogne, on a legitimate mission, on the excavations, doing research on everything about this closely related cousin's existence on earth, so much of it right there in southwestern France.

"I could think of nothing more exciting," I wrote back, "than to write such a book."

Life was truly magical. My return was certain. I'd somehow find a way. You see, you do. And this time, the Neandertals were calling me home. I saw my life pass before my eyes.

I think you'll come back here to live.

If something is going to happen, it is going to happen, just take your time.

It's the capacity of floating that makes life better.

Wherever you go, remember, you are always connected to all that matters. •

ABOUT THE AUTHOR

Photo by Steve Mullen

Born and raised in the Colorado Rockies while traveling across three continents as a child to visit relatives in Iran, travel writer Beebe Bahrami was drawn to anthropology as an adult. This training immersed her deeply into the cultures, languages, peoples, prehistories, and histories of the Mediterranean world. It is in these geographies, especially of France and Spain, that she writes most, especially on travel, food and wine, the outdoors and nature, spirituality, archaeology, and cross-cultural themes. Passionate for trekking, for over two decades she also has walked and written extensively on numerous routes of the pilgrimage road, the Camino, through southern France and northern Spain.

Author of other travel books — *The Spiritual Traveler Spain: A Guide to Sacred Sites and Pilgrim Routes, Historic Walking Guides Madrid*, and *Café Neandertal: Excavating Our Past in One of Europe's Most Ancient Places* — Beebe also has written for *Wine Enthusiast, Archaeology, The Pennsylvania Gazette, Perceptive Travel, Expedition, The Bark, Michelin Green Guides,* and *National Geographic* books. Several of her essays have won awards in Travelers' Tales' annual travel writing contest.

Nomadic in temperament, it was nonetheless the southwest of France, with Sarlat and the Dordogne at the center, that called to Beebe to make it home. This journey is captured here, in *Café Oc*, and though she still is dedicated to exploring the world at the pace of the spirit, on foot, this is something delightfully supported by life in France.

To view her writing portfolio, please visit www.beebebahrami.weebly.com.

www.ingramcontent.com/pod-product-compliance
Lightning Source LLC
Chambersburg PA
CBHW040624240426
43666CB00020BA/2909